Women, Peace and Security and International Law

In 2000, the UN Security Council adopted the ground-breaking Resolution 1325 on Women, Peace and Security (WPS) placing women at the centre of the agenda, thanks to years of campaigning. The Resolution recognises the differential impact of armed conflict on women and men, draws attention to the 'inextricable links between gender equality and international peace and security' and stresses the 'important role of women in the prevention and resolution of conflicts and in peace-building'. But what exactly is the WPS agenda and what is its content? What are its implications for peace and for security? And what does it mean for international lawyers? Through the narratives of women's activism and of international law this book seeks to make the WPS agenda better known to international lawyers and to ask whether it is, or could become, an international legal regime that conforms and responds to the realities of women's lives.

CHRISTINE CHINKIN is the author of many articles on international law, in particular on the human rights of women; co-author of *The Boundaries of International Law: a Feminist Analysis* (2000, with Hilary Charlesworth), *The Making of International Law* (2007, with Alan Boyle) and of *International Law and New Wars* (2017 with Mary Kaldor). She has been an expert witness at the Inter-American Court of Human Rights, scientific adviser to the drafting committee for the Council of Europe Convention on Preventing and Combating Violence against Women and Domestic Violence (Istanbul Convention).

Hersch Lauterpacht Memorial Lectures

Recent books in the Hersch Lauterpacht Memorial Lecture Series

Stephen M. Schwebel, Luke Sobota and Ryan Manton *International Arbitration: Three Salient Problems*

Mary Ellen O'Connell *The Art of Law in the International Community*

Yuval Shany *Questions of Jurisdiction and Admissibility before International Courts*

W. Michael Reisman and Christina Skinner *Fraudulent Evidence before Public International Tribunals: The Dirty Stories of International Law*

Andrés Rigo Sureda *Investment Treaty Arbitration: Judging Under Uncertainty*

Ralph Zacklin *The United Nations Secretariat and the Use of Force in a Unipolar World: Power v. Principle*

John H. Jackson *Sovereignty, the WTO, and Changing Fundamentals of International Law*

Jan Paulsson *Denial of Justice in International Law*

Francisco Orrego Vicuña *International Dispute Settlement in an Evolving Global Society: Constitutionalization, Accessibility, Privatization*

Martti Koskenniemi *The Gentle Civilizer of Nations: The Rise and Fall of International Law 1870–1960*

Thomas M. Franck *Recourse to Force: State Action against Threats and Armed Attacks*

Mohamed Shahabuddeen *Precedent in the World Court*

Antonio Cassese *Self-Determination of Peoples: A Legal Reappraisal*

Women, Peace and Security and International Law

CHRISTINE CHINKIN
London School of Economics and Political Science

CAMBRIDGE
UNIVERSITY PRESS

CAMBRIDGE
UNIVERSITY PRESS

University Printing House, Cambridge CB2 8BS, United Kingdom

One Liberty Plaza, 20th Floor, New York, NY 10006, USA

477 Williamstown Road, Port Melbourne, VIC 3207, Australia

314–321, 3rd Floor, Plot 3, Splendor Forum, Jasola District Centre, New Delhi – 110025, India

103 Penang Road, #05–06/07, Visioncrest Commercial, Singapore 238467

Cambridge University Press is part of the University of Cambridge.

It furthers the University's mission by disseminating knowledge in the pursuit of education, learning, and research at the highest international levels of excellence.

www.cambridge.org
Information on this title: www.cambridge.org/9781108483476
DOI: 10.1017/9781108692076

First published 2022

A catalogue record for this publication is available from the British Library.

ISBN 978-1-108-48347-6 Hardback

Contents

Acknowledgements

This book was written with the support of both an Arts and Humanities Research Council grant called 'A Feminist International Law on Peace and Security' and a European Research Council (ERC) grant under the European Union's Horizon 2020 research and innovation programme (Grant Agreement No. 786494).

Documents

Treaties

Convention for the Pacific Settlement of International Disputes, The Hague, 29 July 1899

Convention for the Pacific Settlement of International Disputes, The Hague, 18 October 1907

Treaty of Versailles, 28 June 1919, Part I, Covenant of the League of Nations; Part XIII, Constitution of the International Labour Organization

ILO Convention No. 3 on maternity protection, 1919

ILO Convention No. 4 on night work for women, 1919

General Treaty for Renunciation of War as an Instrument of National Policy, Paris, 27 August 1928

Charter of the United Nations, San Francisco, 26 June 1945

Statute of the International Court of Justice, San Francisco, 26 June 1945

Charter of the International Military Tribunal, London, 8 August 1945

Constitution of the United Nations Educational, Scientific and Cultural Organization, London, 16 November 1945

Charter of the International Military Tribunal for the Far East, Tokyo, 19 January 1946

Convention on the Prevention and Punishment of the Crime of Genocide, New York, 9 December 1948

North Atlantic Treaty, Washington D.C., 4 April 1949

Convention against Torture and Other Cruel, Inhuman or Degrading Treatment or Punishment, New York, 10 December 1984

United Nations Convention on the Rights of the Child, New York, 20 November 1989

Comprehensive Cambodian Peace Agreement, Paris, 23 October 1991

Convention on the Prohibition of the Development, Production, Stockpiling and Use of Chemical Weapons and on their Destruction, Geneva, 3 September 1992

General Framework Agreement for Peace for Bosnia and Herzegovina, Dayton, initialled 21 November 1995; signed, Paris, 14 December 1995

Convention on the Prohibition of the Use, Stockpiling, Production and Transfer of Anti-personnel Mines and on their Destruction, Oslo, 18 September 1997

Statute of the International Criminal Court, Rome, 17 July 1998

Optional Protocol to the Convention on the Elimination of All Forms of Discrimination against Women, New York, 6 October 1999

Protocol to Prevent, Suppress and Punish Trafficking in Persons Especially Women and Children, supplementing the United Nations Convention against Transnational Organized Crime, New York, 15 November 2000 (Palermo Protocol)

Optional Protocol to the Convention on the Rights of the Child on the sale of children, child prostitution and child pornography, New York, 25 May 2000

Optional Protocol to the Convention on the Rights of the Child on the involvement of children in armed conflict, New York, 25 May 2000

Agreement on Provisional Arrangements in Afghanistan pending the Reestablishment of Permanent Government Institutions, 5 December 2001 (Bonn Agreement)

Protocol to the African Charter on Human and Peoples' Rights on the Rights of Women in Africa, 11 July 2003 (Maputo Protocol)

Council of Europe Convention on Preventing and Combating Violence against Women and Domestic Violence, Istanbul, 11 May 2011

Arms Trade Treaty, New York, 2 April 2013

Treaty on the Prohibition of Nuclear Weapons, New York, 2017

United Nations Security Council Resolutions

Security Council resolution 661, 6 August 1990, *Iraq-Kuwait*
Security Council resolution 678, 29 November 1990, *Iraq-Kuwait*
Security Council resolution 688, 5 April 1991, *Iraq*
Security Council resolution 794, 3 December 1992, *Somalia*
Security Council resolution 1261, 30 August 1999, *Children and Armed Conflict*
Security Council resolution 1265, 17 September 1999, *Protection of Civilians in Armed Conflict*
Security Council resolution 1325, 31 October 2000, *Women and Peace and Security*
Security Council resolution, 1373, 28 September 2001, *Threats to international peace and security caused by terrorist acts*
Security Council resolution 1645, 20 December 2005, *Post-conflict peacebuilding*
Security Council resolution 1674, 28 April 2006, *Protection of Civilians*
Security Council resolution 1820, 19 June 2008, *Women and Peace and Security*
Security Council resolution 1888, 30 September 2009, *Women and Peace and Security*
Security Council resolution 1889, 5 October 2009, *Women and Peace and Security*
Security Council resolution 1894, 11 November 2009, *Protection of Civilians*
Security Council resolution 1918, 27 April 2010, *Somalia*
Security Council resolution 1960, 16 December 2010, *Women and Peace and Security*
Security Council resolution 1973, 17 March 2011, *Libya*
Security Council resolution 1975, 30 March 2011, *Côte d'Ivoire*
Security Council resolution 2106, 24 June 2013, *Women and Peace and Security*
Security Council resolution 2122, 18 October 2013, *Women and Peace and Security*
Security Council resolution 2171, 21 August 2014, *Conflict prevention*
Security Council resolution 2220, 22 May 2015, *Small arms*
Security Council resolution 2242, 13 October 2015, *Women and Peace and Security*
Security Council resolution 2125, 18 November 2013, *Somalia*

Security Council resolution 2250, 9 December 2015, *Maintenance of international peace and security*

Security Council resolution 2253, 17 December 2015, *Threats to international peace and security caused by terrorist acts*

Security Council resolution 2272, 11 March 2016, *Peacekeeping operations*

Security Council resolution 2282, 27 April 2016, *Post-conflict peacebuilding*

Security Council resolution 2286, 3 May 2016, *Protection of Civilians in Armed Conflict*

Security Council resolution 2331, 20 December 2016, *Maintenance of International Peace and Security*

Security Council resolution 2349, 31 March 2017, *Peace and Security in Africa*

Security Council resolution 2388, 21 November 2017, *Maintenance of International Peace and Security*

Security Council resolution 2457, 27 February 2019, *Cooperation between the United Nations and regional and subregional organizations in maintaining international peace and security – Silencing the guns in Africa*

Security Council resolution 2467, 23 April 2019, *Women and Peace and Security: Sexual Violence in Conflict*

Security Council resolution 2493, 29 October 2019, *Women and Peace and Security*

United Nations General Assembly Resolutions

General Assembly resolution 217A, 10 December 1948, *Universal Declaration of Human Rights*

General Assembly resolution 2625, 24 October 1970, *Declaration on Principles of International Law concerning Friendly Relations and Cooperation among States in accordance with the Charter of the United Nations*

General Assembly resolution 3318 (XXIX), 14 December 1974, *Declaration on the Protection of Women and Children in Emergency and Armed Conflict*

General Assembly resolution 33/73, 15 December 1978, *Declaration on the Preparation of Societies for Life in Peace*

General Assembly resolution 37/63, 3 December 1982, *Declaration on the Participation of Women in Promoting International Peace and Co-operation*

General Assembly resolution 39/11, 12 November 1984, *Declaration on the Right of Peoples to Peace*

General Assembly resolution 40/108, 1 December 1985, *Implementation of the Nairobi Forward-looking Strategies for the Advancement of Women*

General Assembly resolution 48/104, 20 December 1993, *Declaration on the Elimination of Violence against Women*

General Assembly resolution 51/77, 20 February 1997, *The Rights of the Child*

General Assembly resolution 56/83, 12 December 2001, Annex: *Responsibility of States for Internationally Wrongful Acts*

General Assembly resolution 60/1, 24 October 2005, *World Summit*

General Assembly resolution 60/146, 16 December 2005, *Basic Principles and Guidelines on the Right to a Remedy and Reparation for Victims of Gross Violations of International Human Rights Law and Serious Violations of International Humanitarian Law*

General Assembly resolution 60/180, 20 December 2005, *The Peacebuilding Commission*

General Assembly resolution 60/251, 15 March 2006, *Human Rights Council*

General Assembly resolution 64/289, 21 July 2010, *System-wide Coherence*

General Assembly resolution 66/290, 25 October 2012, *Follow-up to paragraph 143 on human security of the 2005 World Summit Outcome*

General Assembly resolution, 69/293, 19 June 2015, *International Day for the Elimination of Sexual Violence in Conflict*

General Assembly resolution 70/1, 21 October 2015, *Transforming our world: the 2030 Agenda for Sustainable Development*

General Assembly resolution 70/262, 2016, *Review of the United Nations Peacebuilding Architecture*

General Assembly resolution 71/56, 13 December 2016, *Women, Disarmament, Non-proliferation and Arms Control*

General Assembly resolution 71/189, 19 December 2016, *Declaration on the Right to Peace*

UN General Assembly resolution 71/248, 21 December 2016, *International, Impartial and Independent Mechanism to assist in the Investigation and Prosecution of those Responsible for the Most Serious Crimes under International Law committed in the Syrian Arab Republic since March 2011*

1

The Women, Peace and Security Agenda

1.1 Introduction

This book is an updated and lengthened version of the lectures that I gave in the Lauterpacht Centre for International Law in October 2016 as part of the Lauterpacht lecture series, which was founded in 1983 to celebrate the unique contribution to the development of public international law made by Sir Hersch Lauterpacht. In keeping with the lecture series, I sought connections between my work as a feminist international lawyer and that of Sir Hersch Lauterpacht in his long career as an academic and scholar, a barrister and judge at the International Court of Justice and, as recounted by Sir Robert Jennings, a 'remarkable' teacher.[1] In the simplest, logistic terms, he was a lecturer at the London School of Economics prior to taking up his chair at Cambridge and he also lectured at the University of Michigan,[2] both places where I hold academic appointments.

But the first of the three words of my title – 'women' – is not immediately and apparently connected to the work of Sir Hersch Lauterpacht. Despite what has been called his 'novel, even in his time daring, belief in the position of the individual as a subject of international law',[3] Lauterpacht also maintained the 'internalized

[1] Sir Robert Jennings, 'Hersch Lauterpacht: A Personal Recollection', 2 *European Journal of International Law* (1997) 301–4.

[2] Elihu Lauterpacht, *The Life of Hersch Lauterpacht* (Cambridge University Press, 2010) 307.

[3] Chaim Herzog, 'Sir Hersch Lauterpacht: An Appraisal', 2 *European Journal of International Law* (1997) 299.

public/private political/unpolitical divide, so characteristic of classic liberalism'.[4] This divide is at the core of feminist critiques of law, including international law.[5] But I think that it would be wrong to assume from this that Lauterpacht rejected any public role for women: although, from his letters to his wife Rachel, it is evident that Lauterpacht enjoyed the 'traditional gender structures' of a marriage in the first half of the twentieth century, there was also '[t]he paradox ... that Hersch accepted ... an invitation from the Wellesley College, Massachusetts, to become visiting professor [in 1941] to teach *girls* international law and international politics'.[6] In Sir Hersch's own words, 'there are hundreds of girls [there]',[7] at least some of whom were plainly engaging in educational activities across that divide. And, when arguing for an international Bill of Rights, Lauterpacht admitted that a 'declaration of the rights of man is incomplete without an attempt to redress the legal inferiority of women'. However, coming down on the side of pragmatism, he determined that 'existing possibilities' and the 'necessity of not impeding the acceptance of the Bill' meant that he would omit this topic, as well as that of the 'equality of status of aliens' from his work.[8] Lauterpacht's omission was not allowed to go unremarked: in his review of *An International Bill of the Rights of Man*,[9] Philip Jessup noted Lauterpacht's 'curious caution' and considered the 'greatest weakness' of the book to be the efforts 'to lean strongly on the rock of practicality' and to depend upon the 'gradual operation of public opinion'[10] for acceptance of human rights for all. Lauterpacht's caution was possibly misplaced as, in the same year as the publication of his book, the drafters of the UN Charter accepted the objective of 'promoting and encouraging respect for human rights and for fundamental freedoms for all without distinction as to race, sex, language, or religion'.[11] This was followed by the creation of the Commission on the Status of Women by the Economic and

[4] Reut Yael Paz, 'Between the "Public" and the "Private"', 22 *European Journal of International Law* (2011) 863.

[5] Hilary Charlesworth and Christine Chinkin. *The Boundaries of International Law: A Feminist Analysis* (Manchester University Press, 2000) chapter 2.

[6] Paz (*supra* n 4) 867. [7] Lauterpacht (*supra* n 2) 149. [8] Ibid., at 255.

[9] Sir Hersch Lauterpacht, *An International Bill of the Rights of Man* (1945; republished Oxford University Press, 2013).

[10] Philip Jessup, 'Review', *39 American Journal of International Law* (1945), 847–50.

[11] United Nations Charter, 1945, article 1. Article 8 provides that '[t]he United Nations shall place no restrictions on the eligibility of men and women to

Social Council at the insistence of women that a sub-commission of the Commission on Human Rights was inadequate to address the inferior status of women.[12] And, in 1948, the Universal Declaration of Human Rights was adopted by the General Assembly, which again includes a commitment to non-discrimination on the basis of sex.[13] But, in his hard-headed reasoning for omitting women's equality rights, Lauterpacht was, of course, articulating a dilemma that is often faced by lawyers and academics with an activist policy agenda: which battles do we fight and when do we compromise? Do we go for what we can get or risk losing all in aiming too high, becoming too adrift from public opinion? Do we assume that by advocating enhanced conditions for all, those who are most disadvantaged will equally benefit? In his recognition of the tension between pragmatism and seeking to fulfil higher aspirations, I am inclined to think – hope – that Sir Hersch Lauterpacht would be generally supportive of the subject of my lectures: 'Women, Peace and Security and International Law'.

The terminology that would have been familiar to Sir Hersch Lauterpacht, and on which he commented in the context of the drafting of the UN Charter, is that of 'peace and security', a phrase that as 'international peace and security' is repeated over twenty times throughout that document.[14] It is the conjunction of 'women' with 'peace and security' that is new, and, in 'making strange what appears familiar',[15] it is perhaps jarring to some people. Certainly, even a quarter of a century ago, this grouping of words would have been surprising. The previously more commonly accepted wording with respect to women in the international landscape was 'equality, development and peace', the core objectives of the four world conferences on women convened by the United Nations between 1975 and 1995.[16] That contested cold war terminology has now

participate in any capacity and under conditions of equality in its principal and subsidiary organs'.

12 Hilkka Pietilä, *The Unfinished Story of Women and the United Nations* (UN, Non-Governmental Liaison Service, 2007).

13 UN General Assembly resolution 217A, 10 December 1948, *Universal Declaration of Human Rights*, article 2.

14 UN Charter, 1945, preamble and articles 1 (1), 2 (3), 11, 12, 15, 18, 23, 24, 26, 33, 34, 37, 39, 42, 43, 48, 52, 73, 99.

15 Sandra Harding, *Whose Science? Whose Knowledge?: Thinking from Women's Lives* (Cornell University Press, 1991) 150.

16 Mexico City, 1975; Copenhagen, 1980; Nairobi, 1985; Beijing, 1995.

given way to that of 'gender equality and empowerment', the full title of UN Women[17] and 'Women, Peace and Security', the Security Council agenda that is generally understood as stemming from its landmark resolution 1325, unanimously adopted in October 2000.[18] Together, these keywords encapsulate contemporary UN policy towards women.

UN Security Council resolution 1325 recognised the differential impact of armed conflict on women and men, drew attention to the 'inextricable links between gender equality and international peace and security',[19] and stressed the 'important role of women in the prevention and resolution of conflicts and in peace-building'.[20] It was located squarely within the purposes and principles of the UN Charter, but in its centring of women it was groundbreaking. Although there was no follow-up resolution until the adoption of resolution 1820[21] in 2008, resolution 1325 has become entrenched in ways unusual for a Security Council resolution. In conjunction with the further eight resolutions that have followed resolution 1820,[22] it now has its own acronym (WPS), has generated a huge literature – academic,[23] non-governmental organisation (NGO) 'grey literature',[24] policy-based briefings – and has been the explicit subject of at least three major UN reports[25] and referred to in

[17] UN Women, the United Nations Entity for Gender Equality and the Empowerment of Women, was established by UN General Assembly resolution 64/289, 21 July 2010, *on system-wide coherence*, paras 49–90.

[18] UN Security Council resolution 1325, 31 October 2000, *Women and Peace and Security*.

[19] UN Women, *High-level Review on Women, Peace and Security: 15 years of Security Council resolution 1325*, at www.unwomen.org/en/news/in-focus/women-peace-security.

[20] UN Security Council resolution 1325 (2000), preamble.

[21] UN Security Council resolution 1820, 19 June 2008.

[22] UN Security Council resolution 1888, 30 September 2009; UN Security Council resolution 1889, 5 October 2009; UN Security Council resolution 1960, 16 December 2010; UN Security Council resolution 2106, 24 June 2013; UN Security Council resolution 2122, 18 October 2013; UN Security Council resolution 2242, 13 October 2015; UN Security Council resolution 2467, 23 April 2019; UN Security Council resolution 2493, 29 October 2019.

[23] This includes Sara E. Davies and Jacqui True (eds.) *The Oxford Handbook of Women, Peace and Security* (Oxford University Press, 2019), which runs to 898 pages.

[24] 'Grey literature' is defined by Wikipedia as 'materials and research produced by organizations outside of the traditional commercial or academic publishing and distribution channels'.

[25] *Women, Peace and Security*, study submitted by the Secretary-General pursuant to Security Council resolution 1325 (2000) (United Nations, 2002); Elisabeth Rehn

others.[26] It is referenced in other Security Council thematic and country-specific resolutions. The UN Secretary-General has described it as 'clearly one of the top priorities of the United Nations as a whole'.[27] There is an annual open debate on WPS at the Security Council where progress in the implementation of resolution 1325 is reviewed; the debate on the High-level Review of resolution 1325 in October 2015 saw a record-breaking 110 statements made across 2 different days. Centres on Women, or Gender, Peace and Security have been established in universities in Europe, North America, Africa and Australia. It appears high-flying, 'almost a talisman for those involved, or outsiders interested in questions of women and war, and women and peacemaking',[28] and a significant success story in bringing women from the margins of international affairs into its mainstream: after all, what can be more mainstream than the Security Council's primary responsibility for the maintenance of international peace and security?[29]

But what exactly is the WPS agenda and what is its content? What are its implications for peace and for security? Are the successes that are claimed real or are they illusory, disguising real gaps and ambiguities? Are its precepts widely accepted or does what, until recently, has been consensus within the Security Council conceal divisions and contestations? And, in particular for these chapters, what does WPS mean to or for international lawyers? It is noticeable that much

and Ellen Johnson Sirleaf, *Women, War and Peace: The Independent Experts' Assessment on the Impact of Armed Conflict on Women and Women's Role in Peace-Building* (UNIFEM, 2002); Radhika Coomaraswamy and others, *Preventing Conflict, Transforming Justice, Securing the Peace: A Global Study on the Implementation of Security Council Resolution 1325* (United Nations, 2015) [hereinafter *Global Study*].

26 Report of the High-level Independent Panel on Peace Operations, *Uniting our strengths for peace: politics, partnership and people*, A/70/95–S/2015/446, 17 June 2015; para 31; Report of the Advisory Group of Experts on the Review of the Peacebuilding Architecture, *Challenge of sustaining peace*, A/69/968; S/2015/490, 29 June 2015, paras 51 and 77.

27 Secretary-General's remarks at the Security Council's Open Debate on Women, Peace and Security, 29 October 2019, at www.un.org/sg/en/content/sg/statement/2019–10-29/secretary-generals-remarks-the-security-councils-open-debate-women-peace-and-security-delivered.

28 Victoria Brittain, 'Women in War and Crisis Zones: One Key to Africa's Wars of Underdevelopment' (Crisis States Programme Working Papers Series, No. 1, 2002) at www.lse.ac.uk/international-development/Assets/Documents/PDFs/csrc-working-papers-phase-one/wp21-women-in-war-and-crisis-zones.pdf.

29 UN Charter, 1945, article 24.

of the academic literature on WPS comes from scholars in disciplines such as international relations, political science, international development, political economics, gender studies, and peace and conflict studies but that there is much less interest in the subject shown by international lawyers.

So the limited aim of my Lauterpacht lectures and of this book is to make the WPS agenda better known to international lawyers, both its positives and its flaws, and to raise some underlying questions: has WPS become embedded into international law? Even can it be said to constitute a special regime or sub-discipline of international law in the same way as 'human rights law', 'WTO law', 'EU law', 'humanitarian law' or 'space law'?[30] Is it a 'functionally oriented'[31] international legal regime that conforms and responds to the realities of women's lives? And, from another perspective, does this supposedly woman-friendly space on the international agenda in reality bring women's experiences into international law and what difference does, or could, that make? While I am hopeful that Sir Hersch Lauterpacht might be supportive of the topic, I am also mindful of his own warning about *An International Bill of the Rights of Man.*[32] He wrote 'that this is a kind of book which draws upon itself almost uniformly adverse criticism. It will be assailed by the orthodox as going too far; by the progressive as being too conservative and evasive; by the lawyers as being revolutionary; by the laymen as being too legalistic; and so on.'[33] This may also be true of asserting WPS as an appropriate topic for consideration by international lawyers.

In this first chapter, I outline the substantive and institutional contents of the ten WPS resolutions and, in Chapter 2, I consider the status of these thematic resolutions in international law. Chapters 3 and 4 discuss the concepts of 'women and peace' and 'women and security' within the resolutions and more broadly within the context of international law. Finally, Chapter 5 places WPS alongside other issues in international law and relations, both those that have emerged contemporaneously with WPS, such as the Responsibility to Protect and human security, as well as some that

[30] Report of the Study Group of the International Law Commission, Fragmentation of International Law. *Difficulties arising from the Diversification and Expansion of International Law,* A/CN.4/L.682, 13 April 2006, para 129.

[31] Ibid., at para 133. [32] Lauterpacht (*supra* n 9). [33] Lauterpacht (*supra* n 2) 255.

have since come more to the fore, including climate change. It ends by considering whether there is an existing, or perhaps emergent, special regime of international law: women, peace and security.

1.2 Towards the Adoption of Security Council Resolution 1325 (2000)

As already stated, the WPS agenda is most immediately understood as an initiative of the UN Security Council that commenced in October 2000 with the adoption of resolution 1325. The resolution was widely celebrated by women activists as, for the first time in its history, the male-dominated and conservative Security Council had devoted a full session to debating women's experiences during and after conflict.[34] It urged states and institutions to take measures to bring those experiences into decision- and policy-making about prevention, management and resolution of conflict and its aftermath. By bringing women onto the Security Council's agenda for the maintenance of international peace and security, it seemed that a door had been opened for women to have a role in the decision-making and operations of the Council, for defining the intersection between gender and security[35] and possibly for contributing to 'idealism' and 'progress' in international law.[36]

But starting the story in 2000 belies another story, that of the long history of the women's peace movement, of women's activism and lobbying before and throughout the twentieth century across international borders within both their own networks and the traditional arenas of international relations. The International Congress of Women, held in The Hague in 1915, is a better starting point.[37] In the midst of World War I, when travel to and across Europe was deemed unsafe, from 28 April to 1 May 1915, over 1,100 women

[34] Carol Cohn, Helen Kinsella and Sheri Gibbings, 'Women, Peace and Security: Resolution 1325', 6 *International Feminist Journal of Politics* (2004) 130–40.

[35] Laura McLeod, 'The Women, Peace and Security Resolutions: UNSCR 1325 to 2122', in Jill Steans and Daniela Tepe-Belfrage (eds.) *Handbook on Gender in World Politics* (Edward Elgar, 2016) 271.

[36] Hersch Lauterpacht, 'The Grotian Tradition in International Law', 23 *British Yearbook of International Law* (1946) 1–53, 48.

[37] This is also a late starting date. In tracing the origins of women's activism and human rights, Arvonne Fraser goes back at least as far as the early fifteenth century; Arvonne Fraser, 'Becoming Human: The Origins and Development of Women's Human Rights', 21 *Human Rights Quarterly* (1999) 853–906.

from Europe and North America gathered in the Netherlands at The Hague to discuss how peace might be brought about.[38] Many governments were hostile to such an initiative; for instance, out of the 180 women who sought to go to The Hague from the UK, only 24 received passports. Further, ferries were deliberately cancelled, meaning that even those with passports were unable to cross the Channel. Two of the only three British representatives at The Hague were already in Europe and the third travelled from the United States.

The representatives of over 150 organisations from 12 countries were members of the International Women's Suffrage Alliance who 'developed a unique vision in which peace, gender equality and human rights were intimately entwined'.[39] They adopted 20 resolutions that drew upon proposals that had been previously worked on within national associations and were subsequently signed on to by 88,784 women. The twenty resolutions protested against the 'madness and horror of war' and rejected the idea that war can ever be made safe for women.[40] They put forward principles for a 'permanent peace', urging governments to settle future disputes through conciliation and arbitration[41] and advocating universal disarmament, as well as women's political enfranchisement. Adopting resolutions was not of itself sufficient; they needed to be disseminated to those in power. To this end, the final resolution delegated 'envoys to carry the message … to the rulers of the belligerent nations of Europe and to the President of the United States'.[42] The Congress also established an organisation – the

[38] C. Althusain, 'International Congress of Women of 1915' at www.peacepalacelibrary.nl/2015/02/international-congress-of-women-of-1915/.

[39] Helen McCarthy, 'Women, Peace and Transnational Activism, a Century On: Introduction' (Queen Mary University of London, 30 March 2015) at www.historyandpolicy.org/dialogues/discussions/women-peace-and-transnational-activism-a-century-on.

[40] Resolutions adopted by the International Congress of Women, The Hague, Holland, 1 May 1915 at https://wilpf.org/wp-content/uploads/2012/08/WILPF_triennial_congress_1915.pdf.

[41] Convention for the Pacific Settlement of International Disputes, The Hague, 29 July 1899 and Convention for the Pacific Settlement of International Disputes, The Hague, 18 October 1907 both made provision for mediation and arbitration. Unlike at the Women's Congress, there were no women delegates at the diplomatic conferences at The Hague in 1899 and 1907.

[42] Resolutions adopted by the International Congress of Women (*supra* n 40).

International Committee of Women for Permanent Peace[43] – to carry forward the message and to arrange for a second Congress to take place at the same time as any peace conference between the powers.[44] Following the Hague Congress, most women returned to their own countries, spread the messages and engaged in local activities, while those so designated met with political leaders to convey the resolutions to them.

In accordance with the final resolution adopted in The Hague, the women met again after the end of the war at the second Congress in Zurich in May 1919 and while the Peace Conference was in session. The resolutions adopted in Zurich[45] were telegraphed to the peacemakers in Paris. They expressed the 'deep regret' of the Congress at the terms of the peace proposed at the Conference in Paris, which 'so seriously violate the principles upon which alone a just and lasting peace can be secured'. The Congress recorded its satisfaction that the ideas for the League of Nations (envisaged by the first Women's Congress in The Hague[46]) were now widely accepted, endorsed certain aspects of the proposed League Covenant but regretted other proposals and urged the acceptance of nine conditions for the avoidance of future wars. These included open membership for states, reduction of armaments for all member states and adherence to self-determination in territorial adjustments. Included among *additional principles to strengthen the League* was 'establishment of full equal suffrage and the full equality of women with men politically, socially and economically'. This last was bolstered by the call for a Women's Charter to be included in the Peace Treaty, to recognise 'that the status of women, social, political and economic is of supreme international importance'.

43 In 1919, this became the Women's International League for Peace and Freedom (WILPF), now the oldest women's peace and human rights non-governmental organisation (NGO).

44 *Rapport du Congrès International de Femmes* (Women's International League for Peace and Freedom Congress, Zurich 1919) at https://wilpf.de/docs/Congress-of-Zurich-Fertig.pdf.

45 Ibid., at 241 ff.

46 The resolutions adopted at The Hague included the proposal for a 'permanent International Conference holding regular meetings in which women should take part, to deal not with the rules of warfare but with practical proposals for further international cooperation among the states'. Resolutions adopted by the International Congress of Women (*supra* n 40).

The women who met at The Hague and at Zurich offered a vision of an international organisation that would work openly, where 'peoples of the nations would have a direct democratic influence', and that would transcend national interests.[47] They were not perfect and were in many ways products of their own time and class.[48] Nor were they under any illusions that their resolutions would be heeded. In the words of one delegate: 'In Paris no one will care what we decide here',[49] but their critique of the international order continues to resonate today. Their radical vision for a progressive international legal order was accompanied by ongoing work for the advancement of women. Throughout the period of the League of Nations and the early years of the International Labour Organization,[50] women continued to lobby for social justice, for peace, disarmament and indeed for a 'new international order'.[51] They also continued to address matters of particular importance to women – labour conditions for working women, suppression of human trafficking, nationality rights of married women, to name just a few – thereby maintaining visibility and their belief that women must be central to international affairs.

Turning to the UN era, 'women's participation in promoting world peace' was taken up in the First World Conference on Women in Mexico City in 1975[52] – the UN's International

[47] Jo Vellacott, 'A Place for Pacifism and Transnationalism in Feminist Theory: The Early Work of the Women's International League for Peace and Freedom', 2 *Women's History Review* (1993) 23–56, 35.

[48] E.g. resolutions adopted at The Hague included reference to 'primitive peoples' and those in Zurich to 'backward races'. In its early years, WILPF worked with the International Labour Organization on combating racism and continues to do so.

[49] Dr Anita Augspurg cited Vellacott (*supra* n 47) at 39.

[50] Created by the Treaty of Versailles, 28 June 1919, Part XIII, Constitution of the International Labour Organization.

[51] Sheri Labenski, '"The World Is Not Organised for Peace": Exploring the 1924 "New International Order"', blog post (28 May 2019) at https://blogs.lse.ac.uk/wps/2019/05/28/the-world-is-not-organised-for-peace-exploring-the-the-new-international-order/.

[52] 'Encouraging more active participation by women in intergovernmental and non-governmental organizations working for the strengthening of international peace and co-operation ... Urges Governments ... [t]o provide women with equal opportunities with men to represent their countries in all international forums where the issues of international peace and co-operation are discussed and in particular in the meetings of the organizations of the United

Women's Year. Four years later, the Convention on the Elimination of All Forms of Discrimination against Women (CEDAW)[53] confirmed the instrumental linkage between women and peace and security; on the one hand affirming in its preamble that 'strengthening of international peace and security ... will promote social progress and development and as a consequence will contribute to the attainment of full equality between men and women' and on the other expressing states' conviction that 'the cause of peace require[s] the maximum participation of women on equal terms with men in all fields'.

The Convention, however, had no substantive provisions directly relevant to women and armed conflict or to violence against women more generally. The rhetorical trend continued through the identification of women and peace as a major area for UN activity by the Third World Conference on Women in Nairobi in 1985 at the end of what had become the designated UN Decade for Women.[54] But it was in the following decade that gender-based violence against women – omitted from CEDAW[55] – was brought directly into international affairs, including into relevant regimes of international law, international humanitarian law (IHL),[56] human rights law and the increasingly important international criminal law. A significant step forward was made at Vienna in 1993 where the World Conference on Human Rights asserted that '[v]iolations of the human rights of women in situations of armed conflict are violations of the fundamental principles of international human rights and humanitarian law. All violations of this kind, including in particular murder, systematic rape, sexual

Nations and all conferences on disarmament and international peace and other regional bodies.'

Report of the World Conference of the International Women's Year, Mexico City, 19 June–2 July 1975 at www.un.org/womenwatch/daw/beijing/otherconferences/Mexico/Mexico%20conference%20report%20optimized.pdf.

53 New York, 18 December 1979, UNTS 1249, 13.

54 Report of the World Conference to Review and Appraise the Achievements of the United Nations Decade for Women: Equality, Development and Peace, Nairobi, 15–26 July 1985 (United Nations, 1986) para 13 provides a feminist understanding of peace; see, further, chapter 3.

55 Gender-based violence against women was brought into CEDAW by the CEDAW Committee in its General Recommendation No. 19, Violence against women, 11th session, 1992.

56 Rape and other forms of sexual violence had long been included within IHL; see chapter 4.

slavery, and forced pregnancy, require a particularly effective response.'[57] Against the backdrop of the violence of the 'new wars'[58] of the early 1990s in the former Yugoslavia, Somalia, Haiti, Rwanda and elsewhere and reports of the incidence of associated sexual violence, women's organisations pressed for more systematic inclusion of women's experiences in decision-making about armed conflict. There was success in the adoption of *Women and armed conflict* as a Critical Area of Concern at the Fourth World Conference on Women in Beijing in 1995. The Beijing Platform for Action – the blueprint for women's advancement – asserts that '[p]eace is inextricably linked with equality between women and men and development'.[59] It reiterates the wording of the Vienna Declaration with respect to violations of women's human rights in armed conflict constituting violations of both IHL and human rights.[60] Increased participation by women in conflict resolution at decision-making levels and the protection of women in armed conflict or living under foreign occupation are set out as Strategic objective E. 1. Governments, international and regional organisations are to 'take action to promote equal participation of women and equal opportunities for women to participate in all forums and peace activities at all levels'.[61] In an echo of women's demands in 1915 and 1919 (and in recognition of the leading role played by women in the peace movement), the Beijing Platform for Action also looks for reduction in excessive military expenditure and regulation of armaments and posits that governments 'work actively towards general and complete disarmament under strict and effective international control'.[62] Further, it seeks promotion of 'women's contribution to fostering a culture of peace'.

Following Beijing, women activists sought to ensure appropriate implementation by states and international institutions. But this was slow; especially galling was that the Dayton Peace Agreement – the high-profile peace agreement that was brokered by the United States to bring an end to the war in Bosnia and Herzegovina and

[57] World Conference on Human Rights, Vienna Declaration and Programme of Action, 25 June 1993, II, para 38.

[58] Mary Kaldor, *New and Old Wars: Organised Violence in a Global Era* (Polity Press, 3rd ed. 2012).

[59] Fourth World Conference on Women, Beijing Declaration and Platform for Action, 1995, para 131.

[60] Ibid., at para 132. [61] Ibid., at para 142 (a). [62] Ibid., at para 143 (f) (i).

was concluded only just over two months after Beijing in November 1995[63] – included no local women in the negotiations.[64] The lengthy document made only very limited reference to women and girls despite the high publicity given to detentions of women and girls and repeated crimes of sexual violence committed against them during that conflict.[65] Women in NGOs[66] and activists initiated campaigns, formed partnerships and coalitions,[67] worked through regional meetings preparing for Beijing + 5, sought member state support through the Commission on the Status of Women and collaborated with the United Nations Development Fund for Women (UNIFEM) for endorsement of their demands. Attention turned to the Security Council. The then Council members were lobbied and the case for a Security Council resolution presented at an '*arria*' formula meeting chaired by Ambassador Patricia Durrant, Permanent Representative of Jamaica. Relevant documentation was provided to back up the women's arguments.[68] Bangladesh secured the issue onto the Council's agenda during its presidency and subsequently Namibia took the lead, in line with the interest it had already shown in hosting a meeting on 'Mainstreaming a Gender Perspective in Multidimensional Peace Support Operations' in May 2000.[69]

The journey towards the adoption of resolution 1325 was thus made over nearly a century, through women's activism for peace and securing their own political and economic status, institutional

63 General Framework Agreement for Peace for Bosnia and Herzegovina, Dayton, initialled 21 November 1995, signed, Paris, 14 December 1995.

64 Only one woman participated at Dayton – from the UK Foreign and Commonwealth Office.

65 The 1957 Convention on the Nationality of Married Women and CEDAW are listed as human rights treaties applicable in Bosnia and Herzegovina; General Framework Agreement for Peace for Bosnia and Herzegovina, Annex Four, Constitution of Bosnia and Herzegovina; Annex Six, Agreement on Human Rights.

66 Leading NGOs were International Alert, the Women's International League for Peace and Freedom, The Hague Appeal for Peace, Amnesty International and the Women's Commission for Refugee Women and Children; Sanam Naraghi Anderlini, 'Civil Society's Leadership in Adopting 1325 Resolution', in Sara E. Davies and Jacqui True (eds.) *The Oxford Handbook of Women, Peace and Security* (Oxford University Press, 2019) 38–52, 44.

67 Especially important was the NGO Coalition on Women and International Peace and Security.

68 Anderlini (*supra* n 66) 38–52, 46.

69 Windhoek Declaration, on the 10th Anniversary of the United Nations Transitional Assistance Group, Windhoek, Namibia, 31 May 2000.

manoeuvring and bringing objectives first articulated through their own channels into the soft law instruments of global summit meetings. While success in achieving resolution 1325 owes much to the story outlined here, it must also be admitted that the timing was propitious. The end of the cold war had opened a window for social reform movements, as seen in the outcomes of the global summits held throughout the 1990s.[70] It had also contributed to the outbreak of so-called 'new wars' in Africa, the former Yugoslavia, Haiti, the Caucuses and elsewhere that were characterised by extreme violence against civilian populations, including sexual violence.[71] In response, the Security Council had already, by 2000, adopted thematic resolutions with respect to children and armed conflict and the protection of civilians in armed conflict. It had established the ad hoc international criminal tribunals for former Yugoslavia and Rwanda and agreed the hybrid court for Sierra Leone, with crimes of sexual violence included within the jurisdiction of these newly created tribunals. In 1998, the Rome Statute of the International Criminal Court (ICC) had been adopted, advancing international criminal law with more detailed provisions relating to the prosecution of multiple forms of crimes of sexual violence.[72] Measures directed toward enhancing civilian protection, individual criminal accountability and gender equality had already to some extent shifted the Council away from a focus on state security to one that takes account of the violence that is targeted at peoples – human security[73] – and brought humanitarian concerns into its decision-making.[74] In this

[70] In addition to the Vienna World Conference on Human Rights and the Beijing Fourth World Conference on Women, other global summits convened in the 1990s include: UN World Summit for Children, New York, 1990; UN Conference on Environment and Development, Rio de Janeiro, 1992; UN International Conference on Population and Development, Cairo, 1994; World Summit for Social Development, Copenhagen, 1995.

[71] Christine Chinkin and Mary Kaldor, *International Law and New Wars* (Cambridge University Press, 2017) chapter 1.

[72] Rome Statute of the International Criminal Court, 1998, articles 7 (1) (g) and (h); 8 (2) (b) (xxi) and (xxii); 8 (2) (e) (vi).

[73] The Security Council did not designate its measures in these terms, but institutional and academic writing in the 1990s was exploring the concept of human security; Chinkin and Kaldor (*supra* n 71) chapter 11.

[74] E.g. UN Security Council resolution 688, 5 April 1991 ('magnitude of human suffering'); UN Security Council resolution 794, 3 December 1992 ('magnitude of the human tragedy', 'deterioration of the humanitarian situation').

sense, civil society found fertile ground in advocating for what became resolution 1325.[75]

However, as we can see with hindsight, 2000 was a pivotal moment when a more human rights-based approach to security seemed possible; less than twelve months after the adoption of resolution 1325, the terrorist attacks of 11 September 2001 in New York and Washington were committed, leading to heightened national security concerns especially in the United States. The attacks greatly reduced the post-cold war optimism in the values of the so-called liberal peace – democracy, human rights and rule of law – the framework into which 1325 had readily fitted. More stringent measures to tackle terrorism[76] and the military interventions into Afghanistan (2001) and Iraq (2003) followed quickly after. An environment of hegemonic masculinity,[77] militarism and security defined in terms of national security against terrorist acts came to prevail. The radical and transformative peace agenda that was the start of the journey towards resolution 1325 was inevitably at odds with this changed geopolitical landscape. The tension between the goals of those who campaigned for what became resolution 1325 and the conservative, militaristic Security Council with the primary responsibility for the maintenance of international peace and security will be considered throughout the book. But, first, the content of the ten WPS resolutions will be described in more detail.

1.3 The WPS Resolutions 2000–2019

1.3.1 The Four Pillars of WPS

So what is the content of the ten successive and accumulative resolutions that form the WPS agenda? The texts are rich and detailed and have become progressively longer in both their preambles and their operative paragraphs. Some resolutions repeat and progress issues addressed in their predecessor resolutions while other issues are introduced in one resolution and disappear

[75] Christine Chinkin, 'Adoption of 1325 Resolution', in Sara E. Davies and Jacqui True (eds.) *The Oxford Handbook of Women, Peace and Security* (Oxford University Press, 2019) 26–37, 33.

[76] E.g. UN Security Council resolution, 1373, 28 September 2001.

[77] R. W. Connell and James W. Messerschmidt, 'Hegemonic Masculinity: Rethinking the Concept', 19 *Gender and Society* (2005) 829–59.

from subsequent resolutions or make only sporadic reappearances. Security Council resolutions are intensely negotiated and the changing membership of the ten non-permanent member states means that different states have been engaged in the process over the years. Some resolutions have been at the behest of a permanent member state (for example resolution 1820 (2008) was sponsored by the United States, resolution 2106 (2013) by the UK) while others have been brought forward by non-permanent member states wishing to make a lasting mark during their Council membership (for example resolution 2122 (2013) by Azerbaijan, resolution 2467 (2019) by Germany and resolution 2493 (2019) by South Africa). These factors all contribute to the lack of orderly progression between the resolutions. This section cannot recount the many issues, nuances and swings in language across the ten WPS resolutions. However, it deals in some more detail with the first two WPS resolutions, 1325 (2000) and 1820 (2008), and then highlights some aspects of the later resolutions. Ultimately, there can be no substitute for reading them.

Resolution 1325 has three main substantive themes: gender balance, gender mainstreaming (or taking a gender perspective) and ending perpetrator impunity. Gender balance is about numbers. Resolution 1325 urges states to ensure women's representation and participation in all stages and at all levels in institutions and mechanisms for conflict prevention, management and resolution. The Secretary-General is urged to appoint more women as UN special representatives and envoys and to enhance the role and contribution of women in United Nations field-based operations. In making women's participation and representation in international affairs its leading objective, resolution 1325 is reminiscent of the demands made consistently by women campaigners from the International Women's Congress in The Hague in 1915 through to Beijing eighty years later. The latter is expressly noted in the preamble, but the former is not.

Taking a 'gender perspective' is taking account of what are called the 'special needs of women and girls' in post-conflict processes, repatriation, resettlement, rehabilitation, reintegration and state-building, in particular measures that ensure the protection of and respect for human rights of women and girls, as they relate to the constitution, the electoral system, the police and the judiciary. Resolution 1325 also expresses the Council's willingness to 'incorporate a gender perspective' into peacekeeping operations. It emphasises the responsibility of states for prosecution of those responsible for genocide, crimes against humanity and war crimes, including those relating to sexual and other violence against women and girls, and thus for ending impunity for these crimes. In acknowledgement of what is often a controversial issue in peace negotiations, the resolution stresses the need to exclude these crimes from amnesty provisions. This last provision is, however, weakened by the inclusion of the weasel words: 'whenever feasible'.

Subsequent WPS resolutions have both complemented and in some ways detracted from resolution 1325. In the next WPS resolution, 1820, adopted in 2008, attention shifted explicitly to sexual violence and protection of women and girls from such violence. The resolution expounds that when sexual violence is used or commissioned as a tactic of war in order to deliberately target civilians, or as part of a widespread or systematic attack against civilian populations, it can significantly exacerbate situations of armed conflict and may impede the restoration of international peace and security. Accordingly, 'effective steps to prevent and respond to such acts of sexual violence can significantly contribute to the maintenance of international peace and security'. It suggests some such steps, including a series of preventive measures relating especially to military vetting, discipline and command responsibility, and repeats its calls to states to prosecute and punish perpetrators of crimes of sexual violence as war crimes, crimes against humanity and genocide and to exclude these crimes from amnesties, but this time omitting the condition of feasibility. It affirms the Council's intention to take into account the appropriateness of targeted sanctions against those who commit such crimes. In this, it differs from resolution 1325, which had indicated that the Council would take into account the impact of sanctions mandated under UN Charter article 41 on the civilian population. In contrast, resolution 1820 turns to the potential imposition of sanctions on those who commit sexual violence in armed conflict. Resolution 1820 is also linked to another agenda, that for combating sexual exploitation and abuse (SEA) by UN peacekeepers. It reinforces the 'zero tolerance' policy instigated by the Secretary-General[78] and urges troop-contributing states to take preventive measures.

[78] Secretary-General's Bulletin, *Special measures for protection from sexual exploitation and sexual abuse*, ST/SGB/2003/13, 9 October 2003.

The subsequent WPS resolutions tend to amplify one or other of these two narratives of the women's movement through the twentieth century: either calling for enhanced participation by women in a variety of additional institutions and mechanisms[79] or seeking further means of prevention of and protection against conflict-related sexual violence. Resolutions 1889 (2009), 2122 (2013) and 2242 (2015) are especially oriented towards the former and resolutions 1888 (2009), 1960 (2010), 2106 (2013) and 2467 (2019) towards the latter. Resolution 2122 (2013) has a somewhat different tone from the other WPS resolutions in that it is primarily addressed to the Council itself in expressing its own intention to do more to implement the earlier resolutions.

A further theme of immediate relief and more long-term recovery for survivors is present across the resolutions. Survivors' welfare is first addressed in resolution 1820 (2008) where, in general terms, relevant parties are urged to support the development of systems to provide 'sustainable assistance' to victims of conflict-affected sexual violence. Resolution 1888 (2013) is more specific in encouraging states to 'increase access to health care, psychosocial support, legal assistance and socio-economic reintegration services for victims of sexual violence, in particular in rural areas', as well as more generally 'to build national capacity in the judicial and law enforcement systems'. Similar provisions are included in the subsequent resolutions with the more specific, but intermittent, inclusion of livelihood support. Resolution 2106 (2013) goes further than the other resolutions in its recognition that 'timely assistance' is needed for survivors and, accordingly, United Nations entities and donors are urged 'to provide non-discriminatory and comprehensive health services, including sexual and reproductive health'.[80] This language, implicitly accepting the vital need for abortion services for women survivors of sexual violence, was both celebrated and contested. It has not been repeated in the operative paragraphs of later resolutions, although the preamble of resolution 2122 (2013) is

[79] E.g. UN Security Council resolution 1889 (2009) in political and economic decision-making, aid management and planning, in good offices of the Secretary-General; UN Security Council resolution 2122 (2013) at senior levels as United Nations mediators and within the composition of United Nations mediation teams; UN Security Council resolution 2467 (2019) in transitional justice programmes.

[80] UN Security Council resolution 2106 (2013) para 19.

explicit, noting 'the need for access to the full range of sexual and reproductive health services, including regarding pregnancies resulting from rape, without discrimination'.

Taking the resolutions together, it is often asserted that there are four substantive pillars relating to women in armed conflict that comprise the WPS agenda: women's participation and representation; prevention of sexual violence in conflict and prevention of conflict; protection against sexual violence in conflict; and relief and recovery. This structure is helpful, but it is not the only one applied to the WPS agenda. Another analysis is that WPS comprises four themes: gender-based violence; access to decision-making; peacekeeping operations; and disarmament, demobilisation and reintegration (DDR).[81] Whatever categorisation is preferred, it should not be adhered to too strictly as there are no definitive demarcations between topics and there is considerable overlap among them.

1.3.2 Women's Empowerment

CEDAW moves beyond the earlier UN human rights instruments that prohibit discrimination on, inter alia, grounds of sex to the more progressive and positive obligation that states parties take appropriate measures for the 'full development and advancement of women'.[82] This is for women's benefit – to guarantee their exercise and enjoyment of human rights and fundamental freedoms on a basis of equality with men. In the Beijing Declaration, states went further, dedicating themselves 'unreservedly' to enhancing the 'empowerment and advancement of women all over the world'.[83] This was also given substance for it was understood as contributing 'to the moral, ethical, spiritual and intellectual needs of women and men, individually or in community with others and thereby guaranteeing them the possibility of realizing their full potential in society and shaping their lives in accordance with their own aspirations'.[84]

Much of the focus of the WPS agenda is on the protection of women and their 'special needs' rather than on their empowerment.

[81] Malathi de Alwis, Julie Mertus and Tazreena Sajjad, 'Women and Peace Processes', in Carol Cohn (ed.) *Women and Wars* (Polity Press, 2013) 169–93, 183.

[82] CEDAW, article 3. [83] Beijing Declaration, 1995, para 7. [84] Ibid., at para 12.

Even provisions urging women's participation and representation are phrased instrumentally in that they are said to be important for the 'prevention and resolution of conflicts and in peace-building' rather than for women's advancement. Empowerment does not enter the WPS lexicon until the preamble of resolution 1888 (2009) where it is instrumentally recognised that 'promotion and empowerment of women and . . . support for women's organizations and networks are essential in the consolidation of peace'. Resolution 1889 (2009) softens this instrumentality by stressing that women's empowerment in peacebuilding must be addressed as well as their protection. To this end, it urges states, UN bodies, donors and civil society to take women's empowerment into account in planning for post-conflict needs. Similar provisions are included in some of the later resolutions,[85] although instrumentalisation persists and empowerment is not unreservedly exhorted in women's own interests. For instance, in resolution 2122 (2013) it is asserted that women's economic empowerment 'greatly contributes to the stabilization of societies emerging from armed conflict'; resolution 2242 (2015) reaffirms that 'women's and girls' empowerment and gender equality are critical to conflict prevention and broader efforts to maintain international peace and security'. Resolution 2467 (2019) changes the language somewhat in asserting gender equality and women's empowerment (political, social and economic) to be critical to prevention of and responses to conflict-affected sexual violence, as well as to their meaningful participation in peace processes and conflict prevention. In resolution 2493 (2019), states are called upon to provide aid for the furtherance of gender equality and women's economic empowerment.

Throughout the resolutions where the Security Council champions women's empowerment, it is not clarified what is meant by the term. Is it economic, social or political empowerment, or all three? The Council does not refer to the expansive understanding of empowerment jointly crafted by the CEDAW Committee and the Committee on the Rights of the Child (CRC).[86] Central to

[85] Women's empowerment is not included in UN Security Council resolutions 1960 (2010) and 2106 (2013).

[86] Joint General Recommendation No. 31 of the Committee on the Elimination of Discrimination against Women/General Comment No. 18 of the Committee on the Rights of the Child on harmful practices, CEDAW/C/GC/31-CRC/C/GC/18, 14 November 2014, paras 61–9.

empowerment in the view of the two expert Committees is the state obligation to 'challenge and change patriarchal ideologies and structures' that prevent the enjoyment of human rights: 'Women can be empowered only by winning the battle against those opposed to their empowerment.'[87] Women and girls must therefore be equipped with the training and skills to make freely their own informed choices about their lives. The importance of personal autonomy is also key to Naila Kabeer's discussion of empowerment, which highlights 'the ability to make strategic life choices where this was previously denied'. Empowerment is a process, not a goal. It encompasses three interconnected elements: 'acquiring and accessing resources (material and social); individual and collective agency (through a process of reflection and action); and achievements (the outcomes of choices) all of which interact with structural inequalities and underlying distribution of power'.[88] Kabeer's explanation, like that of the CEDAW Committee and the CRC, highlights that economic enhancement of itself does not constitute empowerment and indeed is limiting if it fails to take account of the other factors. Education and training are important, as is the availability of 'safe spaces' where women and girls can talk freely about their aspirations and fears. The empowerment of individual women should not be equated with addressing the collective situation of women or redressing societal power imbalance.[89] In resolution 2242 (2015), the Security Council welcomed the emphasis on women's empowerment and gender equality in the General Assembly's adoption of the Sustainable Development Goals (SDGs),[90] thus recognising the nexus between these two agendas. But this is not continued in the two resolutions adopted in 2019, resolution 2467 and resolution 2493. Nor does the Council provide

87 Abraham D. Sofaer, '"Mainstreaming" Women through U.N. Security Council Resolutions: Comments on a Paper by Haynes, Cahn, & Ni Aoláin', 11 *Santa Clara Journal of International Law* (2012) 219–23, 223.

88 Naila Kabeer, 'Resources, Agency, Achievements: Reflections on the Measurement of Women's Empowerment', 30 *Development and Change* (1999) 435.

89 Andrea Cornwall, panel presentation, 'Reconciliation, Empowerment and Transformation', Convention of the UKRI GCRF Gender, Justice and Security Research Hub, Colombo, January 2020.

90 UN General Assembly resolution 70/1, 25 September 2015, *Transforming our world: the 2030 Agenda for Sustainable Development.* SDG 5: 'Achieve gender equality and empower all women and girls.'

its own blueprint for attainment of women's empowerment, entrusting work on this front to UN Women.[91]

1.3.3 A Changed Peace and Security Environment

In 2013, the Security Council invited the Secretary-General to commission a global study as preparation for a high-level review of the progress made in implementing resolution 1325.[92] The ensuing independent *Global Study* provided a detailed analysis of the full range of issues encompassed within the WPS agenda within the context of changes since 2000 in the nature of conflict, of security and of peace.[93] It also addressed the woeful level of funding that states had committed to implementing WPS and showed that rhetorical support was not matched by action. Resolution 2242 was adopted following the promised High-level Review where a plethora of speakers voiced their support for resolution 1325 and the subsequent resolutions. Resolution 2242 both expands the WPS agenda and, to some extent, realigns the original emphasis in resolution 1325 on women's participation and conflict prevention. It links WPS as a cross-cutting theme to other contemporary, global security concerns such as increasing flows of refugees and internally displaced persons (IDPs), health pandemics and the impact of climate change. But the resolution makes minimal reference to what the *Global Study* had understood as the changed nature of peace, which demands inclusivity and justice and which privileges human rights. It recognises within the preamble that human rights are essential to implementation of resolution 1325 and reaffirms the human rights obligations of states and all parties to conflict. The operative paragraphs, however, do not build on this and address human rights only through encouragement to states to include them within their National Action Plans (NAPs).

[91] Hilary Charlesworth and Christine Chinkin, 'The New United Nations "Gender Architecture": A Room with a View?' 17 *Max Planck Yearbook of United Nations Law* (2013) 1–60.

[92] UN Security Council resolution 2122 (2013) para 16: 'Invites the Secretary-General, in preparation for the High-level Review to commission a global study on the implementation of resolution 1325 (2000), highlighting good practice examples, implementation gaps and challenges, as well as emerging trends and priorities for action.'

[93] *Global Study* (*supra* n 25) at 20–25.

That said, resolution 2242 (2015) does break new ground in addressing another change in the security environment that poses a further threat to women in armed conflict. In 2014, the military attacks by the Islamic State in Iraq and the Levant (ISIL, ISIS or Daesh) across Syria and Northern Iraq, especially the genocidal killings and abductions of the Yazidi peoples, had shocked and alarmed the United Nations. The Secretary-General's 2015 Report on Conflict-affected Sexual Violence[94] had highlighted the perpetration of sexual violence by non-state armed groups, including those pursuing extremist ideologies, and the need to destroy the capacity of such groups. ISIS, Al-Shabaab, Boko Haram, Ansar Dine and Al-Qaida affiliates were particularly identified. Resolution 2242 echoes the gravity of this concern and includes threats to international peace and security caused by terrorist acts as another cross-cutting theme. The Council recognised that many acts of terrorism and violent extremism are gendered in the targeting of women and girls and the denial of their human rights to health, education and participation in public life. Sexual and gender-based violence is part of the strategic objectives and ideology of some terrorist groups that use it deliberately as a way to increase their power. Sexual violence as a tactic of terror now sits alongside it as a tactic of war. The resolution calls for greater integration by states and the United Nations of their WPS agendas with those for counterterrorism and countering violent extremism.

In 2016, the Security Council addressed human trafficking for the first time. It recognised the linkage between human trafficking, especially of women and girls, and armed conflict, in particular with the strategies and ideologies of terrorist and extremist groups. It affirmed that those who had been trafficked by terrorist groups should be classified as victims of terrorism and as such be eligible for official support and redress. This recognition is not explicitly accorded to victims of sexual violence as a tactic of war, or other victims of trafficking, thereby apparently creating a hierarchy of victims. Surprisingly, the Council did not directly align human trafficking with the WPS agenda.[95]

[94] Report of the Secretary-General, *Conflict-related sexual violence*, S/2015/203, 23 March 2015, para 8.

[95] UN Security Council resolution 2331, 20 December 2016, *Maintenance of International Peace and Security* reiterates 'the critical importance of all Member States fully implementing relevant Security Council resolutions, ... as well as

WPS resolution 2467 (2019) was adopted in the still further changed geopolitical environment of 2019 largely (but not exclusively) associated with the US administration of President Trump.[96] The rise of populism and of right-wing governments across the globe has seen a retreat from the multilateralism, treaty obligations and commitment to human rights associated with liberal internationalism. There has also been a use and abuse of gender ideology to assert 'family values', rejection of women's sexual and reproductive rights and lethal attacks on women's human rights defenders.[97] Negotiations were highly charged and contested. Unlike all previous WPS resolutions, 2467 was not adopted unanimously, with Russia and China both abstaining. The United States threatened to veto the resolution unless certain compromises were made. The resolution makes no direct mention of women's sexual and reproductive rights.

Like resolution 2242 (2015), resolution 2467 stresses sexual violence as a tactic of terror as well as a tactic of war. It seeks cooperation between the Counter-Terrorism Committee Executive Directorate (CTED), the Counter Terrorism Committee, the UN Office on Drugs and Crime, the Special Representative of the Secretary-General (SRSG) on Sexual Violence in Conflict and UN Women in including details of how member states are addressing trafficking by terrorist groups and its linkages with conflict-affected sexual violence into CTED's country assessments. The Council thus seeks to bring together the UN's machinery for combating terrorism, organised crime and conflict-affected sexual violence with its body for the empowerment of women, UN Women. This mix has the benefit of promoting coherent agendas, but it risks subordinating gender equality to these other agendas and prioritising a criminal-law orientation to combating trafficking to the detriment of a human rights approach.

2242 (2015), which expresses concern that acts of sexual and gender-based violence are known to be part of the strategic objectives and ideology of certain terrorist groups'. See also UN Security Council resolution 2388, 21 November 2017, *Maintenance of International Peace and Security*.

96 Jack Goldsmith and Shannon Togawa Mercer, 'International Law and Institutions in the Trump Era', 61 *German Yearbook of International Law* (2018) 11–39.

97 Report of the Special Rapporteur on the situation of human rights defenders, *Situation of women human rights defenders*, A/HRC/40/60, 10 January 2019.

Resolution 2467 is also innovative.[98] It embraces for the first time the need for a 'survivor-centred' approach to preventing and responding to sexual violence in armed conflict; it engages the language of rights in urging states to recognise the 'equal rights of all individuals affected by sexual violence in armed conflict, including women, girls and [for the first time] children born of sexual violence in armed conflict'; it is the first WPS resolution since 1325 to incorporate CEDAW directly into the operative paragraphs; it provides more detail with respect to ensuring survivors' access to justice and suggests a number of reforms that could be undertaken at the national level to strengthen the fight against impunity. Six months later, UN Security Council resolution 2493 (2019) again refers to CEDAW only in the preamble. The wording of this last resolution, introduced by South Africa, was again contested, but the resolution was nevertheless adopted by consensus. The resulting text is bland. It is primarily concerned with setting the scene for the twentieth anniversary of the adoption of resolution 1325 in 2000. As in resolution 2467, there is no place for explicit inclusion of women's sexual and reproductive rights.[99] Following the resolution's adoption, the United States took the unusual step of making a statement[100] that it could not 'accept references to "sexual and reproductive health," nor any references to "safe termination of pregnancy" or language that would promote abortion or suggest a right to abortion'. This major denial of women's rights is exacerbated by the context of conflict-affected sexual violence, which makes offensive the suggestion that abortion is not an acceptable form of family planning. Resolution 2493 does, however, call upon states to promote women's rights, including civil, political and, exceptionally, economic rights.

[98] Christine Chinkin and Madeleine Rees, Commentary on Security Council Resolution 2467: Continued State Obligation and Civil Society Action on Sexual Violence in Conflict (LSE Centre for Women, Peace and Security and Women's International League for Peace and Freedom, 2019) at www.lse.ac.uk/women-peace-security/assets/documents/2019/reports/WPS-Commentary-Report-online.pdf.

[99] Language in resolution 2467 (2019) can be interpreted as upholding its continuation; Chinkin and Rees (*supra* n 98).

[100] US Mission to the UN, Explanation of Vote on the Adoption of UN Security Council Resolution on Women, Peace and Security at https://usun.usmission.gov/explanation-of-vote-on-the-adoption-of-the-un-security-council-resolution-on-women-peace-and-security/.

1.3.4 Institutional Measures

The WPS agenda is directed at states, UN agencies, donors and civil society. Alongside the substantive provisions, a number of institutional reforms have been progressed since 2000. These include the creation of new positions, most significantly the mandating of the Secretary-General's Special Representative (SRSG) on Conflict-related Sexual Violence to bring coherence and leadership, to coordinate UN mechanisms and to engage in advocacy.[101] The SRSG reports annually to the Security Council on overall trends with respect to conflict-related sexual violence and on the situation in specific places, including some not on the Council's agenda. This is significant as it extends the reach of the WPS agenda beyond the Council's remit and was prefigured in resolution 1325, which contained no such limitation. The reports include an annex of listed people and groups, parties to armed conflict, who are 'credibly suspected of committing or being responsible for acts of rape or other forms of sexual violence'. This serves an initial purpose of 'naming and shaming', but the Council has also expressed an intention to use the lists as the basis for further, more focused engagement including the possibility of sanctions.[102] In subsequent resolutions, the Council has urged its sanctions committees to 'apply targeted sanctions against those who perpetrate and direct sexual violence in conflict'[103] and to ensure sexual violence and gender expertise within the committees.[104] The Council has brought criteria relating to serious sexual violence now into sanctions regimes in the Central African Republic, Libya, Somalia and South Sudan.[105] The UN deploys teams of experts on sexual violence and the rule of law to conflict zones where there are concerns about sexual violence, to work with the national authorities in strengthening the rule of law and in addressing perpetrator impunity.[106] The teams report to the

[101] UN Security Council resolution 1888 (2008).
[102] UN Security Council resolution 1960 (2010).
[103] UN Security Council resolution 2106 (2013); see also UN Security Council resolution 2467 (2019) paras 10 and 11.
[104] UN Security Council resolution 2242 (2015).
[105] Report of the Secretary-General, *Conflict-related Sexual Violence*, S/2019/280, 29 March 2019, para 30.
[106] UN Security Council resolution 1888 (2009).

SRSG but seek to foster local responsibility for addressing conflict-affected sexual violence.[107] Women protection advisers have been located within the position of gender advisers in UN peace operations and senior gender advisers within the SRSG's office.[108] The Council has particularly called for budgeting for and recruitment of gender posts in political missions and peacekeeping operations.[109]

Another task given to the Secretary-General by the Council is that of determining indicators and establishing arrangements for monitoring, analysis and reporting on conflict-affected sexual violence and collecting country-specific data. Statistical data are important for providing a baseline, measuring progress and acquiring a snapshot of the situation, but there is also an institutional bureaucratic aspect to the WPS agenda. Indicators are sought and success and failure are measured in terms of numbers of, for instance: allegations of sexual exploitation by peacekeepers; women participants in peace processes, in UN military and security positions; gender advisers or women protection officers appointed to UN missions; references to women in peace agreements; women parliamentarians; countries (or other bodies) with NAPs; or violations of women's and girls' human rights included in the periodic reports by UN peacekeeping or political missions to the Security Council. Technical assistance and training are suggested as remedial measures. Statistical data can provide useful information about the progress (or lack of progress) made by states and other bodies in implementing the resolutions, but numbers do not tell us how women and girls (or men and boys, or those who reject the gender binary) are experiencing peace or (in) security in conflict-affected areas.

The Council has also looked at its own practices and has instituted new processes. In response to the criticism that it fails to

107 United Nations Team of Experts, Rule of Law/Sexual Violence in Conflict, January 2019 at www.un.org/sexualviolenceinconflict/wp-content/uploads/1_2019twopagerforwebsite.pdf.

108 In UN Security Council resolution 2467 (2019), the Council welcomed the efforts made by the SRSG on Conflict-related Sexual Violence, the Team of Experts on Rule of Law and Sexual Violence in Conflict, Women Protection Advisers, and other relevant United Nations entities 'in seeking time-bound commitments and implementation plans by all parties to conflict to prevent and address all acts and forms of sexual violence in conflict and post-conflict situations'.

109 UN Security Council resolution 2242 (2015).

ensure consistently and rigorously that it is fully informed about and can respond appropriately to the relevant in-country issues,[110] it has set up an Informal Expert Group on WPS with UN Women as the Secretariat.[111] This Group enables the Council to receive information from country experts, facilitating a more systematic approach within its own work and providing for greater oversight and coordination of implementation efforts. In resolution 2242 (2015), it expressed its intention to become more accessible to civil society, thereby seeking to reduce the top-down effect of its resolutions.[112] It receives briefings in New York on country-specific situations and – at least in theory – includes consultations with local and international women's groups when on in-country-missions.[113]

From at least the time of resolution 1820 (2008), greater institutional attention has been given to working with civil society to progress the WPS goals (somewhat ironically given that WPS was in its origins a civil society initiative). Resolution 1820 urges states, UN entities and the financial institutions to support local civil society networks in providing assistance to victims of conflict-affected sexual violence. Resolution 2467 (2019) welcomes briefings from civil society on local conditions. It also encourages capacity-building of civil society groups so as to further the community-level protection mechanisms that are formed in conflict situations. Resolution 2493 (2019) calls for support for civil society and encourages the creation of secure environments in which, inter alia, women community leaders, women peacebuilders, political

110 The NGO Working Group on WPS had criticised the Council's level of knowledge of conflict zones about which it is making decisions, especially with respect to women: 'The flow of WPS-related information ... is often absent or superficial, resulting in incomplete and insufficient understanding of the gender dimensions of the conflict and broader conflict dynamics.' NGO Working Group on WPS, *Mapping Women, Peace and Security in the UN Security Council: 2015*, 10 May 2016 at www.womenpeacesecurity.org/.

111 UN Security Council resolution 2242 (2015) para 5 (a).

112 UN Security Council resolution 2242 (2015) para 5 (c). Four years later the Council welcomed the way that this process has enlightened it; UN Security Council resolution 2467 (2019) para 21.

113 UN Security Council resolution 2467 (2019) 'expresses its intention to make better usage of periodical field visits to conflict areas, through the organization of interactive meetings with the local women and women's organizations in the field about the concerns and needs of women in areas of armed conflict ... engage with victims, affected communities and civil society, including women's organizations'.

actors and human rights defenders can carry out their work free from interference, harassment and threats.

WPS is an international agenda that must be implemented at national level. To this end, the Security Council has welcomed the development of NAPs,[114] which were first commended in a presidential statement.[115] Denmark prepared a NAP in 2005 and, as of 2020, there are more than eighty NAPS. Resolution 2467 (2019) encourages states to progress the WPS agenda through fully funded NAPs, reflecting the reality that budgetary allocation is too often omitted. Resolution 2493 weakens this language by suggesting only 'sufficient resources' while encouraging strengthened monitoring and evaluation. The WPS resolutions provide civil society with language and leverage to challenge government action and to pursue the adoption of country NAPs, but the limited traction of thematic resolutions within the Security Council means that they are unlikely ever to occupy the centre stage but will remain subordinate to other political imperatives.

1.4 Omissions from the WPS Resolutions

This account has provided an overview of what is included in the WPS resolutions. But what is just as significant is what has been excluded. Resolution 1325 was campaigned for by some women's NGOs, notably the Women's International League for Peace and Freedom (WILPF), as a peace agenda, but the concept of peace is conspicuously absent. There is no consideration of what peace might or could mean for women, or even mention of some of the main peace concerns of the women in 1915 and 1919: disarmament, militarism and military expenditure. These had not been lost sight of in the intervening years. The preamble to CEDAW affirms the importance of 'general and complete disarmament, in particular

[114] UN Security Council resolution 1889 (2009) '[w]elcom[es] the efforts of Member States in implementing its resolution 1325 (2000) at the national level, including the development of national action plans, and encouraging Member States to continue to pursue such implementation'. This has been repeated in later resolutions.

[115] Statement by the President of the Security Council, S/PRST/2004/40, 28 October 2004: '[T]he Council welcomes the efforts of Member States in implementing resolution 1325 (2000) at the national level, including the development of national action plans'; see also Statement by the President of the Security Council, S/PRST/2005/52, 27 October 2005.

nuclear disarmament under strict and effective international control', and the Beijing Platform for Action asserts the need to reduce military expenditure. There is, however, no mention of the impact of arms in the early WPS resolutions. Later resolutions give preambular acknowledgement of the disproportionate impact of small arms on violence against women and of article 7 of the Arms Trade Treaty,[116] which requires arms-exporting states to take into account the risk of those arms being 'used to commit or facilitate serious acts of gender-based violence or serious acts of violence against women and children'.[117] In 2015, the *Global Study* on implementation of resolution 1325 reported that, in its consultations with women around the world, one message was clear: '[T]he United Nations must take the lead in stopping the process of militarization and militarism that began in 2001 in an ever-increasing cycle of conflict.'[118] The omission of any challenge to militarisation and militarism from the WPS resolutions assumes the importance of military power and potentially military intervention.

The *Global Study* describes WPS as a human rights agenda,[119] but there is limited reference to women's human rights and almost none to economic, social and cultural rights.[120] Delivery of health care, livelihood support and other needs of survivors of sexual violence are described as 'services', not as rights, and, as already suggested, the challenge to sexual and reproductive rights is especially egregious. The impact of the neoliberal economic agenda on armed conflict and violence against women is not addressed.[121] WPS fails to acknowledge the complicity of the states in the global north in policies that uphold the conditions that contribute to conflict and violence. Despite their sponsorship by some states from the global south, the resolutions fail to locate WPS as a postcolonial agenda. These omissions especially weaken the pillar on prevention of conflict (and thus of conflict-related sexual violence)

[116] UN General Assembly resolution 67/234, 2 April 2013, *The Arms Trade Treaty*, article 7 (4).

[117] UN Security Council resolution 2106 (2013); UN Security Council resolution 2467 (2019).

[118] *Global Study*, 17. [119] Ibid., at 15.

[120] UN Security Council resolution 2493 (2019) para 5 '[c]alls on Member States to promote all the rights of women, including civil, political and economic rights'.

[121] Jacqui True, *The Political Economy of Violence against Women* (Oxford University Press, 2012).

and are discussed more fully in Chapter 4. They are all reminders that the Security Council is a political body where the five permanent members – all nuclear-weapon states – hold the veto, understand security in militaristic terms, uphold the demands of multinational corporations and resist challenges to global capitalism and their own power.

1.5 The Concept of 'Women' in International Law

The WPS resolutions constitute a broad agenda that has evolved in a somewhat ad hoc fashion and without clarifying the key concepts – 'women', 'peace' and 'security'. Throughout the resolutions, the understanding of 'women' is not problematised; it is understood through the gender binary of women and girls and men and boys, which raises at least three points for comment.

First is the representation of women and men and thus of femininity and masculinity. It has been observed that since 'women' entered international law as a category, one of three approaches has been taken: protective, corrective and equality.[122] The first presents women as vulnerable, as passive and in need of protection, as for instance in early ILO Conventions,[123] article 27 of the Fourth Geneva Convention[124] and the WPS pillar of protection, with its reference point of women's 'special needs' and appointment of women protection advisers. This approach is silent as to the fact that it is the subordination of women, the pervasiveness of gender stereotypes and structural inequalities that portray women as weak that create situations of vulnerability. It correspondingly presents men as the designated protectors, discounting male violence against women and providing a moral justification for the use of further 'protective' violence. The second approach allows for 'correcting' a perceived wrong against women as in their omission from peace

[122] Natalie Hevener Kaufman, 'International Law and the Status of Women: An Analysis of International Legal Instruments related to the Treatment of Women', 1 *Harvard Women's Law Journal* (1978) 131; Natalie Hevener, 'An Analysis of Gender-Based Treaty Law: Contemporary Developments in Historical Perspective', 8 *Human Rights Law Quarterly* (1986) 70.

[123] E.g. in 1919, the ILO adopted Conventions No. 3 on maternity protection, and No. 4 on night work for women. Both were revised in later years.

[124] Convention Relative to the Protection of Civilian Persons, Geneva, 1949, article 27: 'Women shall be especially protected against any attack on their honour, in particular against rape, enforced prostitution, or any form of indecent assault.'

processes and corrective calls for women's participation. This has the upside of denoting women as active agents who contribute positively to societal change, but it maintains the presumption of women as inherently peaceful (passive) and peacemakers. It also 'corrects' by bringing women into already existing structures and processes without questioning whether it is in fact those that need correcting. This is discussed further in Chapter 3. The third – equality – is the human rights position as exemplified in CEDAW, which is integrated into WPS, at least in resolutions 1325 (2000) and 2467 (2019).[125] However, it is noticeable that, in calling for women's participation and representation, the WPS resolutions do not call for women's 'equal' participation, hence my labelling of this as a 'corrective' rather than an 'equality' stance. Similarly, encouragement of women's empowerment and leadership is a corrective method, but, as with participation, the resolutions offer no concrete measures or timelines for progress toward its achievement.

Where the resolutions use the language of equality, it is as 'gender' (rather than 'sex') equality.[126] This raises the second point. The language of 'gender' is used throughout WPS, not just with respect to equality but in many other ways: 'gender perspective', 'gender balance', 'gender issues', 'gender-biased', 'gender-based violence', 'gender dimensions', 'gender-related', 'gender advisers' and others. 'Gender' has been a controversial concept in international law. CEDAW does not use the term and, in requiring women's equality with men, the Convention is situated squarely within the binary assumption of women/men. But, in identifying gender-based violence as 'violence that ... affects women disproportionately',[127] the CEDAW Committee recognised the concept as relational. The definition of gender was hotly contested in negotiations for the ICC at

[125] After UN Security Council resolution 1325 (2000), CEDAW was not again directly referenced in the operative paragraphs of a WPS resolution until UN Security Council resolution 2467 (2019).

[126] CEDAW, article 1 defines discrimination in terms of sex. The CEDAW Committee subsequently asserted the Convention to be directed at eliminating discrimination on the basis of sex and gender; CEDAW Committee, General Recommendation No. 28 on the core obligations of States parties under article 2 of the Convention on the Elimination of All Forms of Discrimination against Women, CEDAW/C/GC/28, 16 December 2010, para 3.

[127] CEDAW Committee, General Recommendation No. 19, Violence against women, 11th session, 1992.

Rome in 1998. As adopted, the Rome Statute reverts to the binary distinction, as the term 'refers to the two sexes, male and female, within the context of society. The term "gender" does not indicate any meaning different from the above.'[128] The CEDAW Committee returned to the issue in 2010 in its General Recommendation No. 28, where it explained that 'gender' means

> socially constructed identities, attributes and roles for women and men and society's social and cultural meaning for these biological differences resulting in hierarchical relationships between women and men and in the distribution of power and rights favouring men and disadvantaging women. This social positioning of women and men is affected by political, economic, cultural, social, religious, ideological and environmental factors and can be changed by culture, society and community.[129]

The Council of Europe followed this relational and hierarchical reasoning in its Convention on Preventing and Combating Violence against Women and Domestic Violence.[130] The ICC Office of the Prosecutor took notice of these developments and stated that it would interpret the Rome Statute definition so as to take account of social constructions and 'the accompanying roles, behaviours, activities, and attributes assigned to women and men, and to girls and boys'.[131]

The International Law Commission (ILC), the body responsible for the progressive development and codification of international law,[132] at first replicated the Rome Statute definition of gender in its Draft Articles on Crimes against Humanity.[133] Many states and

128 Rome Statute of the International Criminal Court, 1998, article 7 (3).

129 General Recommendation No. 28 on the core obligations of States parties under article 2 of the Convention on the Elimination of All Forms of Discrimination against Women, CEDAW/C/GC/28, 16 December 2010, para 5. See also CEDAW Committee, General Recommendation No. 25, article 4, paragraph 1, of the Convention (temporary special measures), 30th Session (2004), fn 2.

130 Treaty No. 210, Istanbul, 11 May 2011, article 3 (c): '"gender" shall mean the socially constructed roles, behaviours, activities and attributes that a given society considers appropriate for women and men'.

131 Office of the Prosecutor of the ICC, *Policy Paper on Sexual and Gender-Based Crimes* (ICC, 2014).

132 UN Charter, 1945, article 13.

133 ILC, Crimes against Humanity. Texts and titles of the draft preamble, the draft articles and the draft annex provisionally adopted by the Drafting Committee on first reading, A/CN.4/L.892, 26 May 2017, article 3 (3).

NGOs objected that this language was now 'opaque, outdated and not in line with the recent, more inclusive and more gender sensitive definitions of "gender"'[134] and therefore should be abandoned. In the words of Belgium: 'Any text whose definition of gender fails to reflect the current state of international human rights law could marginalize women and lesbian, gay, bisexual, transgender and intersex persons, as well as other groups, and would risk exacerbating the impunity of sexual and gender-based crimes that amount to crimes against humanity.'[135] The ILC heeded these criticisms and the Draft Articles, in their current form, contain no definition of gender, although persecution on the grounds of gender remains as a crime against humanity.[136]

The WPS resolutions show no awareness of this history. They do not define gender and, although the terminology of gender is consistently engaged, the resolutions are in fact gender-specific, applicable to women and girls. The Security Council has no coherent policy of gender: it has tamed gender, conflated women and gender, repeated key buzz words (empowerment, leadership, participation) but failed to unpack their meaning. It has not reflected on the messy and difficult aspects of gender relations or required allocation of sufficient resources to provide for real change in women's lives. In the early resolutions, men and boys are barely referred to.[137] More recently, the importance of 'good' men and boys – those who engage as partners in promoting women's participation – has been recognised by the Council.[138] So, too, has the reality that men and boys are also victims of sexual violence in armed conflict, albeit inconsistently and without amplification,[139] but the complexities of different constructions of masculinity are

[134] ILC, Crimes against Humanity. Comments and observations received from Governments, international organizations and others, A/CN.4/726, 21 January 2019, 32, per Bosnia and Herzegovina.

[135] Ibid., at 31, per Belgium.

[136] ILC, Crimes against Humanity. Texts and titles of the draft preamble, the draft articles and the draft annex provisionally adopted by the Drafting Committee on second reading, Prevention and punishment of crimes against humanity, A/CN.4/L.935, 15 May 2019.

[137] UN Security Council resolution 1325 (2000) encourages all those involved 'to consider the different needs of female and male ex-combatants'.

[138] UN Security Council resolution 2122 (2013).

[139] UN Security Council resolution 2106 (2013) preamble; UN Security Council resolution 2467 (2019) paras 28 and 32.

not addressed.[140] Another omission is that there is no explicit acknowledgement of other gender identities. Despite historic (and contemporary) targeting of LGBTQI people, they are not included in WPS except implicitly, through the encouragement to states to 'adopt a survivor-centered approach' including for 'groups that are particularly vulnerable or may be specifically targeted' in resolution 2467 (2019). Despite the multiple repetitions of the word 'gender', WPS is a women's agenda that, inter alia, seeks to enhance the guarantee of women's and girls' human rights, to secure their access to justice, to eliminate discrimination on the basis of sex and gender, and to promote the empowerment of women and women's leadership. It fails, however, to provide certainty on crucial aspects of the agenda and thus is no blueprint for women's equal citizenship.

However, and third, it is a women's agenda that fails to differentiate among the diverse situations of women or to recognise the impact of multiple and intersecting discriminations. Women's experiences of conflict and its aftermath vary greatly depending upon factors such as whether they are civilians or combatants, their national identity, race, class, economic circumstances, urban or rural location, family situation, whether they are displaced, age, employment, sexuality, gender identity and health. There is within the resolutions some sporadic recognition of diversity among women, for instance as combatants,[141] as women with disabilities,[142] as rural women[143] and as girls. The last are typically mentioned throughout the resolutions

[140] David Duriesmith, 'Hybrid Warriors and the Formation of New War Masculinities: A Case Study of Indonesian Foreign Fighters', 7 (1) *Stability: International Journal of Security and Development* (2018) 16.

[141] E.g. UN Security Council resolution 1325 (2000) para 13 '[e]ncourages all those involved in the planning for disarmament, demobilization and reintegration to consider the different needs of female and male ex-combatants and to take into account the needs of their dependants'.

[142] E.g. UN Security Council resolution 1960 (2010), preamble '[r]eaffirm[s] the importance for States … to increase access to health care, psychosocial support, legal assistance, and socio-economic reintegration services for victims of sexual violence, in particular in rural areas, and taking into account the specific needs of persons with disabilities'.

[143] E.g. UN Security Council resolution 1888 (2009) '[e]ncourages States … to increase access to health care, psychosocial support, legal assistance and socio-economic reintegration services for victims of sexual violence, in particular in rural areas'. This contrasts with the detailed provision for rural women in CEDAW, article 14 and CEDAW Committee, General Recommendation No. 34 on the rights of rural women, CEDAW/C/GC/34, 7 March 2016, para 14.

as 'women and girls' but with no attempt to develop an understanding of why certain offences are committed against female children or what constitute age-appropriate preventive measures and responses. This is also the case with the other categories of women referred to, as there are no recommendations as to measures to be taken to accommodate diverse women. In contrast, in its General Recommendation No. 30 on women in conflict prevention, conflict and post-conflict situations,[144] the CEDAW Committee has provided a more nuanced account of the category 'women' than the Security Council's essentialised approach, noting that women do not form a homogenous group and have diverse experiences and needs,[145] and may be – are – subject to multiple and intersecting forms of discrimination.[146] Intersecting identities are, of course, not just about women and girls as victims; women also bring different strengths and expertise drawn from their life experiences to the multiple tasks of peace and peacebuilding.

1.6 Conclusion

WPS has now been part of the international landscape for two decades. The ten Security Council resolutions have tended to increase in length in both their preambular and their operative paragraphs, to cover a wide range of issues and to fluctuate in their emphases. At certain times, new champions have emerged to sponsor a further resolution. In 2020, the twentieth anniversary of resolution 1325 will likely be marked by another resolution. Many WPS specialists,

[144] CEDAW Committee, General Recommendation No. 30 on women in conflict prevention, conflict and post-conflict situations, CEDAW/C/GC/30, 18 October 2013.

[145] This applies, of course, not just to women but to multiple and intersecting discriminations faced by many people. With respect to women, the UN Committee on the Elimination of Discrimination against Women has explained: 'The discrimination of women based on sex and gender is inextricably linked with other factors that affect women, such as race, ethnicity, religion or belief, health, status, age, class, caste and sexual orientation and gender identity'; General Recommendation No. 28 on the core obligations of States parties under article 2 of the Convention on the Elimination of All Forms of Discrimination against Women, CEDAW/C/GC/28, 16 December 2010, para 18.

[146] CEDAW Committee, General Recommendation No. 30 on women in conflict prevention, conflict and post-conflict situations, CEDAW/C/GC/30, 18 October 2013, para 7.

however, reject the need for a further resolution and argue that what is needed is not more language but implementation of existing resolutions and resistance to their weakening. The NGO Working Group on Women Peace and Security has warned that current attacks on 'core principles of international humanitarian and human rights law, including as they apply to sexual and reproductive rights, and sexual orientation, gender identity and expression, and sex characteristics', all indicate that the twentieth anniversary of WPS is not any 'cause for celebration, but a call to action that addresses the gendered impact of conflict and reaffirms the rights of all women and girls living in conflict-affected communities'.[147]

I agree with this assessment, but my immediate concern as an international lawyer is to ask about the impact of these successive WPS resolutions on international law. The *Global Study* on the implementation of resolution 1325 determined that they now constitute normative standards but are primarily treated as rhetoric rather than as demanding changed behaviours. Do international lawyers in foreign offices or at the UN regard them as imposing legally binding obligations on states and other actors? This is the subject of discussion in Chapter 2.

[147] 2019 Open Letter to Permanent Representatives to the UN: Recommendations on the Security Council Open Debate on Women, Peace and Security (WPS)' (24 October 2019) at www.womenpeacesecurity.org/resource/open-letter-unsc-wps-anniversary-october-2019/.

2

Women, Peace and Security in International Law

2.1 Introduction

I turn now from the brief overview of the substance and institutions of the Women Peace and Security (WPS) agenda to ask what WPS means for international lawyers. The language of the WPS resolutions is not that of international law but primarily that of international relations ('international peace and security'), good governance ('participation', 'monitoring', 'indicators', 'reporting') and development ('empowerment', 'leadership') with subsets of these disciplines such as conflict, security and peace studies. And, of course, the language of gender permeates the resolutions, albeit largely as a synonym for women and girls. The state-centric emphasis of international law is softened by calls for relevant actions by diverse actors as well as states – international institutions, international personnel, men and boys, civil society. The agenda seeks to shape behaviour, policy and decision-making by all these different actors as well as by states, which raises the question of whether the WPS resolutions create binding obligations under international law, which is the subject of this chapter.

The chapter first considers the legal status of UN Security Council resolutions and whether thematic resolutions such as those that comprise the WPS agenda can create legally binding obligations for states. It then asks whether the WPS agenda has attained the status of customary international law and concludes that this is the case for some but not all of its components.

2.2 The Legal Status of Security Council Resolutions

Determination of international legal status is traditionally made by weighing the form of or practice under a supposed rule against the sources of international law as set out in article 38 (1) of the 1945 Statute of the International Court of Justice (ICJ): international conventions (treaties), international custom, general principles of law, judicial decisions and the teachings of the 'most highly qualified publicists'. The last two are described as 'subsidiary sources'.

UN Security Council resolution 1325 (2000) and the follow-up WPS resolutions do not on their face fit directly into the categorisation of sources of international law in article 38 (1). They are not in treaty form and are not therefore legally binding as such. But this is not the end of the story and two issues require consideration: the legal effect of Security Council resolutions and the generation of customary international law.[1]

2.2.1 Existing Treaty Obligations

Before analysing the legal status of Security Council resolutions, it should be emphasised that, in its own terms, UN Security Council resolution 1325 (2000) was at its inception grounded in international law, calling 'upon all parties to armed conflict to respect fully international law applicable to the rights and protection of women and girls, especially as civilians'.[2] It spells out the key instruments of international humanitarian law (IHL),[3]

[1] The discussion in this chapter draws from Christine Chinkin and Madeleine Rees, 'Commentary on Security Council Resolution 2467 Continued State Obligation and Civil Society Action on Sexual Violence in Conflict' (LSE Centre for Women, Peace and Security and Women's International League for Peace and Freedom, 2019), which was written as a policy brief for civil society activists.

[2] UN Security Council resolution 1325 (2000) para 9.

[3] Convention for the Amelioration of the Condition of the Wounded and Sick in Armed Forces in the Field; Convention for the Amelioration of the Condition of Wounded, Sick and Shipwrecked Members of Armed Forces at Sea; Convention relative to the Treatment of Prisoners of War; Convention relative to the Protection of Civilian Persons in Time of War, Geneva, all of 12 August 1949; Protocol Additional to the Geneva Conventions of 12 August 1949, and relating to the Protection of Victims of International Armed Conflicts (Additional Protocol I), Geneva, 8 June 1977 (AP I); Protocol Additional to the Geneva Conventions of 12 August 1949, and relating to the Protection of Victims of Non-International Armed Conflicts (Additional Protocol II), Geneva, 8 June 1977 (AP II).

refugee law,[4] women's rights[5] and children's rights.[6] International criminal law (ICL) is also brought into the resolution through its calling for the relevant provisions of the Rome Statute of the International Criminal Court (ICC) to be borne in mind.[7] Similar language is found in later WPS resolutions, although more often in the preamble than in the operative paragraphs. The Convention on the Elimination of All Forms of Discrimination against Women (CEDAW) and the Convention on the Rights of the Child (Children's Convention), in particular, are not again brought into the body of a resolution until resolution 2467 in 2019.[8] Resolution 2467 also incorporates the 'applicable provisions of international law on the right to an effective remedy for violations of human rights'[9] and acknowledges the Rome Statute.[10] Six months later, the language of international law is weaker in resolution 2493 with CEDAW again located in the preamble, although states are called upon to promote the rights of women.[11] These references to existing international law are, however, general, without any specificity as to which provisions

4 Convention Relating to the Status of Refugees, Geneva, 28 July 1951; Protocol Relating to the Status of Refugees, New York, 31 January 1967.

5 In particular, the Convention on the Elimination of All Forms of Discrimination against Women, New York, 1979 (CEDAW); Optional Protocol to the Convention on the Elimination of All Forms of Discrimination against Women, New York, 1999.

6 United Nations Convention on the Rights of the Child, New York, 1989; Optional Protocol to the Convention on the Rights of the Child on the sale of children, child prostitution and child pornography, 2000; Optional Protocol to the Convention on the Rights of the Child on the involvement of children in armed conflict, 2000. The Optional Protocol to the Convention on the Rights of the Child on a communications procedure was not adopted until 2011.

7 UN Security Council resolution 1325 (2000) para 9.

8 UN Security Council resolution 2467 (2019) para 18 urges 'states to recognize the equal rights of all individuals affected by sexual violence in armed conflict, including women, girls and children born of sexual violence in armed conflict, in national legislation, consistent with their obligations under the Convention on the Elimination of All Forms of Discrimination Against Women and the Convention on the Rights of the Child, as applicable'.

9 UN Security Council resolution 2467 (2019) para 17.

10 UN Security Council resolution 2467 (2019) para 15 'acknowledges the inclusion of sexual and gender-related crimes among the most serious crimes of international concern in the Rome Statute of the International Criminal Court, which entered into force on 1 July 2002'.

11 UN Security Council resolution 2493 (2019) para 5.

of, for example, IHL are the most applicable.[12] The Council also, upon occasion, engages language directly taken from an existing treaty without citing that treaty, as in resolution 2467 when it recognises the right of survivors of sexual violence to be free from 'torture and cruel, inhuman or degrading treatment'.[13]

States' obligations with respect to women's participation in decision-making were not introduced into international law by WPS: requirements for women's equal participation with men are found in CEDAW[14] and the Protocol to the African Charter on Human and Peoples' Rights on the Rights of Women in Africa.[15] Treaty obligations that are brought either directly or indirectly into the WPS resolutions are binding on states parties to those treaties through their accession to or ratification of that treaty, but they do not bind non-parties to the treaty (unless the relevant provisions have achieved the status of customary international law[16]). In this sense, the Security Council's reference to such obligations is irrelevant other than as a reminder that WPS does not exist in an international legal vacuum but operates in conjunction with already existing obligations. It is equally irrelevant for determining legal status whether incorporation of existing law is in the preamble or operative part of a resolution and whether it is consistently or only occasionally repeated.

In summary, in so far as the WPS resolutions reiterate existing treaty law, they are binding upon states parties to the relevant treaties. But the Council goes further and calls for the application of the various regimes of international law (in particular IHL and human rights law) by 'all parties to armed conflict'. In many instances, this includes non-state fighting groups. The Council sidesteps debates about the formal applicability of these laws to

[12] This contrasts with, e.g., UN Security Council resolution 2286, 3 May 2016, *Protection of Civilians in Armed Conflict*, preamble, which recalls the IHL principles of distinction and precaution.

[13] Convention against Torture and Other Cruel, Inhuman or Degrading Treatment or Punishment, New York, 10 December 1984.

[14] CEDAW, articles 7 and 8; see also the Convention on the Political Rights of Women, UN General Assembly resolution 640 (VII), 20 December 1952.

[15] Protocol to the African Charter on Human and Peoples' Rights on the Rights of Women in Africa (Maputo Protocol), 11 July 2003, article 9 (political participation), article 10 (2) (in processes relating to peace).

[16] Vienna Convention on the Law of Treaties, 23 May 1969, article 38.

non-state actors[17] while recognising that such entities may, and in some cases do, commit to organising their activities in compliance with them.[18]

2.2.2 *Thematic Resolutions of the Security Council*

The WPS resolutions do not simply recall existing international law but also contain provisions not found in any treaty, for example the requirement to prosecute crimes against humanity,[19] to exclude sexual violence from amnesties, zero tolerance of sexual exploitation and abuse, and numerous institutional requirements. Do such provisions create legally binding obligations? Under traditional approaches to the sources of international law, there are two possible ways in which positive answers to this question may arise: they may be binding per se as Security Council resolutions or they may have become binding as customary international law or general principles of law.

It is uncontested that Security Council resolutions may (but need not necessarily) create legally binding obligations for member states

[17] Andrew Clapham, *Human Rights Obligations of Non-State Actors* (Oxford University Press, 2006); Andrew Clapham, 'Human Rights Obligations for Non-State-Actors: Where Are We Now?' (15 August 2017) at https://papers.ssrn.com/sol3/papers.cfm?abstract_id=2641390.

[18] Non-state actors may formally enter into a commitment to comply with IHL for the protection of civilians. Geneva Call, an NGO, works with armed groups to sign a humanitarian *Deed of Commitment* to this effect. In 2019, fifty such groups have signed around one hundred different *Deeds of Commitment*. On the law-making potential of such activities, see Anthea Roberts and Sandesh Sivakumaran, 'Lawmaking by Nonstate Actors: Engaging Armed Groups in the Creation of International Humanitarian Law', 37 *Yale Journal of International Law* (2012) 107–52.

[19] IHL requires prosecution only for grave breaches of the Geneva Conventions and Additional Protocol I; ICL brings crimes against humanity into the jurisdiction of the international tribunals but does not demand prosecution. The International Law Commission (ILC) has developed draft articles on crimes against humanity that, if adopted in treaty form, would fill this gap. ILC, Crimes against Humanity. Texts and titles of the draft preamble, the draft articles and the draft annex provisionally adopted by the Drafting Committee on second reading, Prevention and punishment of crimes against humanity, A/CN.4/L.935, 15 May 2019, article 3 (2): 'Each State undertakes to prevent and to punish crimes against humanity, which are crimes under international law, whether or not committed in time of armed conflict.' See also articles 6 (criminalisation of crimes against humanity in national law) and 7 (establishment of national jurisdiction).

when adopted under chapter VII of the UN Charter in accordance with article 25.[20] The WPS resolutions are not adopted under chapter VII; nor are they country specific. They are directed at the generic situation of women's experiences in armed conflict and are what have been termed thematic resolutions, impliedly adopted under UN Charter chapter VI. They form a pattern with other thematic resolutions accepted since the 1990s, notably those relating to children and armed conflict,[21] protection of civilians in armed conflict,[22] youth and peace and security[23] and conflict-associated human trafficking.[24] Those other resolutions, like the WPS resolutions, have had greater input from civil society than is usual for Council resolutions and much of the language and many of the concepts relied upon are similar.

It is sometimes asserted that the crucial factor with respect to the binding nature of Security Council resolutions is whether they have been adopted under UN Charter chapter VI or chapter VII and that article 25[25] applies only to resolutions with respect to Security Council mandated enforcement action. However, it has also been pointed out, including by the ICJ, that article 25 makes no reference to chapter VII and that the critical factor is whether the Council has made 'decisions' that, through article 25, member states have agreed in advance to accept and comply with. The Court in the *Namibia* advisory opinion determined that article 25 could not apply only to chapter VII resolutions with respect to UN enforcement action for if that were the case 'then Article 25 would be superfluous, since this effect is secured by Articles 48 and 49 of the

[20] 'Within the legal framework of the United Nations Charter, notably on the basis of Articles 24, 25 and Chapter VII thereof, the Security Council may adopt resolutions imposing obligations under international law .... Resolution 1244 (1999) was expressly adopted by the Security Council on the basis of Chapter VII of the United Nations Charter, and therefore clearly imposes international legal obligations.' *Accordance with International Law of the Unilateral Declaration of Independence in Respect of Kosovo*, 2010 ICJ Reports (Adv. Op.) 403, para 85.

[21] Resolutions following UN Security Council resolution 1261, 30 August 1999.

[22] Resolutions following UN Security Council resolution 1265, 17 September 1999.

[23] UN Security Council resolution 2250, 9 December 2015.

[24] UN Security Council resolution 2331, 20 December 2016; UN Security Council resolution 2388, 21 November 2016.

[25] UN Charter, 1945, article 25: 'The Members of the United Nations agree to accept and carry out the decisions of the Security Council in accordance with the present Charter.'

Charter'.[26] Adoption under chapter VI or chapter VII is not then of itself determinative of the status of a Council resolution. What is all important is the precise language of any resolution,[27] which must be 'carefully analysed before a conclusion can be made as to its binding effect' on a case-by-case basis. Relevant factors to be taken into account are 'the terms of the resolution to be interpreted, the discussions leading to it, the Charter provisions invoked and, in general, all circumstances that might assist in determining the legal consequences of the resolution of the Security Council'.[28]

In the *Kosovo* advisory opinion, the Court developed further the importance of interpreting every resolution separately to determine its legal effect:

> Security Council resolutions are issued by a single, collective body and are drafted through a very different process than that used for the conclusion of a treaty. Security Council resolutions are the product of a voting process as provided for in Article 27 of the Charter, and the final text of such resolutions represents the view of the Security Council as a body. Moreover, Security Council resolutions can be binding on all Member States . . . irrespective of whether they played any part in their formulation. The interpretation of Security Council resolutions may require the Court to analyse statements by representatives of members of the Security Council made at the time of their adoption, other resolutions of the Security Council on the same issue, as well as the subsequent practice of relevant United Nations organs and of States affected by those given resolutions.[29]

In his Lauterpacht lectures in 2006, Sir Michael Wood examined the role of the Security Council in international law. He rejected what he characterised as the view of some politicians, diplomats and commentators who see the Council solely as a political body and who downplay or write off the function of law in the work of the Council. He discussed what he termed the new development of

[26] *Legal Consequences for States of the Continued Presence of South Africa in Namibia (South West Africa) notwithstanding Security Council Resolution 276 (1970)* 1971 ICJ Reports (Adv. Op.) para 113. [*Namibia Opinion*]

[27] See Sir Michael Wood, 'The Interpretation of Security Council Resolutions', 2 *Max Planck Yearbook of United Nations Law* (1998) 73–95; Sir Michael Wood, 'The Interpretation of Security Council Resolutions, Revisited', at www.ilsa.org/Jessup/Jessup18/Second%20Batch/18757413_020_01_s002_text.pdf.

[28] *Namibia Opinion*, para 114.

[29] *Accordance with International Law of the Unilateral Declaration of Independence in Respect of Kosovo*, 2010 ICJ Reports (Adv. Op.) 403, para 94.

legislative resolutions, that is, resolutions that address a general threat rather than a 'specific situation or dispute'. Without explicitly mentioning thematic resolutions, he considered resolutions not adopted under chapter VII to be 'in any event generally' not legally binding.[30] Thematic resolutions are not routinely incorporated into the Council's country-specific work.[31] Thematic resolutions also remain liable to be subordinated by other political imperatives. In short, as France put it at the Security Council debate at the High-level Review on WPS in October 2015: '[T]he women, peace and security agenda was a political one and should be treated by Member States and the Organization as such.'[32]

This conclusion is supported by the language of the resolutions. As successive resolutions, they should be read accumulatively,[33] but, as discussed in Chapter 1, the language across the ten WPS resolutions varies greatly, with concepts and wording given variable weight. The language is often conceptually imprecise and vague, lacking the certainty of legal obligation. Nor is the terminology of decision-making engaged. Member states negotiate carefully the verbs that introduce a resolution's operative provisions and the most commonly applied in the WPS resolutions are those 'urging', 'encouraging', 'calling upon' or 'requesting' states and other bodies to take certain steps and measures. The Council also 'welcomes' actions taken, 'recalls', 'reaffirms' or 'stresses' earlier resolutions and actions. Its strongest verb with respect to states is 'demands' rather than 'decides'. It has, however, made decisions with respect to its own future actions. In resolution 1888, it 'decided' to include 'specific provisions ... for the protection of

[30] Sir Michael Wood, 'The Legal Framework of the Security Council', lecture delivered 7 November 2006 at www.lcil.cam.ac.uk/sites/www.law.cam.ac.uk/files/images/www.lcil.law.cam.ac.uk/Image/Publications/2006_hersch_lecture_1.pdf.

[31] Swen Dornig, Permanent Mission of Liechtenstein to United Nations, 'Supporting the UN Security Council in Applying Its Thematic Agendas to Its Country-Specific Work', New York, May 2014 at http://lisd.princeton.edu/sites/lisd/files/Commentary_May2014.pdf.

[32] High-level debate on Women, Peace and Security, S/PV.7533, 13 October 2015, 24.

[33] In the *Namibia Opinion*, the ICJ considered the relationship between successive resolutions, stating that before analysing the later resolution it was necessary to consider briefly two earlier resolutions 'since these two resolutions have, together with resolution 276 (1970), a combined and a cumulative effect'; *Namibia Opinion*, para 108.

women and children from rape and other sexual violence in the mandates of United Nations peacekeeping operations',[34] terminology it has not repeated, and in resolution 2242, it 'decided' to integrate WPS across all country-specific situations on the Council's agenda. It consistently 'decides' to remain seized of the issue. Although the general language of the resolutions does not suggest an intention to make the WPS resolutions binding on member states *per se*, it is also the case that states are urged to commit to implementing the WPS agenda and its priorities.[35]

2.2.3 Security Council Resolutions as Generating Customary International Law

Section 2.2.2 suggests that Sir Hersch Lauterpacht's description of the Universal Declaration of Human Rights (UDHR) as constituting 'an aspirational manifesto and some institutional tinkering'[36] is appropriately applied to the WPS agenda. Lauterpacht's opinion was expressed, however, early in the lifetime of the UDHR – a non-binding General Assembly resolution – and there are many proponents of the view that the Declaration has over the years attained the status of customary international law. It should be asked whether aspects of WPS that do not fall within any of the existing regimes of international law might similarly have evolved, or are evolving, into customary international law, either as separate individual principles or even as some holistic package that could be designated as WPS law.

In some resolutions, the Security Council has expressly asserted that it is not establishing customary international law,[37] but in general – including in the WPS resolutions – it is silent as to the legal effect of its exhortations. It is therefore necessary to examine

[34] UN Security Council resolution 1888 (2009) para 12.

[35] UN Security Council resolution 2493 (2019) para 2. The first operative paragraph urges states to implement all the earlier WPS resolutions.

[36] Elihu Lauterpacht, *The Life of Hersch Lauterpacht* (Cambridge University Press, 2010) 260.

[37] E.g. UN Security Council resolution 1918, 27 April, 2010, preamble: 'underscoring ... that resolution 1897 shall not be considered as establishing customary international law'; UN Security Council resolution 2125, 18 November, 2013, para 13: 'underscoring that this resolution shall not be considered as establishing customary international law'. These resolutions are in the context of combating piracy off the coast of Somalia.

whether and, if so, how customary international law may emerge from a Security Council thematic resolution or series of resolutions.

Much less attention has been directed towards the law-generating impact of Security Council resolutions adopted under chapter VI of the UN Charter than that of treaties that have not come into force (either for the specific parties to a dispute or generally) or of General Assembly resolutions.[38] As early as 1950, Sir Hersch Lauterpacht, in a separate opinion in the ICJ, considered the latter. He accepted that General Assembly resolutions, as 'a broad generalisation, . . . are not legally binding upon the Member states', but he did not entirely dismiss their validity. He suggested that while a state is not bound to accept a recommendation, it is 'bound to give it due consideration in good faith' and, if it decides not to give it any legal effect, it is 'bound to explain the reasons for its decision'.[39] Lauterpacht was discussing a particular General Assembly resolution (relating to the administration of a Mandate/Trust territory) rather than a run of successive resolutions on the same subject as was the case of the ICJ in the *Nuclear Weapons* advisory opinion,[40] and his suggestion of good faith is an interesting one that will be returned to.

The ICJ has also considered the law-making impact of the former – a treaty that has not come into force. In the *North Sea Continental Shelf* cases,[41] the Court explained that a multilateral treaty may declare existing customary law or may contribute to the crystallisation of new principles of custom binding on all states including non-parties to the treaty. It affirmed the oft-repeated requirements for determining custom, uniform and consistent state practice and *opinio juris*, although it must be admitted that the Court has not strictly applied these criteria in subsequent cases. Resolutions emanating from

[38] General Assembly resolutions are not of themselves legally binding or constitutive of custom. This is expressed more generically by the ILC: '1. A resolution adopted by an international organization or at an intergovernmental conference cannot, of itself, create a rule of customary international law.' ILC, Draft conclusions on identification of customary international law, with commentaries, A/73/10, 2018, conclusion 12. [ILC, Draft Conclusions]

[39] *Voting Procedure on Questions relating to Reports and Petitions concerning the Territory of South West Africa*, 1955 ICJ Reports (Adv. Op.) 90 (sep. op. Lauterpacht J.).

[40] *Legality of the Threat or Use of Nuclear Weapons*, 1996 ICJ Reports (Adv. Op.) 226. [*Nuclear Weapons Opinion*]

[41] *North Sea Continental Shelf* (*Federal Republic of Germany/Netherlands*) (*Federal Republic of Germany/Denmark*) 1969 ICJ Reports 3, paras 70–81.

international organisations are not equated to treaties that have not come into force, but evidence of practice and *opinio juris* are similarly sought. In the *Nuclear Weapons* advisory opinion, the Court accepted that General Assembly resolutions may have normative value and 'can, in certain circumstances, provide evidence important for establishing the existence of a rule or the emergence of an *opinio juris*'. Contextual and linguistic analysis is required to determine the normative weight of any resolution.[42] In that case, the Court concluded that, despite the annual adoption by the General Assembly of relevant resolutions, the tension between emerging *opinio juris* through those resolutions and the practice of deterrence prevented it from finding a rule of customary international law definitively prohibiting the use of nuclear weapons.[43]

There are two distinct possibilities. The first is that resolutions may influence state behaviour and thus generate the requisite state practice. The second is that they may provide evidence of *opinio juris*. With regard to the first, it is apparent that the Council's action or inaction following a resolution might stimulate behaviours that contribute to developments in general international law. Steve Ratner goes further, arguing that the Security Council has a significant role in the formation of customary international law and that its functions constitute it as a central player. Accordingly, he considers that for those who map the international legal landscape and gauge states' shifting expectations, 'the resolutions and practice of the Council are critical evidence'.[44]

In its study on the identification of customary international law, the International Law Commission (ILC) has specified that '[i]n assessing evidence for the purpose of ascertaining whether there is a general practice and whether that practice is accepted as law (*opinio juris*), regard must be had to the overall context, the nature of the rule, and the particular circumstances in which the evidence in question is to be found'.[45] In making this evaluation with respect to the WPS resolutions, the overall context includes the factors relevant to Security Council resolutions set out by the ICJ in the

42 *Nuclear Weapons Opinion*, para 70. 43 Ibid., at para 73.

44 Steven Ratner, 'The Security Council and International Law', in David Malone (ed.) *The UN Security Council: From the Cold War to the 21st Century* (Lynne Rienner Publishers, 2004) 591.

45 ILC Draft Conclusions, Conclusion 3.

Namibia and *Kosovo* opinions. Sir Hersch Lauterpacht's criterion of good faith is also worth taking into consideration.[46] This would also be a more democratic process – at least among states – than determining a Security Council resolution of itself to constitute legally binding obligations. Indeed, as a matter of policy, extension of the power of the Security Council – an 'unrepresentative and secretive political body' – by according law-making capacity to its thematic resolutions would not be desirable.[47]

The ICJ and the ILC endorse what has been termed the traditional or classic approach to determining customary international law. This conservativism has been criticised in favour of a more modern and flexible methodology.[48] Sections 2.2.3.1 and 2.2.3.2 follow the former approach that requires separate assessment of evidence of state practice and *opinio juris*,[49] evaluating each in the context of WPS. Assessment is not, however, always easy, as resolutions and statements (evidence of *opinio juris*) may stimulate different behaviours (practice), while policy statements may not only indicate intent and belief but can themselves constitute practice.

2.2.3.1 WPS AND STATE PRACTICE

In its list of different forms of state activity relevant for identifying evidence of state practice, the ILC includes 'conduct in connection with resolutions adopted by an international organization or at an intergovernmental conference'.[50] Behaviour associated with the WPS resolutions comes exactly within this categorisation. Perhaps the most striking example of such behaviour is the conclusion by August 2020 by over eighty states of National Action

46 This is supported by UN Charter, 1945, article 2 (2); Wood, 'The Interpretation of Security Council Resolutions' (*supra* n 27) at 89.

47 Dianne Otto, 'Beyond Stories of Victory and Danger: Resisting Feminism's Amenability to Security Council Politics', in Gina Heathcote and Dianne Otto (eds.) *Rethinking Peacekeeping, Gender Equality and Collective Security* (Palgrave Macmillan, 2014) 157–72, 161.

48 E.g. B. S. Chimni, 'Customary International Law: A Third World Perspective', 112 *American Journal of International Law* (2018) 1–46.

49 ILC, Draft Conclusions, Conclusion 3.2.

50 ILC, Draft Conclusions, Conclusion 6.2.

Plans (NAPs)[51] for the implementation of resolution 1325 (2000),[52] a practice that is ongoing. At the open Security Council debate in April 2019 on resolution 2467, over half the speakers committed their state to creating its first ever NAP, modifying an existing NAP or strengthening the implementation of its current NAP, for example through additional funding or investment in monitoring, evaluation and learning methods. Some states noted that they were providing financial or technical support to implementation of other states' NAPs.

The range of states that have adopted a NAP is impressive and satisfies the requirement that practice be 'widespread and representative'.[53] It includes states from the global north (e.g. the UK, the United States, the Scandinavian states), states from the global south (e.g. Burkina Faso, the Philippines, Brazil), 'post-conflict' states (e.g. Bosnia and Herzegovina, Timor Leste) and countries currently conflict-affected (e.g. South Sudan, Afghanistan, Ukraine).[54] Territories of contested legal status – Kosovo and Palestine – have also adopted a NAP. In addition, NAPs have been devolved to further plans at local and zonal levels.[55] This spread satisfies the ICJ's stipulation in the *North Sea Continental Shelf* cases that the practice of the 'most affected' states be assessed.[56] Other significant states, however, have not developed a NAP, for instance countries that are major troop contributors to UN peace operations, such as India, Bangladesh and Jordan, and UN Security Council permanent members China and Russia.

[51] www.peacewomen.org/member-states. For translations of the NAPs, see www.lse.ac.uk/women-peace-security/research/Rethinking-Policy-Advocacy-Implementation.

[52] UN Security Council resolution 1889 (2009) welcomes 'the efforts of Member States in implementing its resolution 1325 (2000) at the national level, including the development of national action plans, and [encourages] Member States to continue to pursue such implementation'.

[53] ILC, Draft Conclusions, Conclusion 8.1: 'The relevant practice must be general, meaning that it must be sufficiently widespread and representative, as well as consistent.'

[54] For a full list of NAPs, see www.peacewomen.org/member-states.

[55] Report of the Secretary-General, *Women, Peace and Security*, S/2019/800, 9 October 2019, para 78.

[56] *North Sea Continental Shelf* (*Federal Republic of Germany/Netherlands*) (*Federal Republic of Germany/Denmark*) 1969 ICJ Reports 3, para 73.

The WPS resolutions are 'meant to be tools' providing a basis for intervening in the various processes they cover.[57] Not surprisingly, then, non-governmental organisations (NGOs) have used NAPs (and more broadly the WPS resolutions) as advocacy tools[58] and as leverage in pushing for gender-sensitive policies and laws with respect to peace and security. There have been mixed results. In some instances, they have generated further state practice through national legislation, appointment of ministerial positions, inclusion in national defence strategies, development of parliamentary committees, national level reporting to parliament or other designated bodies as provided for within NAPs, or mainstreaming into other programmes for promoting gender equality.[59] But, in other instances, NAPS are weakened as evidence of state practice by being poorly drafted or drafted by an international body and thus lacking local ownership or continuity,[60] through their failure to allocate resources,[61] timelines for performance, or responsibility for compliance. Despite their proliferation, the evidence with respect to NAPs as uniform and consistent state practice is inconclusive.

NAPs are not the only potential evidence of state practice with regards to WPS. The United States has exceptionally adopted

[57] Carol Cohn, 'Women and War: Toward a Conceptual Framework', in Carol Cohn (ed.) *Women and Wars* (Polity Press, 2013) 1–35, 34.

[58] Felicity Ruby, 'SC Resolution 1325: A Tool for Conflict Prevention?', in Gina Heathcote and Dianne Otto (eds.) *Rethinking Peacekeeping, Gender Equality and Collective Security* (Palgrave Macmillan, 2014) 173–84.

[59] E.g. the UK NAP is jointly owned by the Foreign and Commonwealth Office (FCO), the Ministry of Defence (MOD) and the Department of International Development (Dfid). The Prime Minister appoints a Special Representative on Preventing Sexual Violence in Conflict; *UK National Action Plan on Women, Peace and Security 2018–2022*, January 2018, at https://assets.publishing.service.gov.uk/government/uploads/system/uploads/attachment_data/file/677586/FCO1215-NAP-Women-Peace-Security-ONLINE_V2.pdf.

[60] Punam Yadav, '1325 – Is That a Taxi Number? Implementation of the National Action Plan on 1325 and 1820 in Nepal' (LSE Centre for Women Peace and Security, Working Paper Series, No. 4, 2017) at www.lse.ac.uk/women-peace-security/assets/documents/2017/wps4Yadav.pdf; Toni Haastrup and Jamie J. Hagen, 'Global Racial Hierarchies and the Limits of Localization via National Action Plans', in Soumita Basu, Paul Kirby and Laura Shepherd (eds.), *New Directions in Women, Peace and Security* (Bristol University Press, 2020) 133–151.

[61] Peacewomen reports that only 43 per cent of NAPs include an allocated budget; at www.peacewomen.org/member-states.

legislation, the Women, Peace and Security Act of 2017,[62] and followed it with a national strategy.[63] Some states have formed an informal, ad hoc advocacy group for implementation of resolution 1325 – the 'Friends of 1325'. Meetings of the Women, Peace and Security Focal Points Network (chaired by a troika of Canada, Namibia and Uruguay) provide opportunities for national and regional focal points and civil society partners to reflect on progress and to share strategies for furthering the agenda.[64] Resolution 1325 has spawned – or is at least associated with – other state initiatives such as the commitment to a feminist foreign policy and the UK's Preventing Sexual Violence in Armed Conflict Initiative (PSVI), co-founded in 2012 by then Foreign Secretary William Hague and Angelina Jolie. This last has generated further practice through the publication of the *International Protocol on the Documentation and Investigation of Sexual Violence in Conflict* – a practical toolkit that is used by state, civil society and institutional investigators. Another practical initiative is the creation of networks of women mediators in the Nordic countries, the Mediterranean and across the Commonwealth to support women's participation in peace processes.[65]

Practice entered into by states or groups of states is bolstered by that of regional and international organisations. This is not directly captured in the ILC Draft Articles on Identification of Customary International Law, but, in his fourth report, Special Rapporteur Sir Michael Wood recorded his view that 'the practice of international (intergovernmental) organizations as such, in certain cases, may contribute to the creation, or expression, of customary international law'.[66] James Crawford, too, has noted that, although '[t]he activities of international organizations do not feature in the sources of international law enumerated in Article 38 of the Statute of the International Court[,] ... they are well placed to

[62] Public Law 115–68—OCT. 6, 2017.

[63] 'United States Strategy on Women, Peace, and Security' (June 2019) at www.whitehouse.gov/wp-content/uploads/2019/06/WPS_Strategy_10_October2019.pdf.

[64] Report of the Secretary-General, *Women, Peace and Security,* S/2019/800, 9 October 2019, para 76.

[65] Ibid., at para 79 discusses the organisation of the Global Alliance of Regional Women Mediator Networks.

[66] Sir Michael Wood, Fourth report on identification of customary international law, A/CN.4/695, 8 March 2016, para 20.

contribute to its development. This is due primarily to the capacity for international organizations to express collectively the practice of member states.'[67]

So how does institutional action on WPS stack up? The annual reports of the Secretary-General on WPS to the Security Council identify trends and provide examples of the practice of states acting through an institution and that of the institution itself. The former includes the growing number of regional and sub-regional action plans for the implementation of WPS.[68] As Laura Shepherd and Paul Kirby have noted, as conflicts do not respect national territorial boundaries, regional collaboration on implementation is appropriate. In this way, Regional Action Plans may open up greater opportunities for women to take on leadership roles in matters of peace and security than at the national level.[69] As examples of the latter, the European Union has adopted a Strategic Approach on *Women, Peace and Security*.[70] NATO has acted since 2007 to promote the role of women in peace and security and, in 2012, established the post of the Secretary-General's Special Representative for Women, Peace and Security.[71] In Africa, impetus is provided by the express mention of UN Security Council resolution 1325 (2000) in the preamble and reiteration of WPS principles in articles 10 and 11 of the Maputo Protocol. The widespread adherence to the Protocol heightens its potential to advance WPS implementation at the national level.[72] The African Union (AU) has created an Office of the Special Envoy

67 James Crawford, *Brownlie's Principles of Public International Law* (Oxford University Press, 9th ed. 2019) 181. See also Isabelle Gunning, 'Modernizing Customary International Law: The Challenge of Human Rights', 31 *Virginia Journal of International Law* (1990–1) 211–48, 222: 'The argument that international organizations should influence custom is based on the premise that the practices of international organizations … constitute a collective state action.'

68 Report of the Secretary-General, *Women, Peace and Security*, S/2019/800, 9 October 2019, para 79.

69 Paul Kirby and Laura Shepherd, 'The Futures Past of the Women, Peace and Security Agenda', 92 *International Affairs* (2016) 373–92, 384.

70 Council of the European Union, *Conclusions on Women, Peace and Security*, Brussels, 10 December 2018. This replaces the 2008 Comprehensive Approach to the EU implementation of the UNSCRs 1325 and 1820 on women, peace and security, at www.consilium.europa.eu/media/37412/st15086-en18.pdf.

71 North Atlantic Treaty Organization, *Women, Peace and Security* (10 July 2019) at www.nato.int/cps/en/natohq/topics_91091.htm.

72 Thelma Ekiyor and L. Muthoni Wanyeki, 'National Implementation of Security Council Resolution 1325 (2000) in Africa: Needs Assessment and

on Women, Peace, and Security and, in 2016, the AU Commission issued a Report on Implementation of the Women, Peace, and Security Agenda in Africa.[73] At the open Security Council debate in April 2019, the AU committed to 50 per cent of its member states having a NAP by 2020. The Economic Community of West African States (ECOWAS), the Intergovernmental Authority on Development (IGAD) and the Pacific Islands Forum are among the regional arrangements that have also developed action plans. In addition to regional NAPs, there are also regional coordination efforts such as the Asia-Pacific Regional Symposium on National Action Plans on Women, Peace and Security.[74]

Institutional practice includes the creation of new gender architecture at the international and regional levels to support implementation of the WPS agenda. At the international level, UN Women has the task of providing input to the Council and member states on integrating WPS, while facilitating the participation of women from civil society in relevant thematic and country-specific meetings and works on peace and security matters in over sixty countries.[75] The Council has mandated new institutional offices, most notably the Special Representative of the Secretary-General (SRSG) on sexual violence in armed conflict.[76] In addition, gender advisers, women protection officers in peace operations and teams of experts to operate within conflict-affected areas have all been instituted. Training programmes on WPS and for gender advisers are offered by states[77] and within NATO. Resolution 2242 (2015) provided for an Informal Experts Group on Women, Peace and Security. Operational since 2016, the Group provides for consultations between the Security Council and local experts on the situation with respect to WPS in countries on the Council's agenda. UN Security Council resolution 2467 (2019) recognised the work of the Informal Experts Group and emphasises that all aspects of the WPS agenda should be addressed in this way. These are only some

Plan for Action', at www.un.org/womenwatch/osagi/cdrom/documents/Needs_Assessment_Africa.pdf.

73 At www.peacewomen.org/sites/default/files/IMplementing%20WPS%20in%20AFrica.pdf.

74 www.peacewomen.org/member-states.

75 Report of the Secretary-General, *Women and Peace and Security*, S/2018/900, 9 October 2018, para 23.

76 The position was mandated by UN Security Council resolution 1888 (2009).

77 E.g. the UK Defence Academy delivered its first Military Gender and Protection Advisers course in November 2018.

of the numerous ways in which WPS principles have shaped the composition and agendas of institutions. While not all innovations have been fully or effectively implemented, it does not alter the reality of significant institutional practice relevant for the identification of customary international law.

Civil society practice has also developed around WPS, for instance through the activities of the NGO Working Group on WPS that was established before the adoption of resolution 1325.[78] The Women's International League for Peace and Freedom allocates through PeaceWomen 'a space for peacemakers to engage, learn and be part of a global movement to advance a holistic Women, Peace and Security Agenda'.[79] In many countries, NGOs work to hold the government to account with respect to its implementation of the WPS agenda, including preparing shadow reports for submission to national parliaments.[80] There are academic centres on Women, Peace and Security or Gender, Peace and Security in the United States, the UK, Australia, Norway and Ghana and associated institutions and university courses elsewhere. In the state-centric framework of international law, civil society actions have never counted for the creation of custom,[81] but they are relevant for the pressure they can put on states and, thus, in their influencing of state practice.

What is not in doubt is the range of actions that have been undertaken around WPS. But, assuming that this provides sufficient evidence of uniform and consistent state practice, is it backed by the requisite level of legal intent to satisfy the requirement for *opinio juris*?[82] This is considered in Section 2.2.3.2.

2.2.3.2 WPS AND OPINIO JURIS

Resolutions and the conduct of international organisations, while not creating legally binding obligations of themselves,

[78] Sanam Naraghi Anderlini, 'Civil Society's Leadership in Adopting 1325 Resolution', in Sara E. Davies and Jacqui True (eds.) *The Oxford Handbook of Women, Peace and Security* (Oxford University Press, 2019) 38–52.

[79] www.peacewomen.org/.

[80] E.g. in the UK, the Gender Action Group for Peace and Security (GAPS) performs this function.

[81] Alan Boyle and Christine Chinkin, *The Making of International Law* (Oxford University Press, 2007) chapter 2.

[82] ILC, Draft Conclusions, Conclusion 9.1.

'may provide evidence for establishing the existence and content of a rule of customary international law, or contribute to its development'.[83] The ILC Draft Articles do not differentiate among international organisations, but the Commentary notes the special attention to be given to General Assembly resolutions 'that may offer important evidence of the collective opinion of its Members'.[84] There seems to be no reason why Security Council resolutions, whether adopted under UN Charter chapter VI or VII, should not similarly evidence the existence of the required intent for a rule of custom.

While acknowledging that the ten WPS resolutions do not use decision-making language and accepting that repetition of itself does not alter the formal legal status of a resolution, 'a series of resolutions may show the gradual evolution of the *opinio juris* required for the establishment of a new rule'.[85] Along with the associated resolutions on protection of children in armed conflict, no other thematic agendas of the Security Council have been so consistently returned to and reinforced through the now annual open debates on WPS and on conflict-related sexual violence during which many states frequently revert to the language of commitment. The earlier WPS resolutions are not replaced or superseded, and later resolutions reaffirm commitment to the 'continuing and full implementation' of the previous resolutions.[86] The notion of 'full' implementation was contested during the negotiations for resolution 2493 (2019). The United States sought to replace 'full' with 'effective' as that country rejects the inclusion of sexual and reproductive rights within WPS. Other states strongly championed 'full' implementation,[87] which was eventually retained.[88]

83 Ibid., at Conclusion 12.2. 84 Ibid., at 147.
85 *Nuclear Weapons Opinion*, para 70.
86 UN Security Council resolution 2467 (2019), preamble; UN Security Council resolution 2493 (2019), preamble and para 1: 'Urges Member States to fully implement the provisions of all previous Security Council Resolutions pertaining to the Women, Peace and Security agenda.'
87 E.g. 'The emphasis on full implementation – and again, I stress "full" – is vital'; UK representative, S/PV.8649, 29 October 2019, 3; see also Belgium, ibid., at 4; Germany, ibid., at 4; France, ibid., at 5; South Africa, ibid., at 15; Dominican Republic, ibid., at 21.
88 UN Security Council resolution 2493 (2019) para 1.

Although the Council does not have the universal membership of the General Assembly,[89] its shifting composition with respect to the ten non-permanent members over the twenty years of WPS resolutions means that many states from a broad regional and geopolitical base have been involved in their negotiation and adoption. Moreover, states from different geographic regions and with different economic status have at different times been lead players in WPS resolutions, including Bangladesh and Namibia (resolution 1325), Azerbaijan (resolution 1889), South Africa (resolution 2493), as well as the UK (resolution 2106), the United States (resolution 1820) and Germany (resolution 2467). These different state sponsors also show that the WPS agenda is not solely at the behest of states in the global north. The WPS resolutions were, until 2019, adopted unanimously with no dissentient voices, but this changed in 2019 when Russia and China abstained from resolution 2467. This might be construed as those states wishing to show their dissent from substantive principles that had already become entrenched or perhaps laying the ground for claiming persistent objection to emergent principles.[90] Another view is that the states did not object so much to the substance of the resolution as to what is perceived as the Council overstretching its authority. At the open debate preceding the adoption of resolution 2467, the Russian delegate stated the importance of not underestimating the 'scope of the Security Council's mandate on combating sexual violence in conflict and of refraining from attempts to broaden its interpretation and take the Council beyond its remit of maintaining international peace and security'.[91] Later in 2019, in the annual debate on WPS, the Russian repeated his country's concerns about the Council overstepping its authority, this time with respect to overloading the resolution with issues relating to human rights, the proper remit of the General Assembly and the Human Rights Council.[92] Nevertheless, Russia (and China) voted for resolution

[89] M. D. Öberg, 'The Legal Effects of Resolutions of the UN Security Council and General Assembly in the Jurisprudence of the ICJ', 16 *European Journal of International Law* (2006), 879–906, 902: 'The GA has the attractive quality of being very broadly representative of the existing states, as well as constituting a centralized, highly convenient means of simultaneously identifying the points of view of all present Member States on a specific topic.' The author nevertheless emphasises that the GA is a political body.

[90] ILC, Draft Conclusions, Conclusion 15.

[91] Security Council, 8514 meeting, 23 April 2019, S/PV.8514, 25.

[92] Security Council, 8649 meeting, 29 October 2019, S/PV.8649, 31.

2493 (2019) and consensus was regained. But that resolution is bland, and unanimity was achieved at a cost to progress in the WPS agenda. Consensus is also undermined by the post-adoption statement by the US representative that the country could not 'accept references to sexual and reproductive health'.[93] Such a publicly made statement seems to be a deliberate denial of *opinio juris*[94] with respect to the inclusion in WPS of sexual and reproductive rights, a stance that was expressly rejected by other states.

The WPS resolutions have not remained in a vacuum but have been explicitly referenced in a host of other instruments and within a range of institutions. Even before the adoption of resolution 1325 (2000), the key principles of what became WPS were adopted in critical area of concern E. in the 1995 Beijing Platform for Action: women and armed conflict.[95] James Crawford has noted: 'The "final act" or other statement of conclusions of a conference of States may be a form of multilateral treaty, but, even if it is an instrument recording decisions not adopted unanimously, the result may constitute cogent evidence of the state of the law on the subject.'[96] The Beijing Declaration and Platform for Action was adopted unanimously at an intergovernmental global summit conference. Global summits proliferated in the 1990s but have fallen out of fashion as a forum for law-making since that time. Perhaps Security Council thematic resolutions have, to some extent, taken their place.

During the two decades since its adoption, resolution 1325 has been endorsed in other fora including the General Assembly, for instance in its World Summit statement of 2005[97] and its adoption of an international day for the elimination of sexual

[93] Ibid., at 3.

[94] The ICJ has affirmed the binding effect of a publicly made and intentional undertaking; *Nuclear Tests* (*New Zealand* v *France*), Judgment, 1974 ICJ Reports 457, para 46. On the same basis, a publicly made denial of any intention to be bound must be effective, at least with respect to that state.

[95] Fourth World Conference on Women, Beijing Declaration and Platform for Action, 1995.

[96] Crawford (*supra* n 67) 39.

[97] UN General Assembly resolution 60/1, 24 October 2005, *World Summit*, para 116: 'We stress the important role of women in the prevention and resolution of conflicts and in peacebuilding. We reaffirm our commitment to the full and effective implementation of Security Council resolution 1325 (2000) of 31 October 2000 on women and peace and security.'

violence – 19 June.[98] The General Assembly's 2015 vision for transforming the world – the Sustainable Development Goals (SDGs) – does not refer explicitly to WPS but has goals relating to women's participation, gender equality, ending sexual violence and the empowerment of women and girls, all core WPS principles.[99] WPS is also incorporated, albeit somewhat inconsistently, into some Security Council decision-making resolutions[100] and other thematic resolutions, for instance on post-conflict peacebuilding,[101] on youth, peace and security,[102] on peacekeeping[103] and on small arms.[104]

Other international institutions have made strong statements of commitment to WPS. The EU has affirmed its own commitment as well as that of its member states to the implementation of WPS in both its internal and external actions and its efforts to integrate WPS into its Common Security and Defence Policy.[105] The Council of the European Commission has also recalled 'the commitments of the European Union and its Member States to the full implementation of the Women, Peace and Security (WPS) agenda'.[106]

Aspects of WPS have been fleshed out in other non-binding, or soft law, instruments such as the (then) G8 Declaration on Preventing Sexual Violence in Conflict adopted in April 2013 and the Declaration of Commitment to End Sexual Violence in Conflict. The former was described by William Hague as a 'historic agreement' by 'some of the world's largest economies and most powerful

[98] UN General Assembly resolution, 69/293, 19 June 2015, *International Day for the Elimination of Sexual Violence in Conflict.*

[99] UN General Assembly resolution 70/1, 21 October 2015, *Transforming our world: the 2030 Agenda for Sustainable Development.*

[100] UN Women reports that 'in 2017, 70.5 per cent of resolutions, 88.8 per cent of presidential statements, and 75.7 per cent of country-specific or regional situations contained provisions on women's peace and security, and in 2016 the percentages were 49.4 per cent, 57.9 per cent and 51 per cent respectively'. UN Women, 'Facts and Figures: Peace and Security', at www.unwomen.org/en/what-we-do/peace-and-security/facts-and-figures#_Security_Council.

[101] E.g. UN Security Council resolution 2282, 27 April 2016, *Post-conflict peacebuilding.*

[102] E.g. UN Security Council resolution 2250, 9 December 2015.

[103] E.g. UN Security Council resolution 2272, 11 March 2016, *Peacekeeping operations.*

[104] E.g. UN Security Council resolution 2220, 22 May 2015.

[105] Report of the Secretary-General, *Women, disarmament, non-proliferation and arms control*, A/73/115, 2 July 2018, 21.

[106] Council of the European Union, *Council Conclusions on Women, Peace and Security*, 3662nd meeting of the Council, Brussels, 10 December 2018.

nations'.[107] The commitments it contained were formally recognised in Security Council WPS resolution 2106 in 2013. This resolution was launched at the start of the 68th session of the General Assembly and is now endorsed by over 150 states worldwide. Another example is the publication of the *Principles for Global Action on Tackling the Stigma of Sexual Violence in Conflict.* Wording followed in resolution 2467 (2019) about the importance of lifting the 'sociocultural stigma' attached to crimes of sexual violence and of shifting it from survivors to the perpetrators of these crimes.[108] There is thus widespread verbal support for at least some aspects of WPS (relating primarily to women's participation and to conflict-affected sexual violence) that has been followed up by some practice such as the adoption of NAPs. These have not been prepared out of 'habit' or 'usage'[109] but through deliberate acts in response to the WPS resolutions[110] and to articulate how states believe that security should be 'gendered in their own contexts'.[111]

Principles consistent with the WPS resolutions have been reiterated in the General Recommendations of the CEDAW Committee on violence against women,[112] on women in conflict prevention, conflict and post-conflict situations,[113] on access to justice[114] and on gender-related dimensions of disasters in the context of climate change.[115] CEDAW Committee General Recommendations (like

[107] 'The Foreign Secretary William Hague, Angelina Jolie and Zainab Hawa Bangura Launch G8 Declaration on Preventing Sexual Violence in Conflict' (11 April 2013) at www.gov.uk/government/news/g8-declaration-on-preventing-sexual-violence-in-conflict.

[108] UN Security Council resolution 2467 (2019) para 28.

[109] The ILC states that practice should be distinguished from 'mere habit or usage'; ILC, Draft Conclusions, Conclusion 9.2.

[110] Michael Wood, Special Rapporteur, Third report on identification of customary international law, A/CN.4/682, 27 March 2015, para 52.

[111] Laura McLeod, 'The Women, Peace and Security Resolutions: UNSCR 1325 to 2122', in Jill Steans and Daniela Tepe-Belfrage (eds.) *Handbook on Gender in World Politics* (Edward Elgar, 2016) 271, 273.

[112] CEDAW Committee, General Recommendation No. 19, Violence against women, 11th session, 1992.

[113] CEDAW Committee, General Recommendation No. 30 on women in conflict prevention, conflict and post-conflict situations, CEDAW/C/GC/30, 18 October 2013.

[114] CEDAW Committee, General Recommendation No. 33 on women's access to justice, CEDAW/C/GC/33, 3 August 2015.

[115] CEDAW Committee, General Recommendation No. 37 on the gender-related dimensions of disaster risk reduction in the context of climate change, CEDAW/C/GC/37, 13 March 2018.

those of the other UN Human Rights Council expert bodies) are not binding of themselves but do provide authoritative interpretations of the legally binding Convention. The CEDAW Committee has described the WPS resolutions as 'crucial political frameworks for advancing advocacy on women peace and security'.[116] At the same time, it requires states to include in their periodic reports details of measures that they have taken to implement the provisions of the Convention, including in conflict prevention, conflict and post-conflict situations. The Committee notes that this consolidates the Convention and the WPS agenda, thereby broadening, strengthening and operationalising gender equality.[117] When states do indeed report on their implementation of WPS, it also consolidates practice in the belief that this is required and can be construed as evidence of *opinio juris.*

The repetition of key WPS principles by states in public fora and through international and regional organisations, coupled with action plans at regional, national and sub-national levels and reporting of pertinent actions, all suggests a level of intent consistent with the required *opinio juris* for a rule of customary international law.

2.2.4 *Enforcement and Implementation of WPS*

It has to be acknowledged that the minimal enforcement provisions in the WPS resolutions weaken claims for their legally binding content. To return to Sir Hersch Lauterpacht – this is what, for him, most undermined the legal effectiveness of the UDHR.[118] From resolution 1888 (2009) onwards, one of the tasks bestowed on the UN Secretary-General has been to devise more effective and

[116] The Committee recognizes that the various thematic resolutions of the Security Council, in particular 1325 (2000), 1820 (2008), 1888 (2009), 1889 (2009), 1960 (2010) and 2106 (2013), in addition to resolutions such as 1983 (2011), which provides specific guidance on the impact of HIV and AIDS on women in conflict and post-conflict contexts, are crucial political frameworks for advancing advocacy regarding women, peace and security.

CEDAW Committee General Recommendation No. 30 on women in conflict prevention, conflict and post-conflict situations, CEDAW/C/GC/30, 18 October 2013, para 25.

[117] Ibid., at para 27.

[118] Hersch Lauterpacht, 'The Universal Declaration of Human Rights,' 25 *British Yearbook of International Law* (1948) 354–81.

efficient ways to ensure monitoring, analysis and reporting on the protection pillar of WPS,[119] but these have remained inadequate. There is no systematic reporting requirement such as that under the UN human rights treaties or the Universal Periodic Review process before the Human Rights Council. This shortfall is to some extent ameliorated by the CEDAW Committee's requirement that states address WPS in their periodic reports to the Committee, which also serves to bring WPS into the Committee's authoritative interpretation of the Convention.[120] But the Committee can only make recommendations; there are no requirements such as temporary special measures to accelerate implementation of WPS,[121] or that states and intergovernmental organisations must refrain from participating in a process where there is inadequate diverse representation. There is no accountability for failure to give effect to the WPS pillars, for instance for excluding women and other civil society organisations from relevant processes relating to conflict prevention, resolution or management.

Nor is there any dedicated Security Council committee such as those on sanctions and counterterrorism to evaluate states' implementation of the WPS agenda and, where appropriate, to demand improved performance. The Security Council has envisaged the possibility of targeted sanctions against persons listed by the SRSG on sexual violence in armed conflict.[122] Resolution 2467 (2019) urges sanctions committees to impose targeted sanctions against perpetrators of sexual violence in conflict and those who direct it. It also reiterates the Council's intention to consider rape and sexual violence as criteria when designating targeted sanctions. In resolution 2493 (2019), the Council requests the Secretary-General to assess the dedicated gender expertise in UN Security Council sanctions committees and how this commitment is met. Sanctions are imposed by the Council in accordance with UN Charter article 41, which is located within chapter VII. The possibility of sanctions within the WPS resolutions thus provides

[119] UN Security Council resolution 1888 (2009); see also UN Security Council resolution 1960 (2010).

[120] CEDAW Committee, General Recommendation No. 30 on women in conflict prevention, conflict and post-conflict situations, CEDAW/C/GC/30, 18 October 2013, paras 25–28.

[121] CEDAW, article 4 provides for temporary special measures to accelerate de facto equality between women and men.

[122] UN Security Council resolutions 1888 (2009), 1960 (2010), 2106 (2013).

a linkage with chapter VII and reinforces that failure to comply constitutes breach of legal obligations, at least with respect to commission of sexual violence.[123]

Nevertheless, the WPS agenda is poorly implemented. The 2015 Global Study on the Implementation of Resolution 1325, *Preventing Conflict, Transforming Justice, Securing the Peace*, considered that lack of implementation of its central pillars is the major weakness of WPS.[124] In 2019, the UN Secretary-General referred to data analysed in an assessment report commissioned by UN Women from which he concluded: 'There remains a stark contrast between rhetoric and reality, where previously agreed commitments have not been matched by action.'[125] The NGO Working Group concluded, with respect to the Council's implementation of its own agenda, that its approach is 'superficial, ad-hoc and inconsistent; subject to the individual efforts of Security Council members rather than being systematically integrated into Council action ... Its approach is defined by a lack of accountability for failure to fully implement all provisions of the ten resolutions that constitute the WPS agenda.'[126] Is this non-implementation violation of existing legal obligation or an indication of insufficient evidence of state practice and *opinio juris* to support any claim that WPS constitutes customary

123 The Secretary-General has noted that 'important advances have been made around Security Council sanctions. Stand-alone designation criteria on sexual violence were included in the sanctions regimes for the Central African Republic, Libya, Somalia and South Sudan.' Report of the Secretary-General, *Conflict-related Sexual Violence*, S/2019/280, 29 March 2019, para 30.

124 Radhika Coomaraswamy and others, *Preventing Conflict, Transforming Justice, Securing the Peace: A Global Study on the Implementation of Security Council Resolution 1325* (United Nations, 2015) 14: 'Obstacles and challenges still persist and prevent the full implementation of the women, peace and security (WPS) agenda.'

125 Report of the Secretary-General, *Women, Peace and Security*, S/2019/800, 9 October 2019, para 5.

126 NGO Working Group on Women Peace and Security, Mapping Women, Peace and Security in the UN Security Council: 2018, 7 November 2019, at https://reliefweb.int/sites/reliefweb.int/files/resources/NGOWG-Mapping-WPS-in-UNSC-2018.pdf. Sarah Kenny Werner and Elena Stavrevska, Where are the Words? The Disappearance of the Women, Peace and Security Agenda in the Language of Country-Specific UN Security Council Resolutions (LSE Centre for Women, Peace and Security and Women's International League for Peace and Freedom, 2020) at https://www.lse.ac.uk/women-peace-security/assets/documents/2020/Report-WILPF-LSE-Web.pdf.

international law? There are different responses to this question with some strong proponents for the legally binding nature of WPS[127] but, equally, some more sceptical commentators.[128]

2.2.5 *WPS: Is It Customary International Law?*

In determining the legal status of the WPS agenda, certain factors should be taken into account, in addition to those of weighing evidence of state practice and *opinio juris*. First, the agenda is broad in scope and covers numerous issues. This requires separate evaluations of legal status to be made of different aspects of the agenda – one single conclusion cannot be sufficient. Second, this is also true of NAPs. They vary enormously in emphasis, in priorities listed and in the degree of detail and concrete actions. There is a marked difference between many NAPs from the states in the global north – primarily donor states – and those in the global south – primarily recipients of aid and other interventions. The former are external-looking, directing attention to states to which aid is given, while the latter are more directed towards the internal constitutional and legal situation. These variations make problematic any conclusion about uniform and consistent practice. Third, many terms repeated throughout the resolutions are undefined and imprecise – 'empowerment', 'gender', 'gender perspective', 'protection', 'security', 'meaningful participation' and many others. This lack of precision undermines the certainty required for legal obligation. Fourth, WPS engages a range of actors – states, non-state parties to armed conflict, international institutions, civil society. Their rights and obligations under international law vary significantly, as well as their capacities and capabilities. This makes difficult any overall evaluation under customary international law.

Fifth, and more controversially, is the methodology for determining customary international law. The WPS agenda has emerged from

[127] E.g. Kwado Appiagyei-Atua, 'United Nations Security Council Resolution 1325 on Women Peace and Security – Is It Binding?' 18 (3) *Human Rights Brief* (2011) 2–6; Dina Francesca Haynes, Naomi Cahn and Fionnuala Ní Aoláin, 'Women in the Post-Conflict Process: Reviewing the Impact of Recent U.N. Actions in Achieving Gender Centrality', 11 *Santa Clara Journal of International Law* (2012) 189–218, 197: Security Council resolutions are 'both determinative and binding as legal, political and normative pronouncements'.

[128] Christine Bell and Catherine O'Rourke, 'Peace Agreements or Pieces of Paper? The Impact of UNSC Resolution 1325 on Peace Processes and Their Agreements', 59 *International and Comparative Law Quarterly* (2010) 941–80.

sustained interaction between civil society (women's activists and NGOs), successive members of the Security Council, with input from like-minded states, and UN entities. Its key principles have been formulated through the resolutions of women's organisations, global summit meetings, the work of expert bodies, treaty provisions and diplomatic negotiations. Practice pursuant to the agenda involves multiple state and non-state actors. This unconventional context problematises the analysis of state practice and *opinio juris* in line with the jurisprudence of the ICJ and the ILC's Draft Conclusions on the Identification of Customary International Law as too formalistic and conservative an approach for an agenda of this sort. Should we instead look to expand the set of norms recognised as customary international law, for instance through understanding its creation as 'an "intensive dialectic process" between different actors of the international society'?[129] Or by giving greater weight to *opinio juris*, thereby minimising the power of leading states to ensure that what is deemed to be custom accords with their interests and favouring what has been termed 'an ethical turn in thinking about CIL'?[130] And is there an argument for greater flexibility and innovation in what should constitute the elements of custom, along the lines of what has been termed humanity's law?[131] One commentator concludes that 'although merely declaratory, such resolutions and related Presidential statements appear to have gained special status among ... Security Council resolutions'.[132] This special status is apparently born out of the shift from the state-centric approach to international law to one that advances 'an entirely distinct approach, centred on the human person'.[133]

These different perspectives merit further consideration, but the caution required in determining the legal status of Security Council

[129] James Crawford, 'The Identification and Development of Customary International Law', Keynote Speech at the Spring Conference of the ILA British Branch, 23 May 2014 (citing P. Allott, 'Language, Method and the Nature of International Law' 45 *British Yearbook of International Law* (1971) 103, 129).

[130] Chimni (*supra* n 48) 3.

[131] Ruti Teitel, *Humanity's Law* (Oxford University Press, 2013).

[132] Rossana Deplano, 'The Use of International Law by the United Nations Security Council: An Empirical Framework for Analysis', at http://law.emory.edu/eilr/recent-developments/volume-29/essays/international-law-united-nations-council.html.

[133] *Jurisdictional Immunities of the State (Germany* v *Italy: Greece intervening)* 2012 ICJ Reports 99 (diss. op. Trindade J.) para 40.

resolutions should also not be discounted.[134] With some hesitation, I venture some conclusions:

(i) Where WPS resolutions reiterate or incorporate existing treaty obligations, they are binding on states parties to those treaties.
(ii) Where WPS principles are reiterated in UN Charter chapter VII country-specific resolutions, they are binding on member states in accordance with UN Charter article 25.
(iii) Where WPS resolutions engage language that has already been accepted as comprising international legal obligation, such legal obligation can be assumed.
(iv) Where aspects of the WPS agenda have already been accepted as constituting customary international law, they are accordingly binding on all states. I suggest that this is the case with respect to:

- fundamental human rights including the prohibition of discrimination on the basis of sex and equality before the law. These norms are constantly reiterated in international and regional human rights treaties, and have been affirmed in human rights jurisprudence, expressly incorporated into international criminal law[135] and accepted by some authorities as constituting *jus cogens*,[136] a peremptory norm of international law;[137]

[134] 'Because the attitude of States towards a given resolution (or a particular rule set forth in a resolution), expressed by vote or otherwise, is often motivated by political or other nonlegal considerations, ascertaining acceptance as law (*opinio juris*) from such resolutions must be done "with all due caution".' ILC, Draft conclusions on identification of customary international law, with commentaries, A/73/10, 2018, 148.

[135] Rome Statute of the ICC, 1998, article 21 (3).

[136] The Inter-American Court of Human Rights has asserted that

> the principle of equality before the law, equal protection before the law and non-discrimination belongs to jus cogens, because the whole legal structure of national and international public order rests on it and it is a fundamental principle that permeates all laws. Nowadays, no legal act that is in conflict with this fundamental principle is acceptable, and discriminatory treatment of any person, owing to gender, race, color, language, religion or belief, political or other opinion, national, ethnic or social origin, nationality, age, economic situation, property, civil status, birth or any other status is unacceptable.

Juridical *Condition and Rights of the Undocumented Migrants* (IACtHR, Adv. Op.) OC-18/03, 17 September 2003, para 101.

[137] Vienna Convention on the Law of Treaties, 23 May 1969, article 53: 'a peremptory norm of general international law is a norm accepted and recognized by

- prohibition of rape and sexual violence in armed conflict. The reiteration of the prohibition of sexual and gender-based violence in international humanitarian law, human rights law and their designation as a war crime and crime against humanity makes a strong case for *jus cogens* status;
- prohibition of gender-based and sexual violence against women in human rights law[138] and states' due diligence obligation to prevent, protect against, investigate, prosecute and punish gender-based violence whenever committed – in conflict or in so-called peacetime; to end perpetrator impunity and secure victims' right to an effective remedy. These reinforce and are reinforced by normative standards relating, inter alia, to the rule of law, access to justice, law reform, protection of victims and witnesses, and reparations.

I do not assert that the entire WPS agenda has legally binding status and I do recognise that there are grey areas; some are substantive. For instance, the concept of 'gender' remains contested. As discussed in Chapter 1, the concept of 'gender' was a latecomer to international law. The human rights treaties, including CEDAW article 1, assert non-discrimination on the basis of 'sex', not gender.[139] The CEDAW Committee has explained that the Convention in fact aims at eliminating discrimination against women on grounds of both 'sex' and 'gender'.[140] Other human rights bodies and experts have recognised the significance of gender in denying equality.[141] The SDGs – a policy

the international community of States as a whole as a norm from which no derogation is permitted'.

138 The CEDAW Committee has determined that the prohibition of violence against women has attained the status of customary international law; CEDAW Committee, General Recommendation No. 35 on gender-based violence against women, updating general recommendation No. 19, CEDAW/C/GR/35, 26 July 2017, para 2.

139 UDHR, article 2; ICCPR, article 2; ICESCR, article 2 (2).

140 CEDAW Committee, General Recommendation No. 28 on the core obligations of States parties under article 2 of the Convention on the Elimination of All Forms of Discrimination against Women, CEDAW/C/GC/28, 16 December 2010, para 2.

141 E.g. 'Gender based assumptions about economic, social and cultural roles preclude the sharing of responsibility between men and women in all spheres that is necessary to equality'; Committee on Economic, Social and Cultural Rights, General Comment No. 16, Article 3: the equal right of men and women

agenda but grounded in the human rights treaties – assert gender equality and women's empowerment. But the human rights bodies are ambivalent about the levels of inequality that are compatible with those treaties. As Philip Alston has argued, a number of steps are required for the international human rights regime to be able to respond meaningfully to extreme inequality, including gender inequality.[142] This ambiguity lies at the heart of WPS; advancing gender equality is proclaimed, but women's sexual and reproductive rights are not unequivocally upheld. Others are procedural or institutional. WPS resolutions call upon donor countries to provide financial and various forms of technical assistance and trainings to women involved in peace processes. They also encourage civil society participation at donor conferences where they can help to ensure that gender considerations are included.[143] As a traditionalist international lawyer, I have to concede that this language is not that of legal obligation; it is unlikely, for instance, that an NGO could demand access to a donor conference on the basis of such wording or that a donor state could be censured for not providing such assistance.

The development of customary international law is a dynamic process. Even if, in a traditional analysis, certain parts of the WPS agenda have not yet attained this status, continued state practice and statements of intent may lead to change. So, too, might more general acceptance of modern methods of determining customary international law that are in accordance with the realities of contemporary international life. Practice under WPS may also contribute to the emergence of customary rules in other areas of law, for instance the so-called *jus post bellum.*[144]

2.3 Conclusion

Resolution 1325 (2000) was widely celebrated as bringing the goals of the women's movement into the Security Council, the body with the primary responsibility for international peace and

to the enjoyment of all economic, social and cultural rights, E/C.12/2005/3, 13 May 2005, para 14.

142 Report of the Special Rapporteur on extreme poverty and human rights, Philip Alston, A/HRC/29/31, 27 May 2015, para 47.

143 E.g. UN Security Council resolution 2242 (2015).

144 Carsten Stahn, Jennifer Easterday and Jens Iverson, *Jus Post Bellum: Mapping the Normative Foundations* (Oxford University Press, 2014).

security. But, as we have seen, there are downsides to the integration of what is predominantly a women's peace and human rights agenda into the very different political environment of the Security Council. Lack of clarity about its legal status and states' obligations provides obstacles to the implementation of the WPS agenda and risks its subordination to other more pressing political priorities. Would it serve the interests of women in armed conflict better if WPS could be renegotiated in treaty form? This would provide greater certainty as to legal status, would clarify the obligations of states that became parties to such a treaty (subject to interpretation) and would provide a surer basis for demands for action.[145] But there would also be downsides. Treaty negotiation risks agreement only on the lowest common denominator of what is acceptable to states; concessions can be made to states that then fail to become parties to the treaty; compromise leads to ambiguous language that does not resolve uncertainties; a robust enforcement mechanism would be unlikely to receive adequate support; different priorities within the WPS agenda would be likely to undermine agreement; a new treaty would impose additional burdens; once negotiated, amendment would be difficult and further progress would be impeded; and this traditional state-centred form of international law-making might completely submerge and tame the innovative and transformative potential of WPS. And, in 2020, the pushback against the language of gender, against women's human rights and, more generally, against human rights would make any such proposal unwise.

The WPS agenda is grounded in a range of existing international legal regimes. It provides a political blueprint for moving towards a multifaceted international legal regime that takes women's lives seriously with its own ethos, language and assumptions – those of transformative feminism. The agenda may be a law in the making, may even be a future subdiscipline of international law, but it is not yet there in its

[145] There are debates about the desirability of a global treaty on combating violence against women. See the discussion in the Special Rapporteur on Violence against Women, Adequacy of the international legal framework on violence against women, A/72/134, 19 July 2017.

entirety. But what it does offer is a Grotian moment in international law. WPS brings together at least three of Sir Hersch Lauterpacht's principal features of the Grotian tradition in international law: the fundamental rights and freedoms of the individual; the idea of peace; and the tradition of idealism and progress.[146] Their interpretation through a feminist lens would enhance all three and further a feminist conception of international peace and security.

[146] Lauterpacht (*supra* n 36) 285.

3

Women and Peace

3.1 Introduction

In Chapter 2, I explored whether the Women, Peace and Security (WPS) agenda creates binding obligations for states and other actors under international law. This chapter and Chapter 4 consider further the concepts enshrined in the Security Council's resolution 1325 (2000): 'women and peace and security'. In Chapter 1, I addressed the Security Council's simplistic understanding of 'women'. This chapter looks at the Council's conceptualisation of 'peace' and Chapter 4 that of 'security', both within the framework of public international law. But this is admittedly an artificial distinction: without security there cannot be peace for any person, regardless of their sex, gender, age or any other categorisation of identity, and without peace there is no security.[1] And militarised security especially denies peace and, for many, fosters feelings of insecurity. I have therefore found it hard to decide what to include in each chapter and have constantly shifted topics between them. Finally, I have decided to adopt the pillars of WPS summarised in Chapter 1: Chapter 3 focuses on peace, primarily women's participatory contribution to peace and Chapter 4 on women's security, understood in WPS primarily as protection against conflict-related sexual violence and conflict prevention.

[1] In the Sustainable Development Goals, peace and security are linked to development: 'Sustainable development cannot be realized without peace and security; and peace and security will be at risk without sustainable development.' UN General Assembly resolution 70/1, 25 September 2015, *Transforming our world: the 2030 Agenda for Sustainable Development*, para 35.

This chapter first outlines the concept of peace in international law through what I have termed a two-pronged approach: the obligation to settle disputes through peaceful means and regulation of the use of force. It weaves into this account aspects of women's peace activism from the time of the Women's Congress in The Hague in 1915 that was discussed in Chapter 1. It recognises the deficiency of the two-pronged approach in that this omits arms control, which was a central demand of women's organisations, notably the Women's International League for Peace and Freedom (WILPF) – the oldest women's peace organisation. It then discusses the concept of peace within human rights law before turning to the narrow approach to peace in the WPS resolutions that concentrates on the call for increased participation by women in conflict prevention, management and resolution. It considers women's exclusion from peace processes and why it is important that this is rectified. Finally, it reflects on women as peacebuilders in conflict-affected societies.

3.2 International Law and Peace

The concept of peace is both continuously present in and strangely absent from mainstream international law. Peace is defined or explained across a range of disciplines by, among others, theologians and philosophers,[2] psychoanalysts,[3] poets,[4] sociologists[5] and pop stars,[6] but only a few international lawyers have made such an attempt.[7] There is no general treaty that defines peace[8] and only

[2] For definitions of peace from a range of disciplines, see J. G. Starke, *The Science of Peace* (Legal Books Pty, 2nd ed. 1986) 5–9.

[3] Rebecca Simpson, 'Hearts and Minds: Einstein and Freud's Quest for Peace' (October 2019) at https://london.ac.uk/senate-house-library/blog/hearts-minds-einstein-freuds-quest-peace.

[4] E.g. *11 Memorable Poems about Peace* at www.thoughtco.com/poems-about-peace-4156702.

[5] E.g. Johan Galtung, 'Violence, Peace, and Peace Research', 6 *Journal of Peace Research* (1969) 167–91.

[6] Perhaps most famously (at least in my age group) John Lennon, 'Imagine'.

[7] E.g. Quincey Wright, a political scientist but also a former president of the American Society of International Law, defined peace as 'the condition of a community in which order and justice prevail, internally among its members and externally in its relations with other communities'; cited in Starke (*supra* n 2) 8.

[8] There have been many bilateral treaties of peace and friendship including those concluded by Britain with indigenous peoples.

a handful of institutional soft law statements. But perhaps there is no need for a legal definition, at least for institutional purposes. After all, former UN Secretary-General Boutros Boutros-Ghali, in his 1992 *Agenda for Peace,* asserted that '[t]he concept of peace is easy to grasp'.[9] He did not elucidate this 'easily grasped' idea, although he did expand his understanding of (in)security.[10] Eight years later, in his report on UN peace operations, Lakhdar Brahimi similarly directed his attention to the doctrine, strategy and decision-making of peace operations[11] without first establishing what constitutes peace, other than as part of the UN's preambular founding purpose of saving 'succeeding generations from the scourge of war'. For lawyers, undefined concepts lack certainty and give rise to misgivings about their legal applicability.

Nevertheless, peace has long been present in international law. In Sir Hersch Lauterpacht's famous reappraisal of the Grotian tradition of international law, he included 'the idea of peace', what he called the pacifist strain that runs through Grotius's work. Lauterpacht considered that 'there breathes from the pages of *De Jure Belli ac Pacis* a disapproval amounting to hatred of war'.[12] Classic writings on international law were divided into the 'Law of War' and the 'Law of Peace',[13] a distinction that was maintained in the ninth edition of *Oppenheim's International Law.*[14] Despite this tradition and the formation of professional societies of international lawyers since the nineteenth century to advance international law as a civilising[15] tool for

[9] Report of the Secretary-General, *An Agenda for Peace: Preventive diplomacy, peace-making and peace-keeping,* A/47/277–S/24111, 17 June 1992, para 12.

[10] See Chapter 4.

[11] Report of the Panel on United Nations Peace Operations, A/55/305; S/2000/809, 21 August 2000. [Brahimi Report]

[12] Hersch Lauterpacht, 'The Grotian Tradition in International Law', 23 *British Yearbook of International Law* (1946) 1–53, 47.

[13] E.g. L. F. L. Oppenheim, *International Law,* vol. I: *Peace* ([1905] 2nd ed. 1912); vol. II: *War and Neutrality* ([1906] 2nd ed. 1912). Sir Hersch Lauterpacht became the editor of Oppenheim's *International Law* in 1935 and was responsible for three editions of volume I on *Peace* and two of volume II on *Disputes, War and Neutrality.*

[14] Volume I: *Peace* was published in 1992; volume 2: *War* has not been published although the same distinction is promised for the 10th edition. Rosalyn Higgins, Philippa Webb, Dapo Akande, Sandesh Sivakumaran and James Sloan, *Oppenheim's International Law United Nations* (Oxford University Press, 2017) introduces a third volume necessitated by the exponential institutional developments.

[15] Martii Koskenniemi, *The Gentle Civilizer of Nations* (Cambridge University Press, 2009).

peace,[16] there are comparatively few works by international lawyers directly on peace.[17] The complexity of contemporary international law is seen now through its many specialised regimes rather than through the binary war/peace divide; nonetheless, peace is central to some of these regimes.[18]

3.2.1 A Two-Pronged Approach

World peace through law[19] has been pursued through both the formation of international institutions[20] and the development of substantive principles.[21] The latter has been primarily through two main prongs or streams: processes for the peaceful settlement of disputes and regulation of the use of force in international relations. This section briefly surveys just some of the key moments in the evolution of these streams, weaving together the two narratives of international law's and women's engagements with peace that later become entwined in WPS.

The Hague Peace Conference of 1899, a diplomatic gathering assembled at the invitation of Tsar Nicolas II, was exceptional in that it was not for the resolution of an ongoing conflict but to make law and to address the growing arms race (in which the Tsar was falling behind).[22] The Conference inspired great public interest

[16] E.g. The Statute of the *Institut de Droit International*, adopted at the Conférence internationale juridique, Ghent, 10 September 1873 has as its purpose to promote the progress of international law including 'by contributing, within the limits of its competence, either to the maintenance of peace, or to the observance of the laws of war'.

[17] See, however, Starke (*supra* n 2).

[18] See Cecilia Baillet and Kjetil Mujezinovic Larsen (eds.) *Promoting Peace through International Law* (Oxford University Press, 2015).

[19] Grenville Clark and Louis Sohn, *World Peace through World Law* (Harvard University Press, 1958) was a famous detailed plan by two international lawyers for the maintenance of international peace involving revision of the UN Charter. See also Hans *Kelsen, Peace through Law* (University of North Carolina Press, 1944).

[20] Mark Mazower, *No Enchanted Palace: The End of Empire and the Ideological Origins of the United Nations* (Princeton University Press, 2009).

[21] Chimni points out that peace through the institutions and substances of international law has long been a project of international lawyers; B. S. Chimni, 'Peace through Law: Lessons from 1914', 3 *London Review of International Law* (2015) 245.

[22] In the Convention for the Pacific Settlement of Disputes, The Hague, 1899, the preamble states that it is animated by 'the sincere desire to work for the

with representatives from the many social movements of the late nineteenth century, including peace and humanitarian organisations, expressing their commitment to its objectives and outcome. Thousands of people sent good wishes, proffered advice through brochures, tracts and letters, and sought information about the proceedings from the press. Their involvement indicates the magnet-like attraction of international conferences and summit meetings for non-state actors who seek access so that they can raise their own concerns and express views that might not otherwise be entertained,[23] a process that was advanced throughout the century and was especially evident at the global summit meetings in the 1990s. In the early years of the twenty-first century, global summits appear to have lost their appeal, perhaps precisely because of the large numbers of civil society actors seeking access.

The Hague Conference's most significant achievement was not with respect to disarmament but in the adoption of the Convention for the Pacific Settlement of International Disputes.[24] This commenced the institutionalisation of processes for the peaceful settlement of disputes and brought into multilateral treaty form good offices and mediation, commissions of inquiry (fact-finding) and the first step towards a permanent arbitral body.[25] Belief in third party dispute resolution processes for preventing war was strongly held and promoted through peace societies including the growing international women's movement.[26] Arbitration was seen by women as especially propitious; the International Council of Women, for instance, pledged 'to take steps in every country to further and by every means in their power the movement towards International Arbitration'.[27]

maintenance of general peace'; the preamble to the Convention for the Pacific Settlement of International Disputes, The Hague, 18 October 1907, repeats this language.

[23] George H. Aldrich and Christine M. Chinkin, 'A Century of Achievement and Unfinished Work', 94 *American Journal of International Law* (2000) 90–8, 98.

[24] Convention for the Pacific Settlement of International Disputes, The Hague, 29 July 1899, 1 Bevans 230.

[25] None of these processes were of course new and variations of third party means of dispute settlement have long formed part of international relations.

[26] By the late nineteenth century, improved communications, education and employment had facilitated the growth of women's organisations across international boundaries, especially within Europe and the United States. Jill Liddington, *The Road to Greenham Common: Feminism and Anti-Militarism in Britain since 1820* (Syracuse University Press, 1989) 34.

[27] Cited in Liddington (*supra* n 26) at 36.

Women actively promoted peacemaking processes during the Boer War that broke out only months after the 1899 Hague Conference. For instance, Emily Hobhouse initiated a Women's Branch of the South African Conciliation Committee that had been founded by Leonard Courtney. She fostered the radical idea that women as well as men could be conciliators. Emily Hobhouse was not satisfied with lobbying and found other ways to promote peace and to challenge her government's conduct of the war. She was active in relief work for women and girls,[28] including for those who were forced into concentration camps by the British, visited and exposed the appalling conditions in the camps and campaigned for an official body to examine and report on them.[29] A commission of women, headed by Millicent Fawcett, was appointed by the government to investigate. It provided a less critical picture[30] than that presented by Emily Hobhouse, but it did lead eventually to some improvements.

This 'Committee of Ladies' was in line with the Hague Convention's recognition of the value of a commission of inquiry, a process for 'elucidating the facts by means of an impartial and conscientious investigation'.[31] As did Emily Hobhouse, women's organisations have long favoured 'seeing for themselves' conditions on the ground and not relying on official accounts. For instance, the first resolution adopted by the Zurich Women's Congress in 1919 was based on the 'famine, pestilence and unemployment' that women attendees had witnessed throughout Europe and that they deplored 'as a disgrace to civilisation'. They called for an end to the blockade and for the alliances that had been formed for the purposes of war to be reconfigured for the distribution of food and other necessities.[32] In another example, WILPF sent a delegation of women to investigate violence in

[28] The South African Women and Children Distress Fund was founded to 'feed, clothe, shelter and rescue women and children ... rendered destitute and homeless by the destruction of property'. Cited in Liddington (*supra* n 26) at 48. This foreshadows the 'relief and recovery' pillar of WPS.

[29] Jennifer Hobhouse Balme, *Agent of Peace: Emily Hobhouse and Her Courageous Attempt to End the First World War* (The History Press, 2015) 12.

[30] The Committee was dubbed the 'Whitewashing Commission' by the Boers; Liddington (*supra* n 26) 55.

[31] Convention for the Pacific Settlement of International Disputes (Hague I), The Hague, 29 July 1899, article 9.

[32] WILPF resolutions, 2nd Congress, Zurich, 1919, at https://wilpf.org/wp-content/uploads/2012/08/WILPF_triennial_congress_1919.pdf.

Ireland between Irish 'rebels' and the British police and to refute reports in the media that attributed violence solely to the Irish. The delegation recommended that political prisoners be released, that the armed forces withdraw and that government be entrusted to locally elected bodies.[33]

These examples of fact-finding by women illustrate that commissions of inquiry have been less prolific in the way envisaged in the Hague Convention, that is, as elucidating disputed facts as a precursor to some other dispute settlement processes.[34] Instead, their significance has been more in providing independent and impartial investigations where there have been allegations of violations of international humanitarian law (IHL) and human rights and to make recommendations. Commissions of inquiry mandated primarily by the UN Human Rights Council have proliferated and their value for these purposes has been affirmed within WPS.[35] Resolution 2467 (2019) encourages the inclusion of investigation of conflict-affected sexual violence within the mandate of such fact-finding bodies and appropriate expertise within their membership.[36] The assumption that fact-finders should concentrate on sexual violence when investigating violations of IHL and human rights against women is less than the whole picture, as was understood by both Emily Hobhouse and the women on their way to Zurich in 1919. The appointment of an all-female official fact-finding mission is a model that could be taken up under the WPS framework, although the appointment of known government supporters to the Committee of Ladies (and not Emily Hobhouse, a vocal critic) shows how such mechanisms are easily undermined. The organising, political lobbying, report writing and active relief work undertaken by women

[33] Jill Liddington, 'The Women's Peace Crusade', in Dorothy Thompson (ed.) *Over Our Dead Bodies: Women against the Bomb* (Random House, 1984) 180–98, 194.

[34] John Merrills, *International Dispute Settlement* (Cambridge University Press, 6th ed. 2017) chapter 3.

[35] E.g. the preamble to UN Security Council resolution 2467 (2019) notes that 'United Nations commissions of inquiry and United Nations fact-finding missions, as appropriate and where relevant, [are established] as mechanisms to verify and investigate allegations of violations and abuses of international human rights law and violations of international humanitarian law, and in accordance with their respective mandates to make recommendations to advance accountability and justice and protection for survivors'.

[36] UN Security Council resolution 2467 (2019) para 8.

during the Boer War all demonstrate women's positive involvement in peace work a century before the adoption of the WPS agenda, in stark relief to the depiction of women primarily as victims of war.

Expanded provisions for the peaceful settlement of disputes were accepted at the second Hague Conference in 1907.[37] The outbreak of World War I put an end to the idea that war would be prevented through recourse to arbitration or other dispute resolution processes or that war could ever be made safe for women.[38] In 1915, the first resolution adopted by the Women's Congress was to protest 'against the madness and the horror of war, involving as it does a reckless sacrifice of human life and the destruction of so much that humanity has laboured through centuries to build up'.[39] The protest was conspicuously against 'war', not against 'the current war'. But faith in law as an antidote to war persisted at least among some on the allied side for whom the war was fought 'in defence of international law' with the goal of a stable post-war order based on international law and a League for Peace.[40] The Peace Treaties did not live up to the women's expectations. Emphasis on territorial division, the continuation of empire and power dynamics between European states, the allocation of blame for the conflict and provision for reparations all 'seriously violate[d] the principles upon which alone a just and lasting peace can be secured'.[41] In expressing their deep regret at the terms of the Treaty of Versailles, women at the 2nd International Women's Congress in Zurich in 1919 protested against multiple factors they deemed antithetical to peace: the tacit sanctioning of secret diplomacy by upholding the terms of secret negotiations;

[37] Convention for the Pacific Settlement of International Disputes, The Hague, 18 October 1907.

[38] Emily Hobhouse was an early proponent of this view and that non-combatant women bear the 'brunt of war'. She published *The Brunt of War and Where It Fell* in 1902; Liddington (*supra* n 26) 52.

[39] Resolutions adopted by the International Congress of Women, The Hague, Holland, 1 May 1915, at http://womhist.alexanderstreet.com/hague/doc1.htm.

[40] Michel Erpelding, 'Introduction: Versailles and the Broadening of "Peace through Law"', in Michel Erpelding, Burkhard Hess and Hélène Ruiz Fabri (eds.) *Peace through Law: The Versailles Peace Treaty and Dispute Settlement after World War I* (Nomos Verlagsgesellschaft, 2019) 11–25, 10.

[41] WILPF resolutions (*supra* n 32).

denial of self-determination; according the 'spoils of war' to the victors; demanding disarmament only of one side; and financial proposals that left a hundred million people living in 'poverty, disease and despair'. Nor did the proposed League of Nations satisfy them. They welcomed the concept of an international organisation that would 'represent the will of the people and promote international cooperation' but regretted that the League Covenant did not incorporate President Wilson's fourteen principles. In their view, it contained provisions that 'would stultify its growth and omits others which are essential to world peace'. Members of WILPF continued their demands for a 'just peace' after the formation of the League of Nations and through the also newly created International Labour Organization (ILO).

In the interwar years, the concept of 'peace through law' persisted through further experiments in legal dispute settlement including the newly created Permanent Court of International Justice and Mixed Arbitral Tribunals,[42] the beginnings of international intervention on behalf of groups of individuals (European minorities and those living in mandate territories) and the growth of the international secretariat. International lawyers framed the constitutionalisation of international governance.[43] Attention also turned to the second prong of substantive law: the regulation of the use of force. The League Covenant made war and the threat of war a matter of concern to the League and member states undertook to submit any matter 'likely to lead to a rupture' to arbitration, judicial process or Council inquiry and not to resort to force until at least three months after action by the relevant body.[44] In 1928, the Kellogg-Briand Pact established the legally binding obligation among states

[42] Erpelding (*supra* n 40) 11–25.

[43] Sir Hersch Lauterpacht's lectures on international law at Cambridge in Lent term 1938 founded international law under the Covenant on the peace schemes of Dubois (1303), Sully (1603) and William Penn (1693). He presented the 'legal organization of peace' in five parts: (i) the duty not to resort to force; (ii) the duty of peaceful settlement; (iii) the duty to accept arbitral or judicial settlement; (iv) the duty to enforce collective decisions; and (v) the duty to participate in the machinery of peaceful change. 'This was a complete constitutionalization of international affairs, a system of Rule of Law writ large.' Martii Koskenniemi, 'Lauterpacht: The Victorian Tradition in International Law', 2 *European Journal of International Law* (1997) 215–63, fn 7.

[44] Covenant of the League of Nations, Paris, 1919, articles 10–12.

parties not to have recourse to war with each other.[45] In the view of two commentators,[46] this was the key moment that effectively ended the use of war as an instrument of national policy. Hathaway and Shapiro argue that the allied response to the military invasions in the 1930s was to punish those aggressive acts and thus to assert the effectiveness of the Pact. Their illegality was endorsed in the inclusion of crimes against peace at Nuremburg and Tokyo.[47]

At the end of World War II, the preamble to the UN Charter contains generalised statements upholding tolerance, good neighbourliness and uniting strength to maintain international peace and security. In essence, however, it continues the two-pronged approach through the obligation to 'settle international disputes by peaceful means in such a manner that international peace and security, and justice, are not endangered'[48] and the prohibition on the use of force in international relations against the territorial integrity and political independence of any state or in any other manner contrary to the Charter.[49] These foundational principles were complemented by the collective security system of chapter VII with the Security Council having bestowed upon it the primary responsibility for the maintenance of international peace and security.[50]

Nonetheless, and as has been much commented on, there are structural flaws made inevitable by the centrality of state sovereignty.[51] There is no recourse to compulsory adjudication of disputes by an independent body.[52] The collective security system has been undermined by geopolitical rivalries and by the threat or use of the veto,[53] while the self-defence exception to article 2 (4)[54]

[45] General Treaty for Renunciation of War as an Instrument of National Policy, Paris, 27 August 1928.

[46] Oona Hathaway and Scott Shapiro, *The Internationalists: How a Radical Plan to Outlaw War Remade the World* (Simon and Schuster, 2017).

[47] Charter of the International Military Tribunal, London, 8 August 1945, article 6 (a); Charter of the International Military Tribunal for the Far East, Tokyo, 19 January 1946, article 5 (a).

[48] UN Charter, 1945, article 2 (3) and chapter VI. [49] Ibid., at article 2 (4).

[50] Ibid., at article 24. [51] Ibid., at article 2 (1).

[52] The Statute of the International Court of Justice, 1945, article 36 limits jurisdiction to cases referred to it by the parties, those cases provided for by treaty binding upon the parties in dispute and cases where the parties have made reciprocal Declarations under article 36 (2).

[53] Ibid., at article 27 (3). [54] Ibid., at article 51.

has opened the way for multiple and extended claims of the legal use of force.[55]

The UN Charter system assumes peace as being in contradistinction to interstate conflict, which it seeks to curtail. Further, its focus is on international (global) peace. It allows for regional action in dealing with local disputes,[56] but internal violence and conflict remain essentially a matter within domestic jurisdiction.[57] The Charter makes no provision for curtailing the violence of colonialism, which shaped and was supported by the structures of international law.[58] The post-Charter world has been characterised by localised and regional conflicts and, to this end, the Charter has contributed to what might be called 'global peace', that is, the absence of global conflict. But by allowing for legal exceptions to the prohibition against force, the Charter has in fact undermined peace and legitimated violence. The same is true of the Geneva Conventions of 1949 and the 1977 Additional Protocols that regulate the conduct of war.[59] In similar fashion, by focusing on prevention of and protection against conflict-affected sexual violence, the WPS resolutions minimise the way in which continued gender-based violence outside conflict denies peace for many women and girls.

3.2.2 International Agencies for Peace

The League of Nations and the United Nations were, from the outset, each engaged in the pursuit of peace in the narrow sense of ending the 'scourge of war'[60] and fostering peaceful settlement of disputes. They have been supplemented by a range of what are

55 Christine Chinkin and Mary Kaldor, *International Law and New Wars* (Cambridge University Press, 2017) chapter 4.
56 UN Charter, 1945, articles 52–54.
57 Similarly, recourse to conflict against the colonial power and violent response was not considered international armed conflict until the adoption of Protocol Additional to the Geneva Conventions of 12 August 1949 and relating to the Protection of Victims of International Armed Conflicts (Additional Protocol I), Geneva, 8 June 1977, article 1 (4).
58 Antony Anghie, *Imperialism, Sovereignty and the Making of International Law* (Cambridge University Press, 2005).
59 Chris Jochnick and Roger Normand, 'The Legitimation of Violence: A Critical History of the Laws of War', 35 *Harvard International Law Journal* (1994) 49–96.
60 UN Charter, 1945, preamble. The Covenant of the League of Nations, 1919, preamble stated that the High Contracting Parties agreed to its terms

now UN agencies, two of which are especially significant in the institutional furtherance of peace and where it might be expected that there would be common ground with WPS.

3.2.2.1 THE INTERNATIONAL LABOUR ORGANIZATION (ILO)

The ILO was created as part of the 1919 'peace package'. Fears stoked by the 1917 Bolshevik Revolution made the Powers in Paris receptive to demands for improved labour conditions for workers. The ILO Constitution spells out that the 'peace and harmony of the world are imperilled' by harsh and unjust conditions of labour and upholds the centrality of 'social justice' for the achievement of a universal and permanent peace.[61] Other 'urgently required' conditions include the protection of children, young persons and women and recognition of the principle of equal remuneration for work of equal value. Despite some strong lobbying, the Constitution fell short of endorsing women's political equality.[62] These aspirational words about peace and progressive social conditions were not necessarily internalised by the peacemakers or by ILO personnel as they commenced their work.[63] In the opinion of an early director, the ILO paid little attention to how it contributed to peace, although WILPF members and other women's bodies continued to press the issue. It was not until World War II made immediately pertinent the association between workers' conditions and peace that the ILO directly addressed the role of labour in the maintenance of security in the transition from war to peace. The Philadelphia Declaration, adopted while World War II was ongoing,[64] reaffirmed the ILO's aims and purposes and the 'truth' of the statement that 'lasting peace can be established only

'[i]n order to promote international co-operation and to achieve international peace and security'.

61 Treaty of Versailles, 28 June 1919, Part XIII, Constitution of the International Labour Organization.

62 Christine Chinkin, 'Enhancing the Impact of International Norms with Special Reference to Women's Labour Rights and the Women, Peace and Security Agenda', in George P. Politakis, Tomi Kohiyama and Thomas Lieby (eds.) *ILO 100 Law for Social Justice* (International Labour Office, 2019) 597–618.

63 Edward Phelan, 'The Contribution of the ILO to Peace', 59 (6) *International Labour Review* (1949) 607–32.

64 Declaration concerning the aims and purposes of the International Labour Organization, Philadelphia, 10 May 1944.

if it is based on social justice'.[65] In 2017, the ILO again explicitly addressed the conditions for peace, affirming the 'importance of employment and decent work for promoting peace',[66] for 'prevention, recovery, peace and resilience with respect to crisis situations arising from conflicts and disasters'.[67] Recommendation 205 makes provision for ensuring that women are not marginalised in conflict and crisis and their aftermath, including, inter alia, through: non-discrimination and equality between women and men in the field of work; paying attention to single-headed households, especially those headed by women or others made vulnerable by conflict; ensuring that women who have assumed expanded responsibilities during conflict are not displaced when the crisis is over; and ensuring 'that women are empowered to effectively and meaningfully participate in decision-making processes in the context of recovery and building resilience, and that their needs and interests are prioritized in strategies and responses, and that the human rights of women and girls are promoted and protected'. ILO recommendation 205 echoes UN Security Council resolution 1325 (2000) in its attention to gender balance and ensuring a gender perspective, but it does not engage directly with the WPS agenda. Nor do the WPS resolutions refer to the relevant ILO standards.

3.2.2.2 THE UNITED NATIONS EDUCATIONAL, SCIENTIFIC AND CULTURAL ORGANIZATION (UNESCO)

Pursuit of a culture of peace is the objective of UNESCO, founded in the wake of war in 1945.[68] The perception of peace within the preamble of the UNESCO Constitution commences with the binary association with conflict but then goes further:

> [S]ince wars begin in the minds of men, it is in the minds of men that the defences of peace must be constructed; . . . That a peace based exclusively

[65] Ibid., at II (a). The provision asserts that 'all human beings, irrespective of race, creed or sex, have the right to pursue both their material well-being and their spiritual development in conditions of freedom and dignity, of economic security and equal opportunity'.

[66] ILO R205 – Employment and Decent Work for Peace and Resilience Recommendation, 2017 (No. 205), Geneva, 106th ILC Session, 16 June 2017.

[67] Ibid., at para 1.

[68] Constitution of the United Nations Educational, Scientific and Cultural Organization, London, 16 November 1945.

upon the political and economic arrangements of governments would not be a peace which could secure the unanimous, lasting and sincere support of the peoples of the world, and that the peace must therefore be founded, if it is not to fail, upon the intellectual and moral solidarity of mankind.

This formulation aspires to a perpetual peace and rejects the position that this is unattainable and that only something less than this is achievable. In any event, it is necessary to 'wage peace'.[69] In 2019, a UNESCO specialist described the organisation as having a 'humanist mission' to 'support people in understanding each other and working together to build lasting peace, including through education, the sciences, culture, communication and information'.[70] Its work includes seeking to 'change mindset through global citizenship education' and fostering 'intercultural and interreligious dialogue'. The WPS resolutions make no mention of the cultural work of UNESCO in seeking to advance a broader understanding of peace that takes account of women. A linkage between WPS and UNESCO could be channelled through the Convention on the Elimination of All Forms of Discrimination against Women (CEDAW) with its requirement for appropriate measures to modify cultural attitudes and behaviours that support the inferiority of either of the sexes.[71] Seeking such structural change must be central to a gendered understanding of peace.

3.2.3 International Law and Disarmament

What is omitted from this two-pronged account of international law and peace is disarmament – the motivation for the 1899 Hague Conference and an objective of WILPF from its origins.[72] The regulation of arms has had a chequered history throughout

[69] Starke (*supra* n 2) 9.

[70] Kostantinos Tararas, Programme Specialist in the Sector for Social and Human Sciences; UNESCO Report of the United Nations High Commissioner for Human Rights, Summary of the intersessional workshop on the right to peace, A/HRC/39/31, 31 July 2018.

[71] Convention on the Elimination of All Forms of Discrimination against Women, 1979, article 5 (a).

[72] The 1915 Women's Congress also considered that the private profits from arms manufacture constituted a 'powerful hindrance to the abolition of war'. Resolutions adopted by the International Congress of Women, The Hague 1915, at https://wilpf.org/wp-content/uploads/2012/08/WILPF_triennial_congress_1915.pdf.

international law and, interestingly, is rarely considered in mainstream accounts or courses in public international law. It is conspicuously absent from Sir Hersch Lauterpacht's outline for foundational topics of international law.[73] Three methods of arms regulation are commonly understood: arms control, non-proliferation and disarmament.[74] The UN Charter divides responsibility for arms control between the General Assembly and the Security Council. Article 11 authorises the Assembly to 'consider the general principles of co-operation in the maintenance of international peace and security, including the principles governing disarmament and the regulation of armaments' and to make recommendations to member states and/or the Security Council. Article 26 places responsibility for 'the establishment of a system for the regulation of armaments' on the Security Council. Since the permanent members are members of the nuclear club and leading global dealers in arms, this responsibility has remained largely ignored. Their position as nuclear powers is cemented by the Non-Proliferation Treaty and their obligation to 'pursue negotiations in good faith on effective measures relating to cessation of the nuclear arms race at an early date and to nuclear disarmament, and on a treaty on general and complete disarmament under strict and effective international control'[75] forcefully resisted.[76] What constitutes 'general and complete disarmament' remains ambiguous. And in the current climate, where the United States has withdrawn from the 1972 Anti-Ballistic Missile Treaty and the 1987 Intermediate-Range Nuclear Forces Treaty with Russia, further real progress seems unlikely.

There have, however, been some successes, for instance with respect to the formation of regional, national and local nuclear

[73] See *supra* n 43. [74] Chinkin and Kaldor (*supra* n 55) chapter 6.
[75] Treaty on the Non-Proliferation of Nuclear Weapons, New York, 12 June 1968.
[76] E.g. the United Kingdom's successful refusal to accept the admissibility of the case brought against it in the ICJ by the Marshall Islands; *Obligations concerning Negotiations relating to Cessation of the Nuclear Arms Race and to Nuclear Disarmament* (*Marshall Islands* v *United Kingdom*) 2016 ICJ Reports 833. In February 2017, the UK added a reservation to its Declaration accepting the compulsory jurisdiction of the Court under the Statute of the ICJ, article 36 (2) to exclude 'any claim or dispute that arises from or is connected with or related to nuclear disarmament and/or nuclear weapons, unless all of the other nuclear-weapon States Party to the Treaty on the Non-Proliferation of Nuclear Weapons have also consented to the jurisdiction of the Court and are party to the proceedings in question'.

free zones and prohibition of specific weapons. The latter include the Landmines Convention,[77] the Chemical Weapons and Biological Weapons Treaties[78] and the Treaty Prohibiting Nuclear Weapons.[79] Legal control of trade in small arms and light weapons has been advanced by the Arms Trade Treaty.[80] There are also regional programmes for the control of arms.

Although the global treaties are weakened by the absence of the major powers from some or all of them and by inadequate provision for monitoring compliance, the contributions of civil society were a major factor in their successful negotiation. A new strategy with respect to weapons control is to highlight the human and humanitarian consequences of weapons use. Thus, the preamble to the Landmines Convention starts with a strong statement about the suffering caused by these weapons 'that kill or maim hundreds of people every week, ... especially children. They remain in place often years after the purported end of conflict[,] inhibiting steps towards reconstruction and peaceful conditions.' The humanitarian disaster aspect is even more explicitly described in the preamble to the Treaty Prohibiting Nuclear Weapons, which details how their use would 'transcend national borders, pose grave implications for human survival, the environment, socioeconomic development, the global economy, food security and the health of current and future generations'. The Treaty also emphasises the disproportionate impact of nuclear fallout on women and girls. This ethical, human rights approach to arms control and its particular relevance to women and girls had already been made in CEDAW, which affirmed that equality between women and men would be advanced by 'general and complete disarmament, in particular nuclear disarmament under strict and effective international control'.[81] The Treaty

[77] Convention on the Prohibition of the Use, Stockpiling, Production and Transfer of Anti-personnel Mines and on their Destruction, Oslo, 1997, preamble.

[78] Convention on the Prohibition of the Development, Production and Stockpiling of Bacteriological (Biological) and Toxin Weapons and on their Destruction, London, Moscow and Washington, 1972; The Convention on the Prohibition of the Development, Production, Stockpiling and Use of Chemical Weapons and on their Destruction, Paris and New York, 1992.

[79] Treaty on the Prohibition of Nuclear Weapons, New York, 2017.

[80] UN General Assembly resolution 67/234, 2 April 2013, *The Arms Trade Treaty*.

[81] Convention on the Elimination of All Forms of Discrimination against Women, 1979, preamble. See also the UN General Assembly resolution 33/73, 15 December 1978, *Declaration on the Preparation of Societies for Life in Peace*.

Prohibiting Nuclear Weapons is innovative in bringing human rights, women's advancement and peace into arms control, but such nexus has also been progressed through the General Assembly, human rights instruments and the global summits for women. These developments are the subject of Section 3.3.

3.3 Human Rights and Peace

At the behest of civil society at San Francisco in 1945, the UN Charter goes beyond the twofold prescriptions of seeking peaceful settlement of disputes and regulating the use of force in another important respect: it introduces human rights guarantees for individuals in place of the minorities protections of the League.[82] Provision for the growth of human rights law and institutions, including women's human rights,[83] allows for a fuller conception of peace than simply the absence of conflict.

But progress in bringing together human rights and peace has been slow. There is no explicit right to peace in either the Universal Declaration of Human Rights (UDHR) or the two 1966 Covenants.[84] The preamble to all three instruments declares that 'recognition of the inherent dignity and of the equal and inalienable rights of all members of the human family is the foundation of freedom, justice and peace in the world'. The assertion in article 28 of the UDHR that 'everyone is entitled to a social and international order in which the rights and freedoms set forth in this Declaration can be fully realized' in effect assumes that human rights cannot be realised in the absence of peace. This all-encompassing entitlement is not found in the Covenants.[85] Despite the preambular linkage between disarmament and women's equality, there is no right to peace in CEDAW. Of the

[82] UN Charter, 1945, articles 1 (3), 55 and 56.

[83] World Conference on Human Rights, Vienna Declaration and Programme of Action, 25 June 1993, I, para 18: 'The human rights of women and of the girl-child are an inalienable, integral and indivisible part of universal human rights.'

[84] International Covenant on Economic, Social and Cultural Rights and International Covenant on Civil and Political Rights, UN General Assembly resolution 2200 A (XXI), 16 December 1966.

[85] There is a similar sentiment in the Declaration concerning the aims and purposes of the International Labour Organization, Philadelphia, 10 May 1944, II (b): '[T]he attainment of the conditions in which this shall be possible must constitute the central aim of national and international policy.'

human rights treaties,[86] only the Banjul Charter (1981) contains an explicit right of all peoples 'to national and international peace and security'.[87] This is furthered in the Maputo Protocol on the Rights of Women in Africa,[88] which provides an expansive understanding of peace. In its preamble, the Maputo Protocol explicitly recalls UN Security Council resolution 1325 (2000). It affirms the right of women in Africa to 'a peaceful existence and ... to participate in the promotion and maintenance of peace'.[89] Article 10 spells out more detail: states' obligation to ensure women's increased participation in 'programmes of education for peace and a culture of peace'; in conflict prevention, management and resolution and decision-making 'to ensure physical, psychological, social and legal protection of asylum seekers, refugees, returnees and displaced persons' at local, regional, national, continental and international levels; in the management of refugee and internally displaced person (IDP) camps and settlements; and in the planning and implementation of post-conflict reconstruction and rehabilitation. It also requires necessary measures for significant reduction in military spending 'in favour of spending on social development in general, and the promotion of women in particular'.

The omission of peace from the UN human rights treaties does not mean that there has been complete silence, and further relevant language is found in international soft law instruments, notably a series of General Assembly resolutions.[90] The cold war reiteration of the principles of the Charter for the Organization's twenty-fifth anniversary preferred the less ambitious terminology of 'friendly

[86] The ASEAN Human Rights Declaration, 19 November 2012, article 38 states:

> Every person and the peoples of ASEAN have the right to enjoy peace within an ASEAN framework of security and stability, neutrality and freedom, such that the rights set forth in this Declaration can be fully realised. To this end, ASEAN Member States should continue to enhance friendship and cooperation in the furtherance of peace, harmony and stability in the region.

[87] African Charter on Human and Peoples' Rights, 27 June 1981, article 23.

[88] Protocol to the African Charter on Human and Peoples' Rights on the Rights of Women in Africa (Maputo Protocol), July 2003.

[89] Maputo Protocol, article 10; see also article 4 (2) (d).

[90] For fuller details of the many General Assembly resolutions, see Djacoba Liva Tehindrazanarivelo and Robert Kolb, 'Peace, Right to, International Protection', *Max Planck Encyclopaedia of International Law* (Oxford University Press, 2006).

relations' and 'cooperation',[91] but nevertheless expressed commitment to the 'peoples of the United Nations' living in peace.[92] The Declaration on the Right of Peoples to Peace,[93] similarly a cold war instrument, went further by proclaiming the 'sacred right to peace' of all peoples on the planet, as well as the fundamental obligation on states to preserve that right. The focus of the Declaration was to eradicate war and 'avert a world-wide nuclear catastrophe'. It reasserts the two familiar pathways to international peace and security: renunciation of the use of force in international relations and peaceful settlement of disputes.

These General Assembly resolutions do not consider what peace might mean for women. The three objectives of the UN's Decade for Women, 1975–85 – 'equality, peace and development' – meant that women's relationship with peace figured in the debates and outcome documents of the global summits. At the first women's conference in Mexico City in 1975, peace was linked to the promotion and protection of human rights for all in conditions of equity and an increased contribution by women towards strengthening world peace.[94] The Conference addressed disarmament, highlighting the cost of the arms race and that such human and financial resources could be more constructively used for peace and development. The Conference called upon women as well as men to 'promote real, general and complete disarmament under effective international control' and to 'maintain vigilance and do their utmost to achieve and maintain international peace'.[95] It also

[91] UN General Assembly resolution 2625, 24 October 1970, *Declaration on Principles of International Law concerning Friendly Relations and Cooperation among States in accordance with the Charter of the United Nations.* The concept of friendly relations draws upon UN Charter, 1945, article 55.

[92] The concept of 'living in peace' echoes UN Charter, 1945, preamble: 'to practice tolerance and live together in peace with one another as good neighbours'. It is found in other instruments; e.g. UN General Assembly resolution 33/73, 15 December 1978, *Declaration on the Preparation of Societies for Life in Peace.* See also the objective that 'people can live in true and lasting peace free from any threat to or attempt against their security'; Conference on Security and Cooperation in Europe, Final Act, Helsinki, August 1975.

[93] UN General Assembly resolution 39/11, 12 November 1984, *Declaration on the Right of Peoples to Peace.*

[94] Report of the World Conference of the International Women's Year, Mexico City, June 1975, E/Conf.66/34, Declaration of Mexico on the Equality of Women and Their Contribution to Development and Peace and Plan of Action, II, para 50.

[95] Ibid., at I, para 30.

emphasised the vital role of women in promoting peace and that they should therefore participate 'equally with men' in relevant decision-making.[96]

A decade later, the Third World Conference on Women agreed a definition that resonates with Johan Galtung's famous distinction between negative and positive peace[97] (and indeed the ILO Constitution with its emphasis on social justice): 'Peace includes not only the absence of war, violence and hostilities at the national and international levels but also the enjoyment of economic and social justice, equality and the entire range of human rights and fundamental freedoms within society.'[98] The Nairobi Conference took place at a time when women's activism against nuclear war had been especially prominent through peace marches and camps, for instance that at Greenham Common and elsewhere in Europe and the United States. The Forward-Looking Strategies noted the unabated arms race, alongside other impediments to peace, and urged that it be halted and that the resources that fuelled it be diverted toward developmental and humanitarian progress. Despite there being an end to the cold war, the World Conference on Human Rights in 1993 did not figure peace strongly, although it did link efforts for the universal observance of human rights with improved conditions for peace and security, as well as social and economic development.[99] In 1995, at Beijing, the Fourth World Conference on Women recognised that '[p]eace is inextricably linked with equality between women and men and development'.[100] As at Mexico City and Nairobi, the Beijing Conference recommended women's participation in decision-making about conflict. Strategic objective E. 2 sought the reduction of excessive military expenditure and arms

[96] Ibid., at I, para 25 and II, para 56: 'Women should have equal opportunity with men to represent their countries in all international forums where the above questions are discussed, and in particular at meetings of the organizations of the United Nations system, including the Security Council and all conferences on disarmament and international peace.'

[97] Galtung (*supra* n 5) 167–91.

[98] World Conference to review and appraise the achievements of the United Nations Decade for Women: Equality, Development and Peace, Nairobi Forward-looking Strategies for the Advancement of Women, A/CONF.116/28/Rev., 26 July 1985, para 13.

[99] World Conference on Human Rights, Vienna Declaration and Programme of Action, 25 June 1993, I, para 6.

[100] Fourth World Conference on Women, Beijing, September 1995, Beijing Declaration, 1995, para 18.

control. In this regard, it recognised the leading role of women in the peace movement and recommended active work toward 'general and complete disarmament under strict and effective international control'.[101] This important step toward international peace and security would release resources for 'social and economic programmes which benefit women and girls'.[102] Beijing and the follow-up Beijing + 5 (held in September 2000) were important forerunners of UN Security Council resolution 1325, adopted in October 2000.

At the 2005 World Summit, the General Assembly resolved to create two new institutions relevant to peace: a Peacebuilding Commission[103] and a Human Rights Council.[104] The former was, in fact, jointly established by the General Assembly and the Security Council,[105] which both took as their starting point that peace, now termed 'sustainable peace', is something that is sought by countries emerging from a different situation called 'conflict': peacebuilding is thus limited to the narrow situation of 'assisting parties to conflicts to end hostilities and emerge towards recovery, reconstruction and development'.

In the mandate for the Human Rights Council, peace does not figure strongly. In the Council's foundational resolution, the General Assembly acknowledged peace and security, along with development and human rights, as the pillars of the United Nations system. It recognised that 'peace and security and human rights are interlinked and mutually reinforcing',[106] but it did not expound further. The Council has, however, located peace within the framework of human rights. It formed an open-ended working group on the subject, which saw contestations as to the desirability and feasibility of a 'right to peace' and held hotly contrasting views that were also expressed in the General Assembly. Some government delegations saw peace as

[101] Fourth World Conference on Women, Beijing, September 1995, Beijing Platform for Action, 1995, para 143 (f) (i).

[102] Outcome of the twenty-third special session of the General Assembly entitled 'Women 2000: gender equality, development and peace for the twenty-first century', 5–9 June 2000 (Beijing + 5) para 99 (k).

[103] UN General Assembly resolution 60/1, 24 October 2005, *World Summit Outcome*, para 97.

[104] Ibid., at para 157.

[105] UN General Assembly resolution 60/180, 20 December 2005, *The Peacebuilding Commission*; UN Security Council resolution 1645, 20 December 2005.

[106] UN General Assembly resolution, 60/251, 15 March 2006, *Human Rights Council*.

a precondition for the enjoyment of human rights and considered that international law, through its prohibition of aggression, is the basis for peace. Other delegations resisted this view, positing that international law provides no basis for a right to peace.[107]

The Declaration on the Right to Peace was adopted by the General Assembly on 2 February 2017.[108] It recognises that peace is more than absence of conflict and entails 'a positive, dynamic participatory process where dialogue is encouraged and conflicts are solved in a spirit of mutual understanding and cooperation, and socioeconomic development is ensured'. Nevertheless, the Declaration is a two-headed beast. On the one hand, it is heavily imbued with the traditional international institutional concerns for the maintenance of international peace and security – state sovereignty, the prohibition of the use of force in international relations, non-intervention, self-determination, an end to foreign occupation and alien domination, and the fight against terrorism. On the other hand, it uses the language of human rights and development so that 'everyone has the right to enjoy peace such that all human rights are promoted and protected and development is fully realized'. Values such as tolerance, dialogue, cooperation and solidarity among all human beings, peoples and nations of the world are extolled as means of fostering peace, and institutions of peace education are promoted for their role in strengthening these values.

But there is a glaring gap in the Declaration: despite women's long history of peace activism, the UN Decade-long objectives of 'equality, development and peace' and the explicit commitment in WPS to 'peace', women are absent from the Declaration. Human rights instruments are listed but not CEDAW. The need for 'special and positive measures, for furthering equal social development and the realization of the civil and political, economic, social and cultural rights of all victims of racism, racial discrimination, xenophobia and related intolerance' is rightly recorded, but there is no such recognition of the harmful consequences for individuals, families and communities of sex and gender-based discrimination, misogyny and patriarchy. Indeed, the only mention of women in the

[107] E.g., Report of the open-ended intergovernmental working group on a draft United Nations declaration on the right to peace on its third session, 26 May 2015, A/ HRC/29/45, paras 24 and 25.

[108] The Declaration was first adopted by the Human Rights Council, A/HRC/32/ L.18, 24 June 2016; UN General Assembly resolution 71/189, 2 February 2017.

Declaration is the instrumentalist assertion 'that the full and complete development of a country, the welfare of the world [no less] and the cause of peace require the maximum participation of women, on equal terms with men in all fields', language drawn from CEDAW without attribution. This omission highlights the disconnect between human rights and security, between the General Assembly and its subsidiary organ, the Human Rights Council, and the Security Council. It fails to identify that continuing gender inequalities and violence against women, 'everyday' violence as well as in conflict, undermine peace and that, while 'tolerance, dialogue and cooperation . . . are [undoubtedly] among the best guarantees of international peace and security', these values must not be misplaced so as to maintain an unequal and oppressive status quo. Women should not be tolerant of the abuses they endure, even if their anger causes social disharmony and threatens peaceful relations. Dialogue must be inclusive; despite endless calls for their participation, women's place in dialogue concerning international affairs remains irregularly implemented at national and international levels.

The Declaration on the Right to Peace locates peace as a human rights entitlement. The General Assembly also views peace as an expression of development, as in its 2015 adoption of the Sustainable Development Goals (SDGs). Under the heading 'peace', the Assembly stated its determination 'to foster peaceful, just and inclusive societies which are free from fear and violence. There can be no sustainable development without peace and no peace without sustainable development.'[109] The SDGs also seek to 'realize the human rights of all and to achieve gender equality and the empowerment of all women and girls'. The 2015 High-level Panel on Peace Operations implicitly recognised this broader understanding of peace in its dedication to three-year-old Nyakhat Pal. It describes her walking for four hours through harsh and dangerous terrain in South Sudan to a UNICEF World Food Programme rapid response distribution centre. When she heard that the UN was providing vaccines, food, water and sanitation supplies – core economic and social rights – she hurried.[110]

[109] UN General Assembly resolution 70/1, 25 September 2015, *Transforming our world: the 2030 Agenda for Sustainable Development.*

[110] Report of the High-level Independent Panel on Peace Operations, *Uniting our strengths for peace: politics, partnership and people,* A/70/95–S/2015/446, 17 June 2015, 6.

3.4 WPS and Peace

The previous sections have outlined international law's complex relationship with peace. The tension between military action to sustain security and human rights as a bulwark for peace, between the New York-based Security Council and the Geneva-based Human Rights Council is the context within which WPS must make its mark. This section considers the concept of peace within WPS.

The word 'peace' appears in UN Security Council resolution 1325 twenty-two times but not as a self-standing concept. On 8 March 2000 – the 'United Nations Day for Women's Rights and International Peace' – the then President of the Security Council, Anwarul Karim Chowdhury from Bangladesh, spoke of a culture of peace and of women as 'peace educators'.[111] His speech was seen as a forerunner of resolution 1325, adopted in October of that year. But his language was not repeated in resolution 1325 where 'peace' is joined with other terms: 'international peace and security', 'peace process', 'peacekeeping', 'peace-building', 'Peace Support Operations', 'peace agreements', 'peace initiatives'. Only once, in the preamble, is there a reference to 'durable peace', but the notion of sustainability is not developed.

Two aspects stand out in the Council's depiction of peace in the WPS agenda. First is that peace is not understood in any holistic sense. It is depicted as the opposite of conflict and is to be made, kept, built and sustained in conflict-affected societies rather than perceived as a process and goal for all societies. There is no wider expression of peace such as that adopted at the Third World Conference on Women in Nairobi (1985) or recognition of the repeated calls for reduction of military expenditure and the availability of arms in the Beijing Platform for Action.[112] WILPF campaigned for resolution 1325 to be a peace resolution that included this part of the Beijing Platform, but it was unsuccessful. This limited perception of peace is additionally disappointing in that, only a year previously, the Council itself had stressed (without terming it peace) 'the need to address the causes of armed conflict in a comprehensive manner in order to enhance the protection of civilians on a long term basis, including

[111] Press Release, SC/6816, 8 March 2000.

[112] Fourth World Conference on Women, Beijing, September 1995, Beijing Platform for Action, Strategic Objective E. 2.

by promoting economic growth, poverty eradication, sustainable development, national reconciliation, good governance, democracy, the rule of law and respect for and protection of human rights'.[113] The Council had also noted how the accumulation of small arms and light weapons can prolong conflict and undermine 'the confidence required for a return to peace'.[114]

The binary between peace/conflict in the WPS resolutions assumes situations called 'conflict' and 'post-conflict', an assumption that is problematic for women. In addition to the 'everyday' violence that women experience, there are circumstances of extreme gender-based violence against women that are not understood as conflict and are thus not the subject of peacemaking. Gender-related killings (femicide) are condemned as human rights violations,[115] and states are reminded of their due diligence obligations to prevent and investigate the violence and to prosecute perpetrators. Transformative reparations that seek to address structural inequalities and prevent repetition have been recommended.[116] But even such extreme violence does not come within the ambit of conflict and thus of WPS. Similarly, just as women experience war differently because of, inter alia, their gender, so are their post-conflict experiences gendered and violent. Gender-based violence against women does not commence with conflict or stop with a formal ceasefire.[117] The forms and locations of gendered violence shift throughout the continuum of what is labelled 'peacetime', 'conflict' and 'post-conflict' so that peace processes 'result in new forms of violence and insecurity, including criminality, gangs and higher rates of sexual and gender-based violence – a perpetual state of no war, no peace, that has

[113] UN Security Council resolution 1265, 17 September 1999, *Protection of civilians in armed conflict*.

[114] Ibid., at para 17.

[115] E.g. Report of the Special Rapporteur on violence against women, its causes and consequences, *Gender-related killings*, A/HRC/20/16, 23 May 2012; Report on Mexico produced by the Committee on the Elimination of Discrimination against Women under article 8 of the Optional Protocol to the Convention, and reply from the Government of Mexico, CEDAW/C/2005/OP.8/MEXICO, 27 January 2005.

[116] E.g. *Velásquez Paiz et al* v *Guatemala* (IACtHR, 19 November 2015); *Linda Lopez Soto et al* v *Venezuela* (IACtHR, 26 September 2018).

[117] CEDAW Committee, General Recommendation No. 30, para 35: 'all forms of gender-based violence, in particular sexual violence escalate in the post-conflict setting'.

detrimental effects on all aspects of political, social and economic development'.[118]

In 2015, the *Global Study on the Implementation of Resolution 1325* reflected on the meaning of peace and how it had changed:

> For decades, peace meant mainly the silencing of guns and the renewal of formal politics as the way of governance. Ceasefires and demobilization were the main focus of peace processes. However, today it is recognized that peace is something far more than the 'absence of violence'. Peace has increasingly meant an inclusive political process, a commitment to human rights in the post-war period and an attempt to deal with issues of justice and reconciliation.[119]

This progressive approach to peace is not captured in the WPS resolution that followed the *Global Study*, resolution 2242 (2015). The two resolutions adopted in 2019, resolutions 2467 and 2493, similarly link peace to peacemaking processes, peace talks and agreements, peacekeeping and peace operations, peacebuilding and peacebuilders, although resolution 2493 does reaffirm the importance of achieving sustainable peace through negotiatory methods.

The second aspect that stands out in the Security Council's account of peace in the WPS resolutions is that women are deemed important peacemakers. Their increased participation in decision-making with regard to conflict prevention and resolution is urged for their 'important role' in these functions. This is the subject of Section 3.5.

3.5 Women and Peacemaking

3.5.1 Women's Participation in Peace Processes

The WPS resolutions do not contribute to substantive understandings of peace. Instead, what they do is urge women's participation

[118] More men than women die 'from all the violence in the world as well as directly from war' but 'on average more women than men die or suffer serious disease as a result of inter-state and internationalised civil wars when the post-conflict period is included'. Donna Pankhurst, 'The Gendered Impact of Peace', in Michael Pugh, Neil Cooper and Mandy Turner (eds.) *Whose Peace? Critical Perspectives on the Political Economy of Peacebuilding* (Palgrave, 2008) 30–6, 32.

[119] Radhika Coomaraswamy and others, *Preventing Conflict, Transforming Justice, Securing the Peace: A Global Study on the Implementation of Security Council Resolution 1325* (United Nations, 2015) [hereinafter *Global Study*] 24.

and representation in processes relating to conflict prevention, management and resolution, thus giving Security Council sanction to what women had long been urging and, more importantly, undertaking in myriad ways. At the beginning of the twentieth century, women were seeking not only national suffrage but also participation in international affairs including in decisions relating to peace. The 1915 International Women's Congress demanded that the negotiated peace include its resolutions. It urged a permanent International Conference that would hold regular meetings where women would take part and consider practical proposals for international cooperation. The Covenant did provide for women's participation in the League of Nations,[120] as did the Charter for the United Nations, albeit in somewhat negative terms in the latter.[121] Women involved themselves in the work of the League in Geneva and in national associations and were active lobbyists, but their formal participation remained limited, as has been the case with the UN.[122]

Demands for and commitments to women's participation have continued both prior to and following the adoption of UN Security Council resolution 1325. CEDAW's preamble states 'that the full and complete development of a country, the welfare of the world and the cause of peace require the maximum participation of women on equal terms with men in all fields'. CEDAW articles 7 and 8 are worded widely, requiring states to take appropriate measures to eliminate discrimination against women in public and private life, including at the international level and in international organisations. This obligation is not limited to processes related to conflict. In 1982, following the entry into force of CEDAW in 1981, the General Assembly repeated that women have an equal right to participate in societal affairs and that measures must be taken to ensure this, which is dependent on

[120] Covenant of the League of Nations, 1919, article 7: 'All positions under or in connection with the League, including the Secretariat, shall be open equally to men and women.' See also Treaty of Versailles, 28 June 1919, Part XIII, Constitution of the International Labour Organization, article 395.

[121] UN Charter, 1945 article 8: 'The United Nations shall place no restrictions on the eligibility of men and women to participate in any capacity and under conditions of equality in its principal and subsidiary organs.'

[122] The Secretary-General has made gender parity a priority of his term of office; UN, System Wide Gender Parity, 6 October 2017, at www.un.org/gender/sites/www.un.org.gender/files/gender_parity_strategy_october_2017.pdf.

a 'balanced and equitable' division of roles within the family and society. Increasing women's participation in society's economic, social, cultural, civil and political affairs will contribute to international peace and security.[123] Eighty years after the resolutions adopted by the Women's Congress at The Hague, the strategic objectives of the Beijing Platform for Action included that governments and international intergovernmental organisations take action 'to promote equal participation of women and equal opportunities for women to participate in all forums and peace activities'.[124] And five years later, women's participation and representation were accepted as a core component of UN Security Council resolution 1325.

The preamble to resolution 1325 reaffirms 'the important role of women in the prevention and resolution of conflicts and in peacebuilding'. It stresses 'the importance of their equal participation and full involvement in all efforts for the maintenance and promotion of peace and security, and the need to increase their role in decision-making with regard to conflict prevention and resolution'. The first operative paragraph follows this up but also weakens it by urging increased (not equal) 'representation of women at all decision-making levels in national, regional and international institutions and mechanisms for the prevention, management, and resolution of conflict'. This language is repeated in subsequent WPS resolutions, notably 1889 (2009) and 2242 (2015). Resolution 2467 (2019) calls upon parties to conflict to ensure 'that women are present and meaningfully participate in political pre-negotiation and negotiation processes'.

Continued calls for women's participation in peacemaking and peacebuilding activities have become routine in a range of UN policy documents and resolutions in the subsequent years. For instance, the 2005 High-level Panel on Threats, Challenges and Change recommended '[g]reater consultation with and involvement in peace processes of important voices from civil society, especially those of

[123] UN General Assembly resolution 37/63, 3 December 1982, *Declaration on the Participation of Women in Promoting International Peace and Co-operation*, article 3; see also UN General Assembly resolution 40/108, 1 December 1985 *on Implementation of the Nairobi Forward-looking Strategies for the Advancement of Women*, para 6.

[124] Fourth World Conference on Women, Beijing, September 1995, Beijing Platform for Action, para 142 (a).

women'.[125] The ensuing Global Summit stressed 'the important role of women in the prevention and resolution of conflicts and in peacebuilding'.[126] In the creation of the Peacebuilding Commission in 2005, the General Assembly and the Security Council separately reaffirmed 'the important role of women in the prevention and resolution of conflicts and in peacebuilding, and stressing the importance of their equal participation and full involvement in all efforts for the maintenance and promotion of peace and security and the need to increase their role in decision-making with regard to conflict prevention and resolution and peacebuilding'.[127] In their review of the UN peacebuilding architecture, the General Assembly and the Security Council each separately recognised 'sustaining peace' as both a goal and a process for societies to achieve a common vision that involved all sections of society.[128] To this end, the important role of women in peacemaking and peacebuilding and the 'substantial link' between their involvement in efforts for conflict prevention, resolution and post-conflict rebuilding and effectiveness and long-term sustainability was reaffirmed.

In 2016, the General Assembly embarked on a series of women-specific resolutions on disarmament, non-proliferation and arms control, which it explicitly links to the WPS agenda.[129] These resolutions call for women's 'full and meaningful' participation in policy-making, planning and implementation, in this instance in matters relevant to disarmament and arms control. In response to the Assembly's request for suggestions from states on 'ways and means of promoting the role of women in disarmament, non-proliferation and arms control',[130] a number of states emphasised promotion of women's participation in security sector activities.

125 High-level Panel on Threats, Challenges and Change, A More Secure World: Our Shared Responsibility, 2005, para 103 (d).

126 UN General Assembly resolution 60/1, 24 October 2005, *World Summit Outcome*, para 116.

127 UN General Assembly resolution 60/180, 30 December 2005; UN Security Council resolution 1645, 20 December 2005.

128 UN General Assembly resolution 70/262, 2016; UN SC resolution 2282, 27 April 2016.

129 UN General Assembly resolution 71/56, 13 December 2016, *Women, disarmament, non-proliferation and arms control.*

130 Ibid.

There is thus widespread – at least rhetorical – agreement about the need for women's participation in matters relating to peace. But three points require emphasis. First is that, throughout these and other instruments, there is an assumption – sometimes explicit, at other times implicit – that increasing the number of women in decision-making about peace (conflict prevention, management and resolution) is good for peace. Women's participation is deemed important more for the maintenance of international peace and security through prevention and resolution of conflict than for enhancing women's rights.[131] Moreover, why this is the case is not explained. Second, there is ambivalence as to whether the requirement is for equal representation (as in CEDAW and some earlier instruments) or merely increased representation (as, for instance, in resolution 1325). Third, there is no guidance as to how enhanced participation is to be achieved or what constitutes 'full and meaningful participation'. There is a danger that women's mere presence might be heralded as success regardless of whether they are able to speak or are listened to. But, more positively, the call for women's participation moves away from the representation of women as passive,[132] as victims in need of protection. The underlying portrayal is of women as active agents, as vital stakeholders whose experiences and expertise can help define realities and who have an important role in constructing a post-conflict society that is committed to sustainable peace. Thus, the participation pillar tempers what might otherwise be the conservative and protectionist discourse of WPS, but only if that participation is implemented, is made to be meaningful and is not simply co-option or instrumentalisation.[133]

131 The CEDAW Committee recommends that states ensure participation by women's and civil society groups that are focused on 'women's issues'; CEDAW Committee, General Recommendation 30, on women in conflict prevention, conflict and post-conflict situations, CEDAW/C/GC/30, 18 October 2013, para 46 (c).

132 Cf.: '[A]longside a necessary focus on women and girls as victims of global conflict has come an important emphasis on them as vital, active agents in peacemaking and peacebuilding.' The Challenge of Sustaining Peace: Report of the Advisory Group of Experts for the 2015 Review of the United Nations Peacebuilding Architecture, 2015, para 51 at https://reliefweb.int/sites/reliefweb.int/files/resources/150630%20Report%20of%20the%20AGE%20on%20the%202015%20Peacebuilding%20Review%20FINAL.pdf.

133 States, the UN and the international community should '[e]nsure that all actors, mediators, Friends Groups, and parties to the conflict guarantee that women's participation in talks is equal and meaningful'; *Global Study*, 58.

3.5.2 Women's Exclusion from Peace Processes

Despite the rhetoric and the constant reiteration of the importance of women's participation in peacemaking, this is one of the least observed areas of WPS at the formal level. The forms of peacemaking recognised by international law are those set out in chapter VI of the UN Charter: article 33 lists 'negotiation, enquiry, mediation, conciliation, arbitration, judicial settlement, resort to regional agencies or arrangements, or other peaceful means of [the disputing parties'] own choice'. These, especially negotiation and mediation, are the processes most commonly pursued in seeking to bring an end to conflict. All stages of the formal, track one peacemaking processes are typically orchestrated by international or regional negotiators – elite males – who bring to the table delegates from the warring parties – 'the men with guns'. These are accompanied by teams from interested states, so-called 'support' or 'contact' groups, a formula that typically excludes women, as well as other civil society representatives. A 2012 study by UN Women found that, in a sample of thirty-one peace processes between 1992 and 2011, women constituted:

- 2 per cent of chief mediators;
- 4 per cent of witnesses and signatories; and
- 9 per cent of negotiators.

While precise statistics vary, the general picture does not. In 2015, the Security Council noted its deep concern at the 'frequent under-representation of women in many formal processes and bodies related to the maintenance of international peace and security'.[134] In 2018, the UN Secretary-General again reported that 'women remain underrepresented and unrepresented in efforts to negotiate peaceful political resolutions to conflict, including in processes designed to create entry points or mitigate the impact of conflict'.[135] A related issue is the under-representation of women in the other processes set out in article 33 of the Charter – international courts and tribunals – but that is beyond the scope of this chapter.

[134] UN Security Council resolution 2242 (2015).

[135] Report of the Secretary-General, *Women, Peace and Security*, S/2018/900, 9 October 2018, para 25.

3.5.2.1 REASONS FOR WOMEN'S EXCLUSION FROM PEACE PROCESSES

A range of reasons is given for women's exclusion when it is considered at all – it may well be that, in many cases, no one even thought about including women. Witnesses to a Select Committee of the UK House of Lords on Sexual Violence in Armed Conflict that reported in 2016 spoke about the multiple and intersecting forms of discrimination such as 'age, background . . . poverty [and] lack of education'[136] that women often face and that exclude them from public life and hence from international affairs. The Foreign and Commonwealth Office (FCO) more pragmatically gave as reasons for the lack of implementation of the WPS agenda 'a lack of political will, resource constraints and enduring social attitudes to the role of women which impede their economic, political and social participation'.[137] Traditional leaders or those from fundamentalist religious groups may oppose women's presence, fearing a challenge to cultural and religious practices or to historical narratives.[138] And international mediators seeking a successful outcome to their negotiations are unwilling to challenge these attitudes. There are also practical obstacles to women's participation, including their 'multiple work burdens',[139] which are often exacerbated post-conflict when social institutions have collapsed and caring for traumatised family members is especially demanding.

Another factor is the nature of peace processes – their militarised, 'informal, secretive and homosocial contexts'.[140] Unequal demands may be imposed on women's groups that seek to participate[141] and

[136] House of Lords, Select Committee, *Sexual Violence in Armed Conflict: A War Crime* (2016), para 170.

[137] Ibid., at para 174.

[138] Thania Paffenholz and others, *Making Women Count – Not Just Counting Women* (UN Women, 2016) gives the example of the Comprehensive National Dialogue Conference for a New Yemen, 18.

[139] Thania Paffenholz, 'What Works in Participation', in Sara E. Davies and Jacqui True (eds.) *The Oxford Handbook of Women, Peace and Security* (Oxford University Press, 2019) 148–60, 150.

[140] Karin Aggestam, 'WPS, Peace Negotiations, and Peace Agreements', in Sara E. Davies and Jacqui True (eds.) *The Oxford Handbook of Women, Peace and Security* (Oxford University Press, 2019) 815–28, 815.

[141] Paffenholz cites research where a UN mediator demanded of women's groups that they represent the diversity of women within the country, a demand that was not made of other civil society organisations. Paffenholz (*supra* n 139) 150.

the length of peace processes and their location far from the conflict zone, such as in Dayton (Bosnia), Rambouillet (Kosovo), Geneva (Syria) or Havana (Colombia), impose other obstacles. Ms Pramila Patten, a former member of the CEDAW Committee and currently the Secretary-General's Special Representative (SRSG) on Conflict-affected Sexual Violence, was graphic in her description to a House of Lords Select Committee of how difficult it is for women to participate in peace processes:

> [I]t has been the NGOs [non-governmental organisations] who have been responsible for bringing the women ... to the processes, which means there is very little security provision. They always have to beg, steal and borrow money in order to get here, whereas the negotiators and the parties are put in secure locations, they are flown, they are looked after and they are given status. It is unrealistic to expect women to have to expose themselves to that degree in a way that the factions do not have to. We need to elevate their status so they are taken seriously.[142]

Gender stereotypes are also engaged to exclude women. Women have been termed too 'emotional' to be able to participate in hard-headed peace talks[143] and it has been said that participation in discussions and decision-making on issues related to society or politics is not 'women's business'[144] and that women are unable to understand the issues. This is despite the long history of women's activism for peace, resistance to conflict, organising and participating in peace crusades,[145] caravans, marches, inter-group dialogues, meetings and debates on issues pertinent to local and international politics and through which they have expressed multiple opinions, ideas and priorities.

142 House of Lords, Select Committee, *Sexual Violence in Armed Conflict: A War Crime* (2016), para 181.

143 Lisa Davis, 'Who's Missing from Syria's Peace Talks?', *Open Democracy* (29 January 2016), at www.opendemocracy.net/5050/lisa-davis/who-s-missing-from-syria-s-peace-talks.

144 Crisis Management Initiative, *The Aceh Peace Process Involvement of Women* (2006).

145 Peace crusades were especially associated with working-class women during World War I, notably in Glasgow and Manchester; Liddington (*supra* n 26) chapter 6.

3.5.2.2 WHY DOES IT MATTER IF WOMEN ARE EXCLUDED?

Having looked at the repeated commitment to women's participation in peace processes throughout the WPS agenda and contrasted it with the reality, two further questions arise: why does the inclusion of women in peace negotiations matter and what difference might it make to the content of peace agreements that must be implemented at the domestic level and thus to the concept of societal peacebuilding if women were included?

The long-term significance of peace negotiations and their potential outcomes for post-conflict societal reconstruction must be emphasised.[146] The first objective is to stop the fighting through a lasting ceasefire and then to determine the contours of the post-conflict state. Contemporary peace processes often result in the adoption of a complex package of agreements that address a range of topics crucial to the rebuilding of a state and state institutions. These include: reconciling conflicting expectations of religious and ethnic minorities; institution and capacity-building; allocation of access to land and other resources; and protecting and facilitating the actions of civil society. Peace agreements seek to set timetables, establish institutions and allocate responsibility for their performance. Christine Bell has identified an emerging practice of peace agreements[147] that seeks to recast the state through the allocation and displacement of internal power.[148] Such agreements simultaneously regulate both external and internal affairs (relations between states and between competing groups within a state) and as such lie at the interface of international and domestic law. The demand for participation therefore 'reaches into the most political of issues, such as whose voices determine the future of a country emerging from conflict'.[149] Negotiating peace only between the warring parties

[146] Aggestam (*supra* n 140) 815–28.

[147] Christine Bell, *On the Law of Peace Agreements and the Lex Pacificatoria* (Oxford University Press, 2008).

[148] UN Security Council resolution 1325 (2000) identifies the constitution, the electoral system, the police and the judiciary as areas where the protection of women's human rights is especially important when negotiating and implementing peace agreements.

[149] Sarah Taylor, *Women, Peace, and Politics at the UN Security Council* (2013), at https://theglobalobservatory.org/2013/07/women-peace-and-politics-at-the-un-security-council/.

simplifies peace processes to the issues raised by them and excluding women reinforces the pre-conflict power structures and denies them any role in planning for and deciding priorities in the post-conflict society. It also risks women's rights being negotiated away. The CEDAW Committee has noted that the 'promotion of gender equality and women's participation in decision-making processes is not seen as a priority and may even be side-lined as incompatible with stabilization goals'.[150]

In light of the window of opportunity for constitutional and societal reconstruction that is offered, it should be unnecessary to have to justify women's participation in negotiations for peace, but their consistent exclusion or under-representation has meant that reasons are proffered. It is striking that arguments are never sought as to why those already wielding power or forcibly seeking it should be included.[151]

Three reasons are frequently asserted for the inclusion of women, but which prevails is unclear and the language shifts. The first reason often given for why women should participate in conflict resolution is that already alluded to – that women are naturally nurturing and caring, inherently peace-loving and, thus, 'good at peace'.[152] Such claims may be made in the name of motherhood,[153] which can be turned into a 'platform [from which] to approach and appeal to powerful men'.[154] This essentialist concept of biological determinism is also strongly contested as having no empirical basis and as being damaging to women as it reinforces gender stereotypes and upholds the sexual division of labour that keeps women in undervalued, low-paid jobs such as those relating to caring. It undermines the objective of presenting women as powerful players and agents of change. It may also limit acceptance of women's political contributions as arising only from their 'womanly instincts' and thus relevant only to

150 CEDAW Committee, General Recommendation 30, on women in conflict prevention, conflict and post-conflict situations, CEDAW/C/GC/30, 18 October 2013, para 43.

151 Taylor (*supra* n 149).

152 Hilary Charlesworth, 'Are Women Peaceful? Reflections on the Role of Women in Peace-Building', 16 *Feminist Legal Studies* (2008) 347–61.

153 Ingrid Sharp, 'The Women's Peace Congress of 1915 and the Envisioning of Women's Rights as Human Rights' (2015) at www.historyandpolicy.org/dialogues/discussions/women-peace-and-transnational-activism-a-century-on.

154 'Cultural essentialism may be inconsistent, but it is powerful'; Charlesworth (*supra* n 152) 358.

issues involving nurturing and mothering.[155] Carol Cohn and Ruth Jacobson have warned that 'for the men who hold power and do not wish to share it, the trope of women's "natural peacefulness" can make it easy to discount the political work women did during the war and to justify their exclusion from the political process during and after the war's end'. The same is not true about men and that they are deemed 'warlike' (in contrast to women's 'peacefulness') does not depoliticize their actions: men's political stances are not reduced to their gender identity in the way that happens for women.[156]

The second reason for including women is simply that it is a matter of state obligation under human rights law, notably CEDAW articles 7 and 8.[157] Third is the illogicality of premising the possibilities of peace on a narrow base that fails to take into account the widest possible range of views, capabilities and lived knowledge of those who, in different situations, endured the conflict. It is an argument that the quality of peace agreements is improved where women have contributed and that their gendered experiences of conflict can help to shift the dynamics and change the conversation to include the importance of everyday life and of wider, shared interests. The CEDAW Committee has explained how what is designated a critical mass of women (30 to 35 per cent participation) impacts on political style and the content of decisions.[158] While emphasising the importance of women's inclusion, the concept of a 'critical mass' can detract from the goal of equality. In the different context of political participation, quotas or other means of achieving 30 per cent participation are regarded as sufficient.

This instrumentalist argument is bolstered by research that offers evidence that peace agreements where women have contributed are more likely to succeed. Peace processes, in general,

[155] Dianne Otto, 'A Sign of Weakness? Disrupting Gender Certainties in the Implementation of Security Council Resolution 1325', 13 *Michigan Journal of Gender and Law* (2006) 113–75, 139.

[156] Carol Cohn and Ruth Jacobson, 'Women's Political Activism in the Face of War and Militarization', in Carol Cohn (ed.) *Women and Wars* (Polity Press, 2013) 102–23, 111–12.

[157] See also CEDAW Committee, General Recommendation No. 23, Political and Public Life, 16th session, 1997; CEDAW Committee, General Recommendation 30, on women in conflict prevention, conflict and post-conflict situations, CEDAW/C/GC/30, 18 October 2013.

[158] CEDAW Committee, General Recommendation No. 23: Political and Public Life, 16th session, 1997, para 16.

do not lead to agreement, and peace agreements widely fail, meaning that there is a reversion to violence and conflict. An oft-cited figure is that 50 per cent of peace agreements fail within five years.[159] The *Global Study* cites research that was carried out between 2011 and 2015 into forty peace processes concluded since the end of the cold war. Findings included that where women's groups had exercised a strong influence on the negotiation process, there was a much higher chance of agreement being reached. Women would push for commencement, resumption or finalisation of negotiations when the momentum had stalled. Women may even resort to mass action to insist on consensus being reached. In further research, examples are given of Liberia, where women who were excluded from the negotiations threatened to undress in full sight of the negotiators unless they reached agreement, and of the forty female delegates in the Democratic Republic of Congo who formed a human chain at the doorways of the negotiation room in Sun City and refused to move until the agreement was signed.[160] These examples also send the message that it is not participation as such that is important but rather the actual pressure that women can exert over the process, including through subverting gender stereotypes. It is not about counting women but about making women count.[161]

A second finding from the forty case studies was that women's strong influence in negotiation processes correlated with a greater likelihood of agreements being implemented. There was not a single incidence of organised women's groups having a negative effect on the process. Indeed, the presence of women strengthened the influence of other actors that had been included in addition to the main warring parties,[162] an observation that is not true for other social actors.

These conclusions are complemented by an analysis of a dataset of 181 peace agreements signed between 1989 and 2011. When controlling for other variables, peace processes that included women as witnesses, signatories, mediators and/or negotiators demonstrated a 20 per cent increase in the probability of a peace agreement lasting at least two years. The percentage increases over time with

[159] *Global Study*, 40. [160] Examples from Paffenholz and others (*supra* n 138) 29.
[161] Paffenholz (*supra* n 139) 149. [162] Paffenholz and others (*supra* n 138).

a 35 per cent increase in the probability of a peace agreement lasting fifteen years.[163] These findings are alluded to in WPS resolution 2242 (2015) where 'the substantial link' between 'women's meaningful involvement in efforts to prevent, resolve and rebuild from conflict and those efforts' effectiveness and long-term sustainability' is noted. If it is accepted – and, admittedly, the database remains small – that processes are often more successful and conflict less likely to resume when women are included, 'it's baffling that women remain the largest group of stakeholders regularly excluded from official peace negotiations. It's also illegal under international law.'[164]

Instrumental arguments have become more prominent than those for women's equal (or equitable) participation rights, not least because the latter have had little sway. It has become fashionable to assert women's participation as the 'smart' as well as the 'right' thing to do. But there should also be caution. First, any assumption that some women can speak for all women[165] discounts differences among women – a critique that can be addressed at the WPS resolutions in general. Women – like men – come from all political parties, religions and ethnic groups, align themselves and share priorities with other participants in conflict and have a multiplicity of standpoints. Warring parties are likely to respond to demands that they include women in their delegations by selecting known women supporters. Constructing a women's coalition as in Northern Ireland or building a common position for women across the conflict divides is a time-consuming and difficult endeavour. Women's meaningful participation requires serious attention to the questions of how to identify appropriate women to participate in peace processes and who should do this, as well as how to

[163] *Global Study*, 42. The study cites as examples of good practice the Peace Agreement between the Government of the Philippines and the Moro Islamic Liberation Front and that between the Government of Colombia and the Revolutionary Armed Forces of Colombia (FARC).

[164] Lisa Davis, 'John Kerry, Where Are Women's Voices in the Syria Peace Talks?', *Open Democracy* (18 December 2015), at www.opendemocracy.net/5050/lisa-davis/john-kerry-where-are-women-s-voices-in-syria-peace-talks.

[165] A nice early example of this critique was the anger expressed at Mrs Pankhurst visiting Russia in 1917 as a representative of British women: 'Does Mrs Pankhurst speak for us? Has her voice ever been raised ... on behalf of the workers of this country against the profiteers or exploiters?'; cited in Liddington (*supra* n 26) 123.

assist those women in preparing for the lengthy and arduous task of peacemaking and what form their participation should take.

Second, participation equates with agency, with capacity to act, which might be construed as shifting onto women the responsibility for achieving sustainable agreement and, thus, the blame for any failure.[166] Instrumentalism is not a sound basis for women's inclusion; if further research were to suggest that there is in fact no benefit to the process to be derived from women's inclusion, would that justify their exclusion? Further, success tends to be measured by the durability of the peace settlement in the narrow sense of there not being a relapse into conflict, while ongoing violence against women and girls in the 'post-conflict' phase is not a measure of failure.[167] Real success is long-term change on the ground with respect to behaviour, attitudes and mindsets, enhancing women's political, economic and social status, peace and security. This cannot be achieved quickly or assessed after only a short period.

The absence of women from peacemaking processes means that issues they deem important for inclusion may not be addressed. Since the adoption of resolution 1325 (2000), more peace agreements negotiated under UN auspices have incorporated references to women and gender, but this is not systematic and may not, in fact, accord with local women's concerns. When asked, women are often clear about their priorities. The first is invariably that the violence should stop and effective steps be taken to determine the fate of disappeared persons. They seek agreements that take clear account of their own context. For instance, in 2001, a parallel women's process – The Afghan Women's Summit for Democracy – was held at the same time as the formal peace process that concluded the Bonn Agreement.[168] At the parallel process, women

[166] Nicola Pratt and Sophie Richter-Devroe, 'Critically Examining UNSCR 1325. on Women, Peace and Security', 13 (4) *International Feminist Journal of Politics* (2011) 489–503, 494.

[167] CEDAW Committee, General Recommendation 30, on women in conflict prevention, conflict and post-conflict situations, CEDAW/C/GC/30, 18 October 2013, para 35: 'For most women in post-conflict environments, the violence does not stop with the official ceasefire or the signing of the peace agreement and often increases in the post-conflict setting.'

[168] Agreement on Provisional Arrangements in Afghanistan pending the Reestablishment of Permanent Government Institutions, 5 December 2001.

urged for equal rights and provisions on education, media and culture, health care, human rights, refugees and internally displaced women.[169] Syrian women activists listed transitional justice and rule of law: '[T]hose who have been forced to leave their homes or the country should be able to return and be compensated[;] those who have committed crimes against or caused harm to the Syrian people should be held accountable, and truth-finding missions should be formed.'[170] Transitional justice processes seek to redress past harms in order to move forward; other objectives are inherently forward-looking, such as 'to build a culture of diversity' and equal citizenship.[171] A South Sudan women's agenda covers quotas for women in constitutional reform processes and in all institutions for resources, finance and economic management; implementing and monitoring the ceasefire; gender sensitisation training; ending sexual violence, psychosocial services for survivors and processes for perpetrator accountability; a land policy review; peace training and peace dialogue for all; and respect for freedom of expression of women and the media.[172]

More eloquent is an expression of priorities from an alternative peace agenda by women displaced both from South Sudan and from Darfur who defined peace to mean

> having security; peace means the right to move without restrictions; peace means love, unity and solidarity; peace is justice, freedom and absence of all forms of discrimination; peace means having a house, a job and land to cultivate, having enough food and being free from diseases; peace means the right to education for our children; peace means freedom of worship; peace means the right to our historical heritage; peace means participation in decisions and plans that affect our lives.[173]

[169] Kavita Ramdas, '"Afghanistan Is Everywhere," Afghan Women Remind Us', *Alliance* (1 March 2002), at www.alliancemagazine.org/feature/afghanistan-is-everywhere-afghan-women-remind-us/.

[170] Razan Ghazzawi, Afra Mohammad and Oula Ramadan, *Peacebuilding Defines Our Future Now: A Study of Women's Activism in Syria* (Badael Foundation and Kvinna Till Kvinna, 2015).

[171] Ibid.

[172] UN Women, 'Women of South Sudan Set Agenda for a Gender-Responsive Peace Agreement' (31 May 2016), at www.unwomen.org/en/news/stories/2016/5/women-of-south-sudan-set-strategic-agenda-for-a-gender-responsive-peace-agreement.

[173] 'Agenda for Peace: A Woman's Agenda for Peace'; cited in Rogaia Mustafa Abusharaf, 'Competing Masculinities: Probing Political Disputes as

These examples suggest that, while there is always need for reference to local conditions during and after the conflict, women's priorities are strikingly consistent and are noticeably more visionary in terms of social justice and cohesion than the provisions of many formal peace agreements. But when women's voices are not heard, or are not listened to, they remain at the peripheries of their societies and their priorities go unaddressed.

3.6 Women and Peacebuilding

A distinction must be made between women's participation in peace processes and the work of women peacebuilders: those who become involved in the former are not necessarily the latter. Peacebuilding is presented as something that can be undertaken only once a peacemaking process has resulted in an agreement, a post-conflict activity dominated by the internationals.[174] But this is a narrow understanding. There is no definitive definition of peacebuilding, but it covers the wide range of activities undertaken at the local level during conflict and in which women are often highly represented in the absence of men who have disappeared, been killed or detained, are away fighting or need to lie low. In Syria, for example, since the outbreak of violence in 2011–12, new and already existing local women's groups have become active within their own communities. Their reasons for so doing are varied: they may be desperate to stop the violence, to seek something that looks like a normal life for themselves and their children or to demand answers about the fate of disappeared loved ones.[175] In interviews, Syrian women saw peacebuilding as a gateway towards reconstructing society and felt obliged to take action.[176]

Acts of Violence against Women from Southern Sudan and Darfur', 7 (2) *Human Rights Review* (2006) 59–74, 71.

174 Boutros Boutros-Ghali made this explicit: 'I consider: preventive diplomacy, peacemaking and peace-keeping – to which I have added a closely related concept, post-conflict peacebuilding.' Report of the Secretary-General, *An Agenda for Peace: Preventive diplomacy, peacemaking and peace-keeping*, A/47/277–S/24111, 17 June 1992, para 6.

175 E.g. the *Mothers of Plaza de Mayo* who have maintained a public presence in seeking answers to the fate of children who disappeared in Argentina's 'dirty war'.

176 Ghazzawi, Mohammad and Ramadan (*supra* n 170).

Activities vary according to the local situation and individual women's circumstances, both of which are subject to constant change. Alongside those actions that are essential to holding communities together are others more directly related to mitigating the violence on a local level and finding ways to survive.[177] Examples from Syria include: negotiating local ceasefires and other agreements; setting up local zones of security and weapon-free areas; working to prevent the recruitment of child soldiers and the proliferation of small arms; organising discussion workshops on the links between Islamic principles and democracy; establishing education programmes for children on coexistence and tolerance.[178] Similar accounts come from other conflict–affected areas.[179] Social media and technology are widely used and new applications constantly emerge.

Not everything that women do is perceived as peacebuilding, and activities such as humanitarian assistance may be dismissed as service provision or women's traditional tasks. But, in the words of one international NGO:

> Women are bringing urgent aid to areas beyond the reach of international agencies who have long since evacuated their staff. In so doing, they offer a vital, peaceful alternative to extremist groups like ISIS, who have won acquiescence from hungry and war-weary communities by providing food and other basics to families made desperate by years of war. When women are able to meet crucial needs for food, water and health care, they bolster their leadership in the eyes of local communities, lending legitimacy to the alternative they represent.[180]

[177] E.g. women in Aceh 'were able to become agents for change, performing negotiations between the two parties involved in the conflict or engaging in efforts to save their husbands, sons or their community. When insecurity forced men to flee their villages, women became the main breadwinners and decision-makers and took over most of the social roles played by men in their community life'; Suraiya Kamaruzzaman, *Agents for Change: The Role of Women in Aceh's Peace Process* (Conciliation Resources, 2008) 70.

[178] Ghazzawi, Mohammad and Ramadan (*supra* n 170).

[179] E.g. in Bougainville, women acted as go-betweens with warring factions, held prayer meetings, peace marches and vigils, organised petitions and established the Bougainville Inter-Church Women's Forum to provide a space for a united women's voice across all church groups. Sister Lorraine Garasu, 'The Role of Women in Promoting Peace and Reconciliation', in Andy Carl and Sister Lorraine Garasu (eds.) *Weaving Consensus: The Papua New Guinea–Bougainville Peace Process* (Conciliation Resources, 2002) 28–31.

[180] Yifat Susskind, 'Salaam and Paz - the word for Peace is Women', at www.opendemocracy.net/5050/yifat-susskind/salaam-and-paz-word-for-peace-is-women.

This understanding of peacebuilding is not necessarily shared by international personnel charged with progressing peace processes. They may instead view such activities as irrelevant or even obstructive.

Peacebuilding activities are dangerous and not easily embarked upon. On the one hand, women may feel that they could be seen as betraying those who have been killed, detained, displaced or in other ways harmed by the war.[181] On the other hand, they may face physical threats or even attacks in their performance. Women peace activists and human rights defenders are increasingly under attack.[182] They suffer physical and online violence that is exacerbated by persistent 'patriarchal attitudes towards women and their involvement in the public domain'.[183] The same activities are also exploited by armed groups and there may be elements of sexual slavery,[184] depending on the context, the degree of coercion and whether there is freely given consent. Other challenges include lack of financial resources in a wartime economy where food and other necessities are hard to come by or dangerous to seek out, women's traditional caring roles making them unable to leave children traumatised by the violence, or wounded relatives, to participate in any activities other than those essential to survival, and lack of training in such skills. Just as women are not naturally peaceful, they are not necessarily naturally good at organising and participating in community activities, either. But violence is not only destructive; it can also create leaders and leadership. The courage of women carrying them out, often, as already noted, in areas where lack of security has caused international agencies to withdraw, is extraordinary.

Women peacebuilders must be supported (but not co-opted) by the international community, but they have merited little attention in the Security Council's WPS resolutions.[185] UN Security Council

181 Ibid.

182 'In the current political climate, in which there is a backlash against human rights, women who defend and promote rights are often the first to come under attack'; Special Rapporteur on the situation of human rights defenders, *Situation of women human rights defenders*, A/HRC/40/60, 10 January 2019, para 7.

183 Ghazzawi, Mohammad and Ramadan (*supra* n 170).

184 E.g. evidence was given in the *Foca* case that women were forced to do 'feminine' household chores like washing, cooking, laundering and cleaning as well as being continually raped; *Prosecutor* v *Kunarac*, IT-96-23-T& IT-96-23/1-T, 22 February, 2001, para 63.

185 In this, the Security Council is not alone. The CEDAW Committee notes that women have a role as 'active agents in both formal and informal peacebuilding

resolution 1325 (2000) refers in the preamble to the important role of women in peacebuilding without any explanation of what it understands by the term. Other references are oblique, such as resolution 2242's (2015) noting of 'the substantial link between women's meaningful involvement in efforts to ... rebuild from conflict and those efforts' effectiveness and long-term sustainability'. Resolution 2467 (2019) recalls civil society's important contribution to peacebuilding but links this only to preventing and responding to conflict-affected sexual violence. It encourages support for capacity-building within civil society groups in order 'to enhance informal community-level protection mechanisms against sexual violence in conflict and post-conflict situations'. Importantly, it appears to recognise that human rights defenders are peacebuilders who are subject to attacks, for it calls upon states 'to condemn acts of discrimination, harassment and violence against civil society'.[186] This strong language of condemnation of violence is, however, weakened in resolution 2493 (2019), which only 'strongly encourages' the creation of 'safe and enabling environments' for women peacebuilders and other civil society actors to continue their work without undue interference.[187] Resolution 2493 (2019) seeks the Peacebuilding Commission's engagement in promotion of women's participation in peacebuilding efforts and calls for it to 'support the participation of women-led peacebuilding organizations, in planning and stabilization efforts in post-conflict reconstruction and recovery'. This misses the point that such peacebuilding activities are not top-down but locally led and they are ongoing throughout conflict and its aftermath, and that women peacebuilders are excluded from decision-making and face daily threats and harms.

3.7 Conclusion

Peace is an understated and narrowly conceived concept throughout the WPS resolutions. It is centred on post-conflict situations rather than on conflict prevention or being recognised as an

and recovery processes' but does not elaborate on what this might entail; CEDAW Committee, General Recommendation 30, on women in conflict prevention, conflict and post-conflict situations, CEDAW/C/GC/30, 18 October 2013, para 6.

186 UN Security Council resolution 2467 (2019) paras 20 and 21.

187 UN Security Council resolution 2493 (2019) para 6.

ongoing process for all societies. In this, the WPS agenda reflects contemporary international law. Within this framework, increased participation is the key method by which the resolutions seek to ensure that women's experiences of conflict are taken into account and addressed. This is a step, an important step, but, of itself, it is insufficient to ensure full consideration of the many and complex ways in which gender must be made core to decision-making about prevention, management and resolution of conflict. In particular, simply enhancing participation by women or any other politically and economically disadvantaged group cannot achieve the re-conceptualisation of power that is necessary to achieve peace.[188] This entails seeking a better understanding of how the elements that create power are interlaced, interactive and interdependent and how power is highly gendered.[189] Peace is not a 'fixed set of practices and procedures leading to some universally defined end called "peace"' that can be achieved through negotiations at a peace process or series of peace processes. Peace and peacebuilding comprise 'multiple ideas, relationships and experiences that are embedded within hierarchies of power and knowledge'.[190] They are essential in all societies whether or not those societies are affected by conflict. Peace is a long-term project that must be entered into through a genuine and equal partnership between the top-down (the Security Council, the international community, national elites) and the bottom-up (local peacebuilders, women and others) and sustained with commitment to equality, especially gender equality.

Chapter 1 discussed the meaning of 'women' in the WPS resolutions and how this excludes men and boys and those to whom gender is a fluid, non-binary status. What is also missing from the resolutions is an understanding of peace that moves beyond human relationships and takes account of the need for humans to live in peace with nature, with the environment and with non-human species. Threats to peace for women, for humanity, for life on the planet and for the planet itself come from climate change and

188 http://wilpf.org/wilpf_statements/wilpf-text-suggestions-to-the-un-declaration-on-the-human-right-to-peace/.

189 Ibid.

190 Devon Curtis, 'The Contested Politics of Peacebuilding in Africa', in Devon Curtis and Gwinyayi A. Dzinesa (eds.) *Peacebuilding, Power and Politics in Africa* (Ohio University Press, 2012) 1–28, 3.

environmental destruction. Climate change has become a root cause of conflict and displacement; it is estimated that there will be more than 200 million climate refugees in the next two decades with catastrophic impact on other species and the continued existence of a habitable planet. Following the 2015 *Global Study*, WPS resolution 2242 noted the impact of climate change as part of the changing peace and security environment and reiterated the Security Council's intention to 'increase attention to women, peace and security as a cross-cutting subject in all relevant thematic areas of work on its agenda'. Unfortunately, and unsurprisingly in the current political climate, this was not repeated in resolutions 2467 or 2493 in 2019. The CEDAW Committee's General Recommendation No. 37 on Gender-related dimensions of disaster risk reduction in the context of climate change shows the way ahead. It is the first analysis by a UN human rights treaty body of the potential gendered threat to women and girls caused by climate change and of how conflict further exposes these risks, with recommendations within a rights-based and gendered framework. It is important that WPS and the work of the CEDAW Committee are more integrated and that the future of WPS includes cooperation and coordination to ensure that the 'peace' of the agenda has at its core the preservation of life in all its forms.

4

Women and Security

4.1 Introduction

In Chapter 3, I explained that international law has no definition of 'peace'. The same is true of 'security', a concept that is essentially left to other disciplines such as international relations, security and conflict studies. International relations scholars examine the causes and consequences of conflict with feminists turning the lens to the forms of insecurity experienced by women in conflict because they are women.[1] International law has sought to regulate conflict, restricting both legal recourse to war (the *jus ad bellum*) and the means and methods through which war may be waged (the *jus in bello*, international humanitarian law (IHL)). These international legal regimes have been scrutinised by feminist scholars to reveal the discipline's biases and blind spots and how they uphold the structures of power.[2] This chapter considers women and security within the framework of international law. It first outlines some of the key instruments and reports that make up the international legal order for the maintenance of international peace and security. It then considers the location of the Security Council WPS resolutions within this framework and their limited conception of security for women and girls that centres on militarised protection from sexual and gender-based violence to the exclusion of the structural

[1] J. Ann Tickner, 'Peace and Security from a Feminist Perspective', in Sara E. Davies and Jacqui True (eds.) *The Oxford Handbook of Women, Peace and Security* (Oxford University Press, 2019) 15–25, 17.

[2] E.g. Gina Heathcote, *The Law on the Use of Force: A Feminist Analysis* (Routledge, 2012).

drivers of insecurity. It then considers the extent to which the WPS agenda has been instrumentalised or co-opted into the Security Council's programme for countering terrorism and violent extremism. It reflects finally on the significant structural bases of insecurity – militarism, inequalities, the ongoing production and circulation of weapons and the impact of the neoliberal economic system. It concludes that, by omitting these, the WPS agenda cannot in fact provide security for women and girls.

4.2 International Law and Security

The two-pronged approach in international law to maintaining international peace that was discussed in Chapter 3 is equally applicable to the counterpart of peace: security. The 'maintenance of international peace and security' is the mantra of contemporary international law. It was an implied goal of both the 1899 and the 1907 Hague Conventions for the Pacific Settlement of Disputes[3] and was brought directly into the 1919 League Covenant.[4] In the preamble to its Charter, the United Nations sets out the aim 'to unite our strength to maintain international peace and security' and this is spelled out as the first purpose of the Organization.[5] The Charter provides for state security from external threat through the principles of state sovereignty, the sanctity of territorial integrity and the political independence of sovereign states and the prohibition of the use of force in international relations.[6] But force can be used 'in the common interest'[7] as determined by the Security Council in exercise of its primary responsibility to maintain international peace and security.[8] As was also flagged in Chapter 3, the primacy of state (national) security was further emphasised through the self-defence exception to the prohibition of force, although

[3] The preamble to the Convention for the Pacific Settlement of Disputes, The Hague, 29 July 1899, and the Convention for the Pacific Settlement of International Disputes, The Hague, 18 October 1907 both state that 'it is expedient to record in an international Agreement the principles of equity and right on which are based the security of States and the welfare of peoples'.

[4] Covenant of the League of Nations, Paris, 1919, preamble: 'The High Contracting Parties in order to promote international co-operation and to achieve international peace and security ... Agree to this Covenant of the League of Nations.'

[5] UN Charter, 1945, article 1. [6] Ibid., at articles 2 (1) and 2 (4).

[7] Ibid., at preamble. [8] Ibid., at article 24 and chapter VII.

formally subordinated to the Security Council's authority through the requirement in article 51 of the Charter that states immediately report to the Council any measures that they have taken in self-defence. Action taken in individual or collective self-defence does not negate the Council's authority to take any measures it deems necessary 'to maintain or restore international peace and security'. Another formal manifestation of its primary responsibility to this end is international law's third approach – the Council's responsibility for formulating plans for the regulation of armaments.[9] International law is ambivalent with respect to arms control. On the one hand, attempts have long been sought to regulate the proliferation and use of weapons, in particular those designated as weapons of mass destruction, while, on the other, the right of states to arm is an essential component of sovereignty.[10] The Charter purports to bind non-member states to these principles in so far as they are necessary for the maintenance of international peace and security[11]

Despite its opening stirring words with respect to 'saving succeeding generations from the scourge of war', the Charter is state-centred and there is little space for individual security. The assumption of the state's exercise of jurisdiction within its territory and other areas under its control assumes state power over individuals. However, the inclusion in very general terms of protection of human rights as a purpose of the UN,[12] coupled with the prosecution of crimes against humanity at Nuremburg and Tokyo, provided the genesis of the international legal regime for protecting the security of human life and well-being against abusive state power.

As has been much analysed, during the cold war, the collective security system was blocked by the threat or use of the veto,[13] the device through which the five permanent members maintain control. Spurious claims of the legality of the use of force led to claims of the death of article 2 (4) of the Charter.[14] At the international

[9] Ibid., at article 26.
[10] E.g. the Arms Trade Treaty, New York, 2013, preamble reaffirms 'the sovereign right of any State to regulate and control conventional arms exclusively within its territory, pursuant to its own legal or constitutional system'.
[11] UN Charter, 1945, article 2 (6). [12] Ibid., at article 1 (3).
[13] Ibid., at article 27 (3).
[14] Thomas Franck, 'Who Killed Article 2(4)? or: Changing Norms Governing the Use of Force by States', 64 *American Journal of International Law* (1970) 809–37.

level, the threat of nuclear warfare was contained by the policies of deterrence and mutual assured destruction, arms limitation talks between the United States and the Soviet Union and the Nuclear Non-Proliferation Treaty.[15] At the local level, protest against the nuclear threat was expressed through peace marches and camps, where women were especially prominent. The international human rights regime became more entrenched following the coming into force of the International Covenant on Civil and Political Rights (ICCPR) and the International Covenant on Economic, Social and Cultural Rights (ICESCR) in 1976, the adoption of further human rights treaties and the growing confidence of human rights institutions.[16]

The end of the cold war allowed for what was optimistically viewed as a 'New World Order' with primacy accorded to the rule of law, democracy and human rights. It opened with the apparent revitalisation of the collective security system in the 1991 military action against Iraq following its invasion of Kuwait,[17] the conclusion of long-standing conflicts in places such as Cambodia,[18] and Namibian independence from South Africa.[19] Security was understood as more multifaceted. In his 1992 Agenda for Peace, former UN Secretary-General Boutros Boutros-Ghali considered that, while the concept of peace was 'easy to grasp', a pattern of contradictions made that of international security more complex.[20] He highlighted aspects of the 'new' dimensions of insecurity – proliferation of weapons of mass destruction, amassing of conventional arms, new racial tensions, revolutions in technology and communications: there had been social progress since the founding of the UN, but it had brought with it destabilisation through 'ecological

15 Treaty on the Non-Proliferation of Nuclear Weapons, Moscow and Washington, 1 July 1968.

16 Samuel Moyn has argued that the international human rights regime emerged in the late 1970s; Samuel Moyn, *The Last Utopia Human Rights in History* (Harvard University Press, 2010). But this fails to take account of the many earlier human rights initiatives especially within the regional frameworks; Philip Alston, 'Does the Past Matter? On the Origins of Human Rights', 126 *Harvard Law Review* (2013) 2043–81.

17 UN Security Council resolution 678, 29 November 1990.

18 *Comprehensive Cambodian Peace Agreement,* Paris, 23 October 1991.

19 Namibian independence was achieved on 21 March 1990.

20 Report of the Secretary-General, *An Agenda for Peace: Preventive diplomacy, peace-making and peace-keeping,* A/47/277–S/24111, 17 June 1992, para 12.

damage, disruption of family and community life, greater intrusion into the lives and rights of individuals'. But early optimism for a time of 'hope and change' gave way to further concerns about security in the face of the eruption of extreme violence in the 'new wars' in Somalia, Rwanda, Haiti, the former Yugoslavia and the Soviet Union.[21] In 2000, and following the failure of the UN to ensure security in Rwanda and Srebrenica, the Brahimi Report emphasised conflict prevention and strategies for peacebuilding operations.[22] Other bodies within the UN argued for centring human security (the 'welfare of peoples' in the words of the Hague Conventions) but with differing emphasis on economic and material well-being[23] or military protection from physical harm.[24] The Security Council adopted its first resolutions on the protection of children[25] and the protection of civilians in armed conflict.[26] This was the security environment into which resolution 1325 was adopted in October 2000.

The message of a changed and changing security environment has continued through the first two decades of the twenty-first century – the span of the WPS agenda – intensified by terrorist attacks, in particular those of 11 September 2001, and violent extremism. Demands for extending the scope of self-defence to encompass pre-emptive response to anticipated attacks by states or non-state actors have been made alongside claims for a further, 'humanitarian' exception to the prohibition against the use of force where individuals' lives are threatened, not by external actors but from within the state, by governments seeking to close down

[21] Report of the Secretary-General, *Supplement to an Agenda for Peace, position paper of the Secretary-General on the occasion of the fiftieth anniversary of the United Nations*, A/50/60; S/1995/1, 25 January 1995. Boutros Boutros-Ghali noted the intra-state nature of such conflicts, their extreme violence towards citizens and the collapse of state institutions that necessitated new forms of peacekeeping operations.

[22] Report of the Panel on United Nations Peace Operations (Brahimi Report), A/55/305–S/2000/809, 21 August 2000.

[23] UNDP, *Human Development Report 1994*.

[24] Christine Chinkin and Mary Kaldor, *International Law and New Wars* (Cambridge University Press, 2017) chapter 11.

[25] UN Security Council resolution 1261, 17 September 1999. The General Assembly had earlier addressed the issue and recommended the creation of a Secretary-General's Special Representative on the impact of armed conflict on children; UN General Assembly resolution 51/77, 20 February 1997.

[26] UN Security Council resolution 1265, 30 August 1999.

protest against their exercise of power.[27] Claims that 'legitimate' use of force is more important than 'legality' have contributed to a destabilisation of the authority of international law itself, despite a strong reassertion of its continuing adequacy by the General Assembly in its 2005 World Summit.[28]

In 2015, the High-level Panel on Peace Operations considered further this security landscape. In language similar to that of 'new wars',[29] it described contemporary security threats: the increased number of civil wars and targeted violent attacks on civilians (including rape and sexual violence), displacement, the mix of organised crime – trafficking in drugs, weapons and people – and conflict exacerbated by shortages of and demands for basic resources. Submissions to the General Assembly as contributions to the Sustainable Development Goals have noted changing threats to security: 'In the last decade the rise of extremism, escalating violent conflict, recurrent and deepening economic crises, food insecurity, natural disasters and the effects of climate change have intensified vulnerability and increased inequalities, including gender inequalities. Furthermore, as the current refugee crisis in the Middle East demonstrates, the situation of refugee and internally displaced women is particularly difficult.'[30] And in the years since the delivery of the Lauterpacht lectures in 2016, there have been further insecurities generated by militarisation and aggressive foreign and domestic policies; continuing violence in, inter alia, Syria, Yemen, Venezuela and the Democratic Republic of Congo; and, especially in the United States, a retreat from the multilateral global order in which WPS is located. There have also been widespread and ongoing protests against ruling elites in many places across the globe from Hong Kong to Chile, further protests against the failure of governments to address the climate and environmental

[27] Chinkin and Kaldor (*supra* n 24) chapters 4 and 5.

[28] UN General Assembly resolution 60/1, 24 October 2005, *World Summit Outcome*, para 79: 'We reaffirm that the relevant provisions of the Charter are sufficient to address the full range of threats to international peace and security.'

[29] Mary Kaldor, *New and Old Wars: Organised Violence in a Global Era* (Polity Press, 3rd ed. 2012).

[30] CEDAW Committee, Contributions to the 2030 Agenda for Sustainable Development (16 May 2016) at https://tbinternet.ohchr.org/_layouts/15/treatybodyexternal/Download.aspx?symbolno=INT%2fCEDAW%2fINF%2f8697&Lang=en.

catastrophe, at times violent response and a closing of civic space for citizen action.

4.3 WPS and Security

The WPS resolutions are strangely muted on the threats to security that have emerged or increased since the adoption of resolution 1325 in 2000 and their impact on women. The implicit human security approach of resolution 1325 is expressed in its concern that 'civilians, particularly women and children, account for the vast majority of those adversely affected by armed conflict'. It refers expressly to the targeting of refugees and internally displaced persons (IDPs) that prevents camps from being places of security. While emphasising the obligations on 'all parties to armed conflict', resolution 1325 implicitly assumes traditional interstate conflict.[31] It calls for 'special measures' of protection for women and girls 'from gender-based violence, particularly rape and other forms of sexual abuse, and all other forms of violence in situations of armed conflict'. The Council makes oblique reference to other harms, for instance by emphasising that programmes for mine clearance and disarmament, demobilisation and reintegration (DDR) should take account of the 'special needs' of women and girls, but it is evident that sexual violence is the major cause and consequence of harm (and thus insecurity) for women that the resolution seeks to address.

Resolution 1325 invited the UN Secretary-General to undertake a study on the impact of armed conflict on women and girls. Two studies were, in fact, produced,[32] detailing multiple conflict-related sources of insecurity for women and girls, including social attitudes and gender stereotypes; increased availability of and access to arms; prescribed gender roles in conflict leading to situations of

[31] UN Security Council resolution 1325 (2000) refers 'in particular' to states' obligations under the 1949 Geneva Conventions and the 1977 Additional Protocols, which are overwhelmingly directed at regulating international armed conflict.

[32] Women, Peace and Security Study submitted by the Secretary-General pursuant to UN Security Council resolution 1325 (2000) (United Nations, October 2002); Elisabeth Rehn and Ellen Johnson Sirleaf, *Women, War, Peace: The Independent Experts' Assessment on the Impact of Armed Conflict on Women and Women's Role in Peace-Building* (UNIFEM, 2002).

vulnerability (for instance gathering fuel or seeking food); different forms of work; flight and displacement; collapsed or collapsing social support systems; detention and disappearance of male relatives. But the next WPS resolution, 1820 in 2008, does not relate to these many and diverse conditions of insecurity. It assumes that security for women and girls requires, above all, protection from the sexual violence that is committed as a tactic of war. The insecurity caused through the inherent violence and social disruption of armed conflict is taken for granted and is not addressed other than through calling upon all parties to comply with their obligations under existing international law – IHL, human rights law, international criminal law, transitional justice and refugee law. Subsequent WPS resolutions also concentrate on protection from sexual violence.[33] Other causes of insecurity receive some – primarily preambular – notice. For instance, resolution 2122 (2013) recognises wider violations of women's human rights and the effects of unequal citizenship rights, gender-biased application of asylum laws, and obstacles facing women in registering and accessing identity documents;[34] resolutions 2106 (2013) and 2122 (2013) implicitly acknowledge the insecurity engendered by the availability of weapons through their noting of the Arms Trade Treaty. The WPS resolutions pay little regard to intersecting bases of insecurity; women in especially vulnerable situations such as those with disabilities, refugees and displaced persons and children born of sexual violence are sporadically mentioned, but there is no systematic appraisal of how women's diverse identities impact upon their security. Nor is there consideration of the various responses needed to restore individual or collective security for differently situated women.

As discussed in Chapter 1, in 2013, the Security Council announced a high-level review of the implementation of resolution 1325 and commissioned a global study to be carried out as preparation. The 2015 *Global Study* has much in common with the High-level

33 See, especially, UN Security Council resolution 1888 (2009); UN Security Council resolution 1960 (2010); UN Security Council resolution 2106 (2013); UN Security Council resolution 2467 (2019).

34 CEDAW Committee, General Recommendation No. 30 on women in conflict prevention, conflict and post-conflict situations, CEDAW/C/GC/30, 18 October 2013 provides a fuller picture of other conflict-affected human rights violations against women.

Panel on Peace Operations that also reported in 2015.[35] The *Global Study* examined the challenge presented by changed conceptions of (in)security. It noted that security is not limited to physical violence but also has 'political, economic and social dimensions. It is both public and private.'[36] In language that links it directly to the international regime for the protection of human rights, the *Global Study* stated that security denotes 'absence of fear but also absence of want'.[37] This echoes the preamble to the 1948 Universal Declaration of Human Rights, which states that 'freedom from fear and want has been proclaimed as the highest aspiration of the common people'. The preamble to the ICCPR affirms that 'the ideal of free human beings enjoying civil and political freedom and freedom from fear and want can only be achieved if conditions are created whereby everyone may enjoy his civil and political rights, as well as his economic, social and cultural rights'. The preamble to the ICESCR is similarly worded.[38] The linkage made by the *Global Study* between WPS and human rights in effect invokes a gendered human security approach. It is therefore not surprising that the *Global Study* also reminds us that 'resolution 1325 was conceived of and lobbied for as a human rights resolution that would promote the rights of women in conflict situations' and that, as such, it forms 'part of the international tradition of human rights'.[39] In the same vein, it rejects the processes of militarisation and militarism and the normalisation of violence that these entail.

Resolution 2242 (2015) was adopted following the high-level review that was informed by the *Global Study*. It notes the changed global context of peace and security, as well as insecurities relating

[35] The High-level Panel on Peace Operations proposed ways to integrate WPS and human rights into peace operations, at 14.

[36] Radhika Coomaraswamy and others, *Preventing Conflict, Transforming Justice, Securing the Peace A Global Study on the Implementation of Security Council Resolution 1325* (United Nations, 2015) [hereinafter *Global Study*] 24.

[37] Report of the Secretary-General, *In larger freedom: towards development, security and human rights for all*, A/59/2005/Add.3, 26 May 2005, includes freedom from fear and freedom from want.

[38] International Covenant on Economic, Social and Cultural Rights, 1966, preamble: 'Recognizing that, in accordance with the Universal Declaration of Human Rights, the ideal of free human beings enjoying freedom from fear and want can only be achieved if conditions are created whereby everyone may enjoy his economic, social and cultural rights, as well as his civil and political rights.'

[39] *Global Study*, 15.

to violent extremism, the increased numbers of refugees and IDPs, the impacts of climate change and the global nature of health pandemics. The only one of these additional causes of insecurity that is expanded upon is that caused by terrorist acts and violent extremism – neither of which is defined. The Council recognises that violent extremism has a differential impact on the lives of women and girls, impinging adversely on their health, access to education and participation in public life. It elaborates that sexual and gender-based violence forms part of the ideology and strategy of some groups committed to violent extremism and denotes sexual violence as an instrument and central tactic of terror as well as of war.[40] In requesting the Counter-Terrorism Committee and the Counter-Terrorism Committee Executive Directorate (CTED) to integrate gender as a cross-cutting issue throughout their activities, the Council seeks a mutually reinforcing approach to advancing WPS and combating violent extremism.

The Council's call in resolution 2242 (2015) for more gender-sensitive research and data into the drivers of the radicalisation of women and the impact of counterterrorism strategies on women's human rights is welcome, but, unfortunately, it was not repeated in resolutions 2467 and 2493 in 2019. Assimilation of the WPS agenda with those for countering violent extremism and terrorism furthers the securitisation of women's experiences in conflict.[41] On the one hand, this might be a positive step. It brings the WPS agenda into the foremost concerns of powerful (global north) states, thereby indicating that WPS is not a marginal sideshow but something that can offer valuable insights into countering the violence of extremism. But, since there is no doubt about which is generally regarded as the more important issue in international affairs, such integration risks WPS being hijacked by or co-opted to this

[40] The Challenge of Sustaining Peace: Report of the Advisory Group of Experts for the 2015 Review of the United Nations Peacebuilding Architecture, 2015, para 14.

[41] 'Security is not an objective condition, but a sustained strategic practice aimed at convincing others that a specific development is threatening and risky, requiring immediate action. The process by which this occurs … is referred to as "securitization"'; Katherine E. Brown, 'The Securitisation of Human Rights', in Jill Steans and Daniela Tepe-Belfrage (eds.) *Handbook on Gender in World Politics* (Edward Elgar, 2016) 255–62.

heightened security agenda.[42] The special rapporteur on human rights and countering terrorism has pointed to the fact that such instrumentalisation of women in the name of security raises ethical concerns that are worsened when programmes are announced as measures for the empowerment of women or for training them in new, beneficial skills while concealing the security dimension.[43] Engaging women and girls in counterterrorism activities can also be dangerous and intrusive, exposing them to risks within their own societies.

Another dimension is the flattening of women's and girls' identities according to their position with respect to terrorist groups, reducing the complexities of their conflict-affected experiences and discounting their rights, whether as suspected *jihadis* or as brought into activities for countering violent extremism. The stripping of British nationality from Shamima Begum is illustrative. Her experiences as a young girl and bereaved mother within Daesh have been overlooked in favour of her identity as a person who travelled to Syria to join the group. There has been little national attention accorded to why such young girls have felt a lack of belonging in their home countries and sought inclusion in a war zone.[44] It obscures what has been called the 'fundamental paradox' at the heart of the securitisation of [WPS]: 'greater gender equality and equity are correlated to less violent, more stable societies, yet (male) political leaders and policy-makers often respond to the threats of violence from other men by disempowering women and undermining their status'.[45] While highlighting that sexual and gender-based violence are 'known to be part of the strategic objectives and ideology of certain terrorist groups, used as a tactic of terrorism'[46] and as

[42] Report of the Special rapporteur on the promotion and protection of human rights and fundamental freedoms while countering terrorism, Human rights impact of policies and practices aimed at preventing and countering violent extremism, A/HRC/43/46, 21 February 2020, para 40: 'The distinct focus on using women as a means of improving counter-terrorism efforts runs the risk of agenda-hijacking, whereby a narrow emphasis on "women" distracts attention from the wider structural realities that produce gender inequality, exclusion and violence.'

[43] Ibid., at para 41.

[44] Azadeh Moaveni, *Guest House for Young Widows Among the Women of ISIS* (Scribe, 2019).

[45] Brown (*supra* n 41) 259.

[46] UN Security Council resolution 2242 (2015) preamble.

an instrument of power, the Council does not recognise that victims of sexual violence are *per se* terrorised and thus victims of terrorist behaviour. To do so would empower the state to confront fundamentalism by opening political space to women[47] on their own terms, allow for 'counter-narratives and counter-strategies and pave the way for reparations and redress'.[48]

Neither of the two WPS resolutions adopted in 2019, resolutions 2467 and 2493, repeat the more expansive indicators of insecurity of resolution 2242 (2015). Resolution 2467 does reiterate the impact of terrorist and extremist behaviours on women and other factors that contribute to the 'disproportionate impact' of sexual violence on women and girls: discriminatory laws and discrimination, gender biased enforcement and application of existing laws, under-representation in decision-making and leadership, harmful social norms and practices, structural inequalities, and lack of availability of services for survivors. The resolution does not go further to show how conflict-related insecurity exists in a continuum from pre-conflict conditions and, unless redressed, persists post-conflict. Six months later resolution 2493 neither reinforces these sources of insecurity for women and girls, nor makes any further contribution to their understanding.

Despite the *Global Study's* urging the WPS resolutions do not affirm WPS as a women's human rights agenda as a counter to securitisation. There is some language of rights in resolution 2467 (2019). It incorporates the Convention on the Elimination of All Forms of Discrimination against Women (CEDAW) and the Convention on the Rights of the Child in operative paragraph 18 and recalls that international law provides for the right to a remedy for human rights violations. Resolution 2493 (2019) relegates CEDAW back to the preamble but does call for the promotion of all women's rights, 'including civil, political and economic rights'. It is not surprising that the Security Council has not responded to a human rights orientation for WPS. The WPS resolutions come within the Security Council's mandate, not that of the General Assembly, the institutional home for human

[47] Sami Thamir Alrashidi, 'Using a Background-Vernacularist Approach to Promote Compliance with CEDAW with Reference to Egypt and Tunisia' (thesis, Flinders University, 2017) 66.

[48] Report of the Secretary-General, *Conflict-related sexual violence*, S/2016/361, 20 April 2016, para 22.

rights.[49] Indeed over-stepping the Council's authority has been an expressed concern for some states, notably Russia and China. But this also raises questions. Was the human rights characterisation by the *Global Study* no more than wishful thinking on the part of its authors, or could WPS represent an institutional shift of human rights into the Security Council? And is this an acceptable shift in the responsibility of the Council? Or is WPS in fact traditional security cloaked with a legitimating veneer of human rights? If the WPS agenda is to be understood as bringing women's lives from the peripheries of international affairs into the mainstream what does it mean that they are brought into the Council's security discourse and what might this institutionalisation and securitisation of women's issues mean for the effective provision of security for women?

Seeing WPS as a human rights agenda also blurs the distinction between external threats to security and internal threats to people within a state's territory. WPS is perceived by many states as a foreign policy initiative that seeks to reduce violence against women and girls in armed conflict between states rather than during non-conflict (or post-conflict) situations such as protection against domestic violence or 'everyday' rape. This is certainly true of the United Kingdom where WPS is located in the Foreign and Commonwealth Office, the Department for International Development and the Ministry of Defence, not the Home Office. The United Kingdom's National Action Plan (NAP) on implementation of resolution 1325 focuses on how WPS priorities can guide its policies toward nine focus countries.[50] Domestic policy is only included with respect to increasing the numbers of women in the armed forces. Despite urging by civil society, the NAP does not address Northern Ireland as a conflict-affected area. Nor does it consider the situation of asylum-seeking women within the UK. Similarly, the US

[49] UN Charter,1945, article 13 (1): 'The General Assembly shall initiate studies and make recommendations for the purpose of: (b) promoting international co-operation in the economic, social, cultural, educational, and health fields, and assisting in the realization of human rights and fundamental freedoms for all without distinction as to race, sex, language, or religion.'

[50] HM Government, 'UK National Action Plan on Women, Peace & Security 2018 to 2022' (January 2018) at https://assets.publishing.service.gov.uk/government/uploads/system/uploads/attachmenfile/file/677586/FCO1215-NAP-Women-Peace-Security-ONLINE_V2.pdf.

WPS Strategy[51] comprises four 'lines of effort', directed toward action to enhance women's participation[52] and protection from violence and exploitation 'around the world', adjusting international programmes to enhance equality and building partnerships with other governments to improve women's participation in processes connected to peace and security. In other countries this external bias is not the case. Afghanistan's NAP,[53] for instance, addresses women's participation in domestic politics, in national peace and security agendas, elections, and judicial structures. It seeks to contribute to combating gender-based violence and enhancing the provision of education opportunities for women in Afghanistan. The Nepalese NAP allocated budgets for projects in the Ministries of Home Affairs and Education and the National Women's Commission.[54] The difference between the 'outward looking' NAPs of (donor) states in the global north and the 'inward looking' NAPs of conflict-affected states in the global south[55] reveal strong differences about which women's security is at issue, the nature of the threats to that security and priorities in addressing those threats and building peaceful societies.

4.4 International Law and Protection from Sexual Violence

The WPS resolutions present the high incidence of gender-based and sexual violence targeted against women and girls as tactics of war and terror as the most prevalent and extreme form of conflict-affected insecurity they experience. Their focus on prevention of

51 'United States Strategy on Women, Peace, and Security' (June 2019) at www.whitehouse.gov/wp-content/uploads/2019/06/WPS-Strategy-FINAL-PDF-6.11.19.pdf.

52 E.g. Council on Foreign Relations, 'How Women's Participation in Conflict Prevention and Resolution Advances U.S. Interests' (October 2016) at www.cfr.org/report/how-womens-participation-conflict-prevention-and-resolution-advances-us-interests.

53 Wazhma Frogh, 'Afghanistan's National Action Plan: A "Wish List of Many Dreams"' (LSE Centre for Women, Peace and Security, Working Paper Series, No. 10, 2017).

54 Punam Yadav, '1325 – Is That a Taxi Number? Implementation of the National Action Plan on 1325 and 1820 in Nepal' (LSE Centre for Women, Peace and Security, Working Paper Series, No. 4, 2017).

55 Laura J. Shepherd, 'Making War Safe for Women? National Action Plans and the Militarisation of the Women, Peace and Security Agenda', 37 (3) *International Political Science Review* (2016) 302.

and protection against such violence accords with longstanding requirements of IHL, human rights law and international criminal law. Indeed, like WPS international law perceives women's security as centred on their sexual identity and thus concentrates on combating sexual violence. This section briefly outlines the relevant international legal regimes.

IHL language has fluctuated between the stronger language of prohibition and that of protection. For instance, the Lieber Code, the instructions given to Union forces in the US civil war, provided that the 'United States acknowledge and protect, in hostile countries occupied by them ... the persons of the inhabitants, especially those of women'. It prohibited under penalty of death 'wanton violence committed against persons in the invaded country, ... all rape, wounding, maiming, or killing of such inhabitants'.[56] At the international level, the 1907 Hague Regulations provide that 'Family honour and rights, the lives of persons, and private property, as well as religious convictions and practice, must be respected.'[57] Article 27 of the Fourth Geneva Convention applicable in international armed conflict requires women to be 'especially protected against any attack on their honour, in particular against rape, enforced prostitution, or any form of indecent assault'.[58] This was followed in almost identical language in Additional Protocol I.[59] However in non-international armed conflict violence to life and person, and outrages on personal dignity, humiliating and degrading treatment are prohibited 'at any time and in any place'.[60] Much of this language demands cessation of sexual violence against civilians in accordance with the IHL principle of distinction.[61] But sexual violence must also be unacceptable against combatants, or those directly participating in conflict as

[56] General Orders No. 100: The Lieber Code, 24 April 1863, articles 37 and 44.

[57] Laws and Customs of War on Land (Hague IV), The Hague, 18 October 1907, article 46.

[58] Convention Relative to the Protection of Civilian Persons, Geneva, 12 August 1949.

[59] Protocol Additional to the Geneva Conventions of 12 August 1949 and relating to the Protection of Victims of International Armed Conflicts, Geneva, 8 June 1977, article 76 (Additional Protocol I).

[60] Convention Relative to the Protection of Civilian Persons, Geneva, 12 August 1949, article 3; Protocol Additional to the Geneva Conventions of 12 August 1949 and relating to the Protection of Victims of Non-International Armed Conflicts (Additional Protocol II), Geneva, 8 June 1977, article 4 (2) (e).

[61] Additional Protocol I, article 51.

a form of unnecessary suffering that can have no military advantage, making deference to the IHL principle of distinction misplaced.

The applicability of IHL rests upon the existence of an international or non-international armed conflict. The newer legal regime of human rights applies to all persons within a state's territory and under its jurisdiction, irrespective of conflict[62] and thus complements IHL. The state is responsible for an international wrongful act, including human rights violations.[63] This conjunction of legal regimes was accepted in the assertion at the 1993 World Conference on Human Rights that 'violations of the human rights of women in situations of armed conflict are violations of the fundamental principles of international human rights and humanitarian law'.[64] And two years later it was repeated at the Fourth World Conference on Women that 'acts of violence against women include violation of the human rights of women in situations of armed conflict, in particular murder, systematic rape, sexual slavery and forced pregnancy'.[65] The CEDAW Committee has since clarified that CEDAW remains applicable in armed conflict and that states must 'exercise due diligence to prevent, investigate, punish and ensure redress for the acts of private individuals or entities that impair the rights enshrined in the Convention'.[66] This last is especially important as human rights law provides the legal basis for reparations to victims and survivors of conflict-affected sexual and gender-based violence as affirmed in WPS resolution 2467 (2019).[67]

[62] The extraterritorial application of human rights law has been the subject of controversy, especially with respect to the actions of foreign military forces in Iraq and Afghanistan; see Marko Milanovic, *Extraterritorial Application of Human Rights Treaties: Law, Principles, and Policy* (Oxford University Press, 2011).

[63] UN General Assembly resolution 56/83, 12 December 2001, Annex: *Responsibility of States for Internationally Wrongful Acts*. State responsibility gives rise to the obligation to make reparation to the victim of the violation of human rights.

[64] World Conference on Human Rights, Vienna Declaration and Programme of Action, 25 June 1993, II, para 38.

[65] Ibid., at para 114.

[66] CEDAW Committee, General Recommendation No. 30 on women in conflict prevention, conflict and post-conflict situations, CEDAW/C/GC/30, 18 October 2013, para 15.

[67] UN Security Council resolution 2467 (2019) '[r]ecalls the applicable provisions of international law on the right to an effective remedy for violations of human rights'.

For international lawyers increased provision for individual criminal liability through the prosecution of alleged perpetrators and/or those in responsible command is an important step toward ending impunity. Despite having been long prohibited, crimes of sexual violence in armed conflict remained largely invisible in the verdicts of the Nuremburg and Tokyo war crimes trials following World War II.[68] In the 1990s women's campaigning ensured their inclusion in the jurisdiction of the *ad hoc* international criminal tribunals for the former Yugoslavia (ICTY) and Rwanda (ICTR), the hybrid Special Court of Sierra Leone, the special courts in Timor Leste and Cambodia, and the permanent International Criminal Court (ICC). The Rome Statute of the ICC spells out that when the other legal conditions are satisfied 'rape, sexual slavery, enforced prostitution, forced pregnancy, enforced sterilization or any other form of sexual violence of comparable gravity' come within the Court's jurisdiction as crimes against humanity[69] and violations of the laws and customs of war in international[70] and non-international armed conflict.[71] Where rape and sexual violence are integral to the attempt to destroy in whole or in part a group as defined in the Genocide Convention[72] it can also be genocidal, as was the case in Rwanda in 1994[73] and against the Yazidi people from 2014 until the military defeat of ISIS.[74] Further, persecution against an identifiable group on the basis of gender is a crime against humanity.[75]

In addition to legal provision, condemnation of and seeking ways to combat sexual violence against women in conflict has become almost a staple item on the agenda of United Nations' organs,

68 See, however, trials held under the auspices of the UN War Crimes Commission; William Schabas, Carsten Stahn, Joseph Powderly, Dan Plesch and Shanti Sattler, 'The United Nations War Crimes Commission and the Origins of International Criminal Justice', 25 *Criminal Law Forum* (2014) 1 (and the articles following).

69 Rome Statute of the International Criminal Court, 1998, article 7 (1) (g).

70 Ibid., at article 8 (b) (xxii). 71 Ibid., at article 8 (e) (vi).

72 Convention on the Prevention and Punishment of the Crime of Genocide, New York, 9 December 1948, article 2.

73 In *Prosecutor* v *Jean-Paul Akayesu*, ICTR-96-4-T, Trial Chamber I, 2 September 1998, the accused was convicted, inter alia, of rape as a crime against humanity, acts that were core to the genocide against the Tutsis.

74 Human Rights Council, '"They Came to Destroy": ISIS Crimes Against the Yazidis', A/HRC/32/CRP.2, 15 June 2016.

75 For international law definitions of 'gender', see Chapter 1.

agencies and special procedures, spawning soft law resolutions,[76] reports,[77] the appointment of high-level experts[78] and attention from human rights treaty bodies.[79] What this brief overview makes clear is that international legal regimes are mutually reinforcing in their prohibition of sexual violence in its different forms in armed conflict.

4.5 WPS and Prevention of and Protection against Sexual Violence

As discussed in chapter two, the WPS resolutions incorporate these legal regimes. The resolutions sometimes refer to gender-based violence and at others to sexual violence. Neither is defined. Gender-based violence has been defined by the CEDAW Committee and this definition must be assumed. Sexual violence has not been authoritatively defined; the Secretary-General has adopted the Rome Statute's approach of listing the different offences and setting out their nexus to conflict:

> rape, sexual slavery, forced prostitution, forced pregnancy, forced abortion, enforced sterilization, forced marriage and any other form of sexual violence of comparable gravity perpetrated against women, men, girls or boys that is directly or indirectly linked (temporally, geographically or causally) to a conflict. This link with conflict may be evident in the profile of the perpetrator (often affiliated with a State or non-State armed group), the profile of the victim (who is frequently a member of a persecuted political, ethnic or religious minority), the climate of impunity (which is generally associated with State collapse), cross-border consequences (such as displacement or trafficking in persons) and/or violations of the terms of a ceasefire agreement.[80]

This fails to capture either the essence of sexual violence, its gendered dimensions (whether committed by or against males or

[76] E.g. General Assembly resolution 3318 (XXIX), 14 December 1974, *Declaration on the Protection of Women and Children in Emergency and Armed Conflict.*

[77] E.g. *Global Study.*

[78] E.g. UN Security Council resolution 1888 (2009) that mandated the creation of the position of Special Representative of the Secretary-General (SRSG) on Sexual Violence in Armed Conflict.

[79] E.g. CEDAW Committee, General Recommendation No. 30 on women in conflict prevention, conflict and post-conflict situations, CEDAW/C/GC/30, 18 October 2013.

[80] Report of the Secretary-General, *Conflict-related sexual violence,* S/2016/361, 20 April 2016, para 2.

females, or those who reject the gender binary), its incidence following the formal end of conflict and that the perpetrator may be a civilian, for instance a family member. In contrast the detailed *The Hague Principles on Sexual Violence,*[81] compiled through consultations with multiple civil society organisations, highlight the complexity, fluidity and contextuality of sexual violence and that it 'encompasses all violations of sexual autonomy and sexual integrity ... often characterized by humiliation, domination, and destruction'.

The logical follow up question is whether legal prohibition has served to protect women and girls from conflict-related gender-based and sexual violence and thus to enhance their security. The disappointing answer is that it has not and that the flurry of international activity has had little effect on its incidence. Precise statistics are impossible due to under-reporting and different understandings of what constitutes such violence, but there is no reason to doubt the continuing veracity of the opinion of practitioners in the field that 'for each rape reported in connection with a conflict, 10 to 20 cases go undocumented'.[82] The SRSG on conflict-related sexual violence details such violence in 19 countries where there is 'credible and verifiable information' and in 2019 the Security Council remains deeply concerned about the 'slow progress' in its elimination.[83]

Despite the reiteration that women and girls must be protected against sexual violence, what that legal obligation entails remains unclear. What protection means and what actions are required to be undertaken and by whom to prevent and protect women and girls against conflict-affected sexual violence has not been clarified. The legal regimes listed above provide different answers. Under IHL protection amounts to the principle of distinction and military training and discipline ensuring compliance with the prohibition of the relevant acts. Under human rights law protection would encompass the full guarantee of women's human rights by the state during conflict and peacetime, as well as the exercise of due diligence with respect to the acts of non-state actors. International criminal law

[81] *The Hague Principles on Sexual Violence* (2019) at https://4genderjustice.org/wp-content/uploads/2019/11/The-Hague-Principles-on-Sexual-Violence.pdf.

[82] Report of the Secretary-General, *Conflict-related sexual violence*, S/2016/361, 20 April 2016.

[83] UN Security Council resolution 2467 (2019).

relies upon the application of criminal justice – functioning courts with jurisdiction, appropriate legislation and effective law enforcement agencies to implement the law.[84] In all three legal regimes there are gaps and inconsistencies.

The WPS resolutions set out some specific means of protection. First is women's full and meaningful participation in all decision and policy-making about conflict and post-conflict.[85] Failing to 'connect and acknowledge the mutually reinforcing nature of women's participation and protection' creates 'a false dichotomy that claims women's protection issues are more important than, and separate from, issues related to women's participation'.[86] Accordingly the discussion about women's participation in chapter three is directly relevant to women's security as well as to the broader issue of sustainable peace. Second is the importance of military order and discipline. Third is ensuring the accountability of perpetrators through criminal prosecution. Fourth is subjecting perpetrators to Security Council sanction. And fifth is protection through peacekeeping operations. These processes are not limited to the WPS resolutions and may be incorporated into UN Charter chapter VII country specific mandates, into resolutions concerning the accountability of peacekeepers, and to those addressing more broadly the protection of civilians in armed conflict. The following section briefly considers these protective measures, except for peacekeeping operations, which is too big a topic for consideration here.

4.5.1 Military Order and Discipline

Assertion of military order is a means to protect against the sexual violence that occurs 'as a manifestation of a lack of discipline and

[84] E.g. *Fatma Yildirim (deceased)* v *Austria*, CEDAW/C/39/D/6/2005, 1 October 2007, para 12.1.2: '[I]n order for the individual woman victim of domestic violence to enjoy the practical realization of . . . her human rights and fundamental freedoms, the political will that is expressed in the aforementioned comprehensive [legal] system of Austria must be supported by State actors, who adhere to the State party's due diligence obligations.'

[85] UN Security Council resolution 2467 (2019): 'women's protection and participation are inextricably linked and mutually-reinforcing as reflected by all previous resolutions on women, peace and security'.

[86] NGO Working Group on WPS, 'Mapping Women, Peace and Security in the UN Security Council: 2015', at http://womenpeacesecurity.org/media/pdf-NGOWG_MappingWPS_PolicyBrief_2015.pdf.

lax command and control'.[87] In resolution 1820 (2008) the Security Council demands that all parties to conflict undertake to enforce appropriate military disciplinary measures, uphold the principle of command responsibility, train troops on the categorical prohibition of all forms of sexual violence against civilians, take into account past actions of sexual violence when deploying armed or security forces and debunk myths that fuel sexual violence. This last complements the jurisprudence of the CEDAW Committee that gendered myths and stereotypes about rape and sexual violence are discriminatory, undermine access to justice and thus impede accountability.[88] Such myths abound including that sexual intercourse with a young girl gives fighting men a special power that supports their military exploits,[89] provides protection against being killed in conflict,[90] or simply that women lie about sex. Later resolutions have added further practical measures such as the need for clear orders to be issued and codes of conduct developed that prohibit sexual violence along with enforcement procedures to ensure accountability for breaching these orders. All credible allegations must be diligently investigated. These stipulations have been supplemented by innovative institutional positions to support militaries in the field and to provide technical expertise.[91] The SRSG on conflict-related sexual violence provides leadership, collects and collates verified information and through her annual reports to the Security Council keeps the issue on the agenda.

Prevention and protection in these terms assumes offences committed by military forces and that enforcing military discipline is the

[87] Report of the Secretary-General, *Conflict-related sexual violence*, S/2016/361, 20 April 2016, para 11.

[88] *Vertido* v *The Philippines*, CEDAW/C/46/D/18/2008, 1 September 2010; *R.P. B.* v *The Philippines*, CEDAW/C/57/D/34/2011, 12 March 2014.

[89] E.g. Watye Ki Gen and CAP International, 'The Lord's Resistance Army's Forced Wife System', at https://wpsncanada.files.wordpress.com/2012/05/wpsn-c-watye-ki-gen-and-cap-international-lra-force-wife-system-publication.pdf.

[90] E.g. 'In DRC, for example, one armed group reportedly committed acts of sexual violence based on a belief that the rape of a virgin conveyed magical powers and invincibility.' Megan Bastick, Karin Grimm and Rahel Kunz, *Sexual Violence in Armed Conflict: Global Overview and Implications for the Security Sector* (Geneva Centre for the Democratic Control of Armed Forces, 2007) 14.

[91] UN Team of Experts Rule of Law/Sexual Violence in Conflict (September 2019) at www.un.org/sexualviolenceinconflict/wp-content/uploads/2013/04/our-work/team-of-experts/TOE-Update-Sept-2019.pdf.

answer. It may also presume offences committed by the other side in the conflict. In a 2017 decision, the ICC appeals chamber confirmed charges against Ntaganda of rape and sexual slavery as crimes against humanity and war crimes committed against a child soldier who was under his command, in the course of the armed conflict in the Democratic Republic of Congo. It affirmed that 'provided there is a nexus to the armed conflict, rape and sexual slavery against any person is prohibited, and that therefore members of the same armed force are not *per se* excluded as potential victims of the war crimes of rape and sexual slavery'.[92] This clarifies this important point, at least in the jurisprudence of the ICC, but not all acts of conflict-related sexual violence are committed by military forces under operational command or as a tactic of war. Other perpetrators include humanitarian workers, private security forces, criminal gangs and civilians, some taking opportunistic advantage of the collapse of social support structures, others engaging in predatory economic activity including people smuggling and trafficking. Forced and early (child) marriage may be instigated by family members as a form of protection for female relatives against random rape, or to provide the family with some financial support through selling a valuable commodity – the girl. The WPS emphasis on military activity fails to capture the complexity of the causes of and motivations for conflict-affected sexual violence and thus fails to provide a holistic agenda.

4.5.2 Criminal Prosecution

International criminal prosecution as a means of prevention of and protection against sexual violence rests upon the presumed deterrent effect of legal accountability[93] and punishment of individual perpetrators or their commanders. The ICTY and ICTR both recorded some successful prosecutions but in the spring of 2020

[92] *The Prosecutor* v *Bosco Ntaganda*, ICC-01/04–02/06–1962, 15 June 2017, judgment on the appeal of Mr Ntaganda against the 'Second decision on the Defence's challenge to the jurisdiction of the Court in respect of Counts 6 and 9'; *The Prosecutor* v *Bosco Ntaganda*, ICC-01/04–02/06, 8 July 2019, para 965.

[93] 'Prosecution is therefore essential to prevention, because it can deter potential perpetrators and contribute to restoring faith in the rule of law.' Report of the Secretary-General, *Conflict-related sexual violence*, S/2016/361, 20 April 2016, para 10.

Ntaganda remains the only accused convicted by the ICC for sexual violence.[94] The vast majority of perpetrators never face trial or punishment in international tribunals that are limited by jurisdictional requirements, practical considerations relating to collection and retention of evidence, and by their inability to address the magnitude of the problem. These factors engender a culture of impunity. Seeking to combat the lack of accountability was a motivating factor behind the UK government's Preventing Sexual Violence in Conflict Initiative (PSVI), which has produced an *International Protocol on the Documentation and Investigation of Sexual Violence in Conflict.*[95] Criminal trials are rarely possible during conflict and may be politically and practically possible only many years later by which time important evidence (even if gathered at the time) may have been lost or may have been inadequately or inappropriately stored. The *Protocol* is a practical tool kit for the collection and collation of evidence in a legally admissible form. The same motivation has inspired the creation by the General Assembly of the International, Impartial and Independent Mechanism (IIIM) to assist in the investigation and prosecution of persons responsible for the most serious crimes under international law committed in Syria since March 2011.[96] As neither Iraq nor Syria are parties to the Rome Statute and the Security Council has not referred the situation, the ICC has no jurisdiction over crimes committed in their territories, including those by ISIS/Daesh. The IIIM is not a court but a mechanism for the collection, preservation and analysis of evidence so it will be available if at some future date trials become possible. Following this example and a report by a UN Human Rights Council Fact-finding Mission,[97] in October 2018 the Human Rights Council decided to establish a similar mechanism with respect to serious

[94] *The Prosecutor* v *Bosco Ntaganda*, ICC-01/04–02/06, 8 July 2019. The first person to be convicted by the ICC for crimes of sexual violence on the basis of command responsibility was acquitted on appeal; *Prosecutor* v *Jean-Paul Bemba Gombo*, ICC-01/05–01/08, 8 June 2018.

[95] *International Protocol on the Documentation and Investigation of Sexual Violence in Conflict Best Practice on the Documentation of Sexual Violence as a Crime or Violation of International Law* (UK FCO, 1st ed. June 2014; 2nd ed. March 2017). The second edition has an expanded scope and includes chapters on sexual violence against children and against men and boys.

[96] UN General Assembly resolution 71/248, 21 December 2016.

[97] Report of the independent international fact-finding mission on Myanmar, A/HRC/39/64, 12 September 2018.

international crimes committed in Myanmar. These innovative responses demonstrate a determination that prosecutions of international crimes should not be frustrated by political unwillingness to allow jurisdiction but nevertheless address only one aspect of the problem – availability of reliable evidence for use in a trial compliant with international standards. In seeking an alternative forum, a case has now been brought by The Gambia against Myanmar in the International Court of Justice (ICJ) claiming the latter's acts against the Rohingya people to be in violation of the Genocide Convention.[98] A ruling against Myanmar would assert the responsibility of the state rather than the criminal liability of any individual.

International tribunals are never going be adequate to reverse the culture of impunity for crimes of conflict-affected sexual violence and attention has also turned to domestic courts. Holding trials of international crimes in domestic courts depends upon crimes being reported, prosecutorial will, effective investigations and security for victims and witnesses. There also need to be operational courts that can ensure fair trials. There are differences of opinion about the suitability of military tribunals for this purpose,[99] also bearing in mind that the regular criminal court system may have ceased to function effectively during conflict and its aftermath. There have been some high profile successes, albeit many years after the commission of the offences. These include the landmark conviction by the Extraordinary African Chambers in the Senegalese court system of former Chadian President Hissène Habré[100] and the conviction of two former military officers from Guatemala who received a combined prison sentence of 360 years for human rights abuses committed during the 1980s. The latter case was the first time such a conviction has been secured within the country where the crimes

[98] *Application of the Convention on the Prevention and Punishment of the Crime of Genocide* (*The Gambia* v *Myanmar*) (Order for provisional measures), 23 January 2020.

[99] Lois Moore and Christine Chinkin, 'The Crime of Rape in Military and Civilian Jurisdictions', in Mark Latimer and Philippe Sands (eds.) *The Grey Zone Civilian Protection between Human Rights and the Laws of War* (Hart Publishing, 2018) 179–206.

[100] In the ICJ, Justice Trindade criticised the delay in the delivery of justice in this case: 'With the persistence of impunity in the present case, the passing of time will continue hurting people, much more than it normally does, in particular those victimized by the absence of human justice.' *Questions relating to the Obligation to Prosecute or Extradite* (*Belgium* v *Senegal*) 2012 ICJ Reports 422, para 145 (sep. op. Trindade, J.).

were committed. In the *Habré* case the late inclusion into the indictment of sexual violence has been credited to the actions of civil society advocates who entered an *amicus* brief setting out to the Court the importance of so doing.[101] Prosecutions in national courts are regularly detailed by the Secretary-General in his annual reports to the Security Council.[102]

Women survivors face particular obstacles in accessing justice for the crimes committed against them that resolution 2467 (2019) addresses in greater detail than the earlier WPS resolutions.[103] To this end states are called upon to: establish victim and witness protection laws; provide, where appropriate, legal aid for survivors; specialised police units and courts to address such crimes; remove procedural impediments to justice for victims such as restrictive limitation periods for filing claims; end discriminatory corroboration requirements, exclusion or discrediting of victims' testimony. These recommendations address both practical measures for making trial processes more amenable to victims and witnesses and challenge the gender stereotypes and biases that make courtrooms hostile places for so many women and LGBTQI persons. The ending of corroboration requirements alone would go a long way to achieving this in the 'coercive circumstances' of conflict.

The WPS resolutions do not question whether criminal justice is always the appropriate response to conflict-affected sexual violence. Alternative or complementary transitional justice processes are given much less space with women's participation within them as

[101] Participants in the Human Rights Center, University of California, Berkeley mobilised a global effort to prepare an *amicus* brief, seeking revision of the charges in light of evidence of sexual violence that had been heard by the Court. The Judges did not directly refer to the brief but appear to have been influenced by it in modifying the charges. Sarah Taylor, 'Women, Peace, and Politics at the UN Security Council', *IPI Global Observatory* (17 July 2013) at https://theglobalobservatory.org/2013/07/women-peace-and-politics-at-the-un-security-council/.

[102] E.g. in 2019, the Secretary-General reported on the work of the High Military Court in the DRC, the trial in Goma of Ntabo Ntaberi Sheka for the alleged mass rape of 387 people in Walikale, and the investigations that are being undertaken into mass rape that occurred near Bossangoa in February 2018. Report of the Secretary-General, *Conflict-related sexual violence*, S/2019/280, 29 March 2019, para 8.

[103] Christine Chinkin and Madeleine Rees, 'Commentary on Security Council Resolution 2467 Continued State Obligation and Civil Society Action on Sexual Violence in Conflict' (LSE Centre for Women, Peace and Security and Women's International League for Peace and Freedom, 2019).

the major recommendation.[104] What is needed at a minimum is listening to the survivors in order to frame a holistic approach to reform of legal and social institutions that are context specific, take account of individual survivors' choices and address the obstacles to securing gender justice in periods of non-conflict, as well as during and post-conflict.[105]

4.5.3 Sanctions

Resolution 1325 was adopted while the sanctions regime instituted against Iraq following its invasion of Kuwait[106] was still in place and its adverse effect especially on women and children causing controversy.[107] As discussed in Chapter 1, resolution 1325 (2000) affirms that in imposing sanctions under UN Charter article 41, the Council was ready to consider the potential adverse impact on the civilian population and to accept humanitarian exceptions. Later WPS resolutions have shifted the emphasis to the potential of targeted sanctions on perpetrators as identified and listed by the SRSG on sexual violence in armed conflict and urging sanctions committees to include commission of sexual violence among the criteria for the designation of sanctions.[108] Imposition of sanctions can have a number of objectives: punishment, securing compliance with the law, exerting pressure to induce behaviour change, deterrence, making an example to deter others. Effectiveness in achieving the required objective depends on a number of variables including the likelihood of sanctions being imposed and complied

104 E.g. UN Security Council resolution 2467 (2019) para 16 '[e]ncourages concerned Member States to ensure the opportunity for the full and meaningful participation of survivors of sexual and gender-based violence at all stages of transitional justice processes, including in decision-making roles, [and] recognizes that women's leadership and participation will increase the likelihood that transitional justice outcomes will constitute effective redress as defined by victims and will respond to important contextual factors'.

105 See CEDAW Committee, General Recommendation No. 33, Women's access to justice, CEDAW/C/GC/33, 3 August 2015.

106 UN Security Council resolution 661, 6 August 1990.

107 Committee on Economic, Social and Cultural Rights, General Comment No. 8, E/C.12/1997/8, The relationship between economic sanctions and respect for economic, social and cultural rights. The Committee emphasised the impact of sanctions on the poor but did not engage in any gender analysis.

108 UN Security Council resolution 1888 (2009); UN Security Council resolution 1960 (2010); UN Security Council resolution 2106 (2013).

with by others. They must also be directed at the wrongful behaviour in question. Sexual violence is high earning and makes a considerable contribution to the political economy of war.[109] The Security Council has expanded the sanctions framework for the suppression of terrorist financing to include ISIL/Daesh and has condemned the abduction of women and children for sexual exploitation and trading and to force the payment of ransoms.[110] In WPS resolution 2242 (2015) it posited the nexus between the gender-based and sexual violence committed by terrorist groups and their use of it as an instrument of power and for financing their activities.[111] In resolution 2467 (2019), the Council urges sanctions committees to apply targeted sanctions within the scope of the designated criteria against the perpetrators of sexual violence in conflict (not limited to the context of terrorism or violent extremism)[112] and expresses its own intention to include rape and sexual violence as designation criteria in sanctions regimes. In his 2019 Report, the Secretary-General recommended that the Security Council integrate conflict-related sexual violence into the work of counterterrorism sanctions committees as well as considering for sanctions designations those who help finance such groups through the sale, trade or trafficking of women and children.[113] Research published by Georgetown University in 2018 found inconsistencies, gaps and delays in the current sanctions system, thereby undermining its effectiveness in protecting against conflict-affected sexual violence.[114] In 2019, the Secretary-General noted that advances have been made with stand-alone designation criteria on sexual violence brought into sanctions regimes in the Central African

[109] Report of the Secretary-General, *on the threat posed by ISIL (Da'esh) to international peace and security and the range of United Nations efforts in support of Member States in countering the threat*, S/2016/92, 29 January 2016.

[110] UN Security Council resolution 2253, 17 December 2015, *Threats to international peace and security caused by terrorist acts*, preamble.

[111] UN Security Council resolution 2242, preamble; para 12 urges the UN to ensure relevant gender expertise in sanctions committees to guarantee their mandate.

[112] UN Security Council resolution 2467 (2019) para 10; UN Security Council resolution 2493 (2019) para 10 (c) seeks only an assessment of progress with respect to inclusion of gender expertise in sanctions committees.

[113] Report of the Secretary-General, *Conflict-related sexual violence*, S/2019/280, 29 March 2019, para 124 (e).

[114] Sophie Huvé, *The Use of UN Sanctions to Address Conflict-Related Sexual Violence* (Georgetown Institute for Women, Peace and Security, 2018).

Republic, Libya, Somalia and South Sudan.[115] However, whether sanctions are an effective tool for combating conflict-affected sexual violence remains unclear, not least because they have as yet been little used for this purpose.

4.5.4 WPS and Protection against Sexual Violence: Some Conclusions

While it is undoubtedly important and contrasts with the earlier near-invisibility of sexual violence in international bodies, emphasis on this aspect of the WPS agenda has its downsides. Resolution 1820 (2008) adopts a reductionist approach to rape and sexual violence in conflict in two ways: it addresses sexual violence only as a tactic and method of war and it prioritises women and girls as its victims. With respect to the former, it narrows the scope of resolution 1325 itself, which calls for protection against 'gender-based violence, . . . and all other forms of violence in situations of armed conflict'. Resolution 2467 (2019), too, demands the cessation of all sexual violence. Recognition of sexual violence as a tactic of war (and subsequently as a tactic of terrorism[116]) was important for the categorical assertion that rape is not an inevitable by-product of conflict but may be a deliberate tactic that can and must be prohibited. But it also risks reducing attention to just this one form of conflict-affected gender-based violence. Although 'civilian' is gender neutral, resolution 1820 repeatedly refers 'in particular to women and girls'. Similarly, resolution 1888 (2009) designates women's protection officers rather than protection officers for all people threatened by sexual violence. WPS has drawn criticism for failing to explicitly include sexual violence against men and boys until resolution 2106 in 2013 and not again until resolution 2467 in 2019.[117] This raises a further shortcoming, the assumption of the gender binary – women and men. The unwillingness of many states to accept diverse sexual and gender identities means that those targeted for their sexual or gender identity are invisible in the WPS resolutions. Reports of targeted attacks by ISIS/Daesh against

[115] Report of the Secretary-General, *Conflict-related sexual violence*, S/2019/280, 29 March 2019, para 30.

[116] UN Security Council resolution 2242 (2015).

[117] The SRSG on sexual violence in armed conflict includes such violence against men and boys in her annual reports to the Security Council.

homosexuals or those suspected of being homosexuals make clear that this a significant omission. Moreover, where homosexuality is criminalised,[118] male victims are at further risk and there are, by definition, no services for male victims of rape.[119] Nor should sexual violence against women and girls, men and boys, and LGBTQI people be addressed as a single package. Greater attention must be given to providing responses that take account of the many and diverse ways in which conflict-affected sexual violence impacts upon different people because of their sexuality and/or gender.[120] The WPS agenda will remain limited unless it accepts that security for all depends on an integral understanding of both the gendered nature of conflict and how this impacts upon targeting and the harms incurred.

It is also important that conflict-affected sexual violence is not perceived as a single-dimensional phenomenon; rather, we must take into account its many contextual variants. While there are the commonalities of extreme violence, denial of autonomy and bodily integrity, as well as the assertion of domination and control, there is a danger in bringing diverse tactics and strategies together under this one rubric. These include those of ISIS/Daesh, which targets identified groups for destruction, notably the Yazidi, killing men and boys and enslaving women and girls;[121] the militia in Sierra Leone that abducted women and girls, often forcing them into marriage as 'bush' wives;[122] the Bosnian Serb militia who detained women and girls in camps and repeatedly raped them;[123] and many instances of rampant militia attacking villages

[118] Sexual violence against men and boys remains under-reported including for fear of social ostracism and of criminalisation as is the case in seventy-eight countries. Report of the Secretary-General, *Conflict-related sexual violence*, S/2016/361, 20 April 2016, para 8.

[119] 'A total of 62 countries still provide no legal protection for male rape victims.' Ibid., at para 9.

[120] Institute for International Criminal Investigations, *Guidelines for Investigating Conflict-related Sexual and Gender-based Violence against Men and Boys*, The Hague, 29 February 2016, at www.gov.uk/government/uploads/system/uploads/attachmenfile/file/546569/PSVI_training_-_violence_against_men_and_boys.pdf.

[121] Human Rights Council, '"They Came to Destroy": ISIS Crimes Against the Yazidis', A/HRC/32/CRP.2, 15 June 2016.

[122] E.g. the facts in *Prosecutor* v *Brima et al.*, SCSL-2004–16-A, Appeals Chamber, 22 February 2008.

[123] E.g. the facts in *Prosecutor* v *Kunarac et al.*, IT-96–23; IT-96–23/1-A, 12 June 2002.

and committing rape and pillage.[124] Such differences have implications for criminal investigation – determining the appropriate charges, prosecution and legal argumentation, including what defences prosecutors might have to meet – for their inclusion in other processes of transitional justice and for appropriate reparations, relief and support measures: a woman who was abducted and 'married' to a militia member, had children with him and was also active in combat has very different needs from a woman in the DRC who was repeatedly publicly gang-raped in an attack on her village; or from a Yazidi child captured, beaten, registered for transfer in a slave-market and subsequently discarded; or from another child who was sexually abused by a peacekeeper in return for food.

The threat and fear of sexual violence adds significantly to the insecurity experienced by women and girls in conflict-affected areas, but the WPS resolutions (and indeed the international legal regimes) should not be taken as determining that this is the only form of insecurity faced in conflict. Focus on sexual violence obscures the importance of addressing other gendered harms that undermine women's security, thereby minimising the likelihood of their being addressed post-conflict. These include: domestic violence during and post-conflict; displacement; separation from and disappearance of male relatives, perhaps entailing curtailed movement and rendering women unable to carry out routine activities such as accessing markets, fuel and water, employment, health services, schools, and land and property in the face of collapsed or suspended support systems. All these situations are often exacerbated by lost, inadequate or inaccessible documentation.[125] Other harms are incurred through discriminatory state laws such as those relating to nationality and statelessness that leave displaced women and their children without any state responsible for their security in the state-centric international system.[126]

[124] E.g. the facts in *Prosecutor* v *Jean-Pierre Bemba Gombo*, ICC-01/05–01/08, 21 March 2016. The conviction was overturned on appeal.

[125] This was reported as a consequence of the fall of Kunduz to the Taliban in September–October 2015; Report of the Secretary-General, *Conflict-related sexual violence*, S/2016/361, 20 April 2016, para. 23.

[126] CEDAW Committee, General Recommendation No. 30 on women in conflict prevention, conflict and post-conflict situations, CEDAW/C/GC/30, 18 October 2013, paras 58–61.

Omission of such harms from the WPS resolutions allows for an assertion that the Security Council is concerned about women's human rights while limiting those rights away from the full panoply of rights, especially economic and social rights. It also portrays gender-based and sexual violence in conflict as exceptional rather than as rooted in gender inequality and as occurring in a continuum from that committed in so-called 'peacetime' through to conflict-related violence. The assumption that there is a distinction between something called 'conflict' and a different situation called 'post-conflict' disregards the reality of continued violence against women following a ceasefire or peace agreement.[127] It sustains the image of women as passive victims with 'special needs', upholding the binary of women in need of protection and men (especially military men) as the designated protectors. This undermines women's agency and runs counter to the realities of sexual violence against men and of sexual exploitation and abuse committed by peacekeepers. It also compromises a more transformative agenda capable of effectively empowering women as agents of change.[128]

The many steps that women initiate for their own and others' security are rendered invisible through a focus on women as victims. Women have set up safe-houses and shelters in the most unforgiving of places. They operate warning systems. Where state security services have failed to provide adequate protection from sexual violence, civil society groups often take over: 'From Uganda to Colombia to Tunisia, civil society organisations are doing critical work in documenting incidents of sexual violence, lobbying for stronger legislation, delivering training, providing care for the victims, and taking initiatives to ensure a more protective environment.'[129] The later WPS resolutions have given some limited recognition to civil society and women's activism that promotes

[127] Ibid., at para 35. For a different form of 'post-conflict' gender-based violence, see Sandra Walklate, '"Seeing" Gender, War and Terror', 18 *Criminology & Criminal Justice* (2018) 617–30, 619 (a woman in France was taken nude through streets crowded with male onlookers to have her head shaved for the 'crime' of having had sexual relations with the enemy).

[128] Paula Drummond, 'Conflict-Related Sexual Violence' in Jill Steans and Daniela Tepe-Belfrage (eds.) *Handbook on Gender in World Politics* (Edward Elgar, 2016) 206–14, 212.

[129] Bastick, Grimm and Kunz (*supra* n 90).

their security and protects their rights. But, rather than presenting this as a priority, resolution 2493 only 'strongly encourages' the formation of 'safe and enabling environments' where women community leaders and peacebuilders can work independently and without interference. That states are also encouraged to address threats, violence and hate speech against these women and those who promote and protect women's human rights is an indicator of the backlash and the increased insecurities faced by women and girls including in post-conflict settings.

4.6 Prevention of Conflict

There is an ambiguity in the WPS agenda as to whether women and girls must be protected from conflict-related gender-based and sexual violence or from armed conflict itself. The women at The Hague in 1915 'opposed the assumption that women can be protected under the conditions of modern warfare' with the necessary corollary that war itself must therefore be prevented.[130] If women – indeed all people – cannot be protected in conflict, then attention must turn to preventing conflict. This is the purpose of UN Charter chapter VI on the pacific settlement of disputes with its array of negotiatory and adjudicative processes. But, despite efforts to promote a 'prevention culture', this has not been readily accepted by states or, indeed, by the UN itself.[131] The inclusion of preventive diplomacy in the 1992 *Agenda for Peace*[132] had little traction against the imperatives of state sovereignty and non-intervention. The General Assembly in its 2005 celebration of sixty years since the founding of the UN solemnly renewed the commitment 'to promote a culture of prevention of armed conflict as a way of addressing

[130] Resolutions adopted by the International Congress of Women, The Hague, Holland, 1 May 1915, at http://womhist.alexanderstreet.com/hague/doc1.htm.

[131] Report of the High-level Independent Panel on Peace Operations, *Uniting our strengths for peace: politics, partnership and people*, A/70/95–S/2015/446, 17 June 2015, 11.

[132] Report of the Secretary-General, *An Agenda for Peace: Preventive diplomacy, peacemaking and peace-keeping*, A/47/277–S/24111, 17 June 1992, para 20: '*Preventive diplomacy* is action to prevent disputes from arising between parties, to prevent existing disputes from escalating into conflicts and to limit the spread of the latter when they occur.'

global security and development challenges'.[133] In his report on the outcome of the 2016 World Humanitarian Summit, then Secretary-General Ban Ki-Moon regretted that lack of recognition of the importance of attending to conflict prevention had resulted in few individual commitments to what he termed a 'core responsibility' to humanity.[134] He considered that 'prevention and conflict resolution remain a laudable ambition rather than a concrete and operational activity that is adequately equipped, financed and championed'.[135] His successor, Antonio Guterres, has again urged the UN to commit to the 'culture of prevention' that was promised in 2005, and to a diplomacy for peace. He also considered that the reviews on peacekeeping operations and on WPS created a 'unique opportunity to develop a comprehensive, modern and effective operational peace architecture, encompassing prevention, conflict resolution, peacekeeping, peacebuilding and long-term development – the "peace continuum"'.[136] Section 4.6.1 considers prevention of conflict in the context of WPS.

4.6.1 WPS and Conflict Prevention

From resolution 1325 (2000) onwards, the WPS resolutions have paid lip service to the importance of women's participation in conflict prevention[137] but less to either immediate preventive measures or long-term structural factors that contribute

133 UN General Assembly resolution 60/1, 24 October 2005, *World Summit Outcome*, para 74.

134 Prior to the World Humanitarian Summit, Istanbul 2015, Ban Ki-moon asserted that '[p]reventing conflicts and finding political solutions to resolve them is the first and foremost responsibility to humanity'. Report of the Secretary-General, *One Humanity: Shared Responsibility*, A/70/709, 31 January 2016.

135 Report of the Secretary-General, *Outcome of the World Humanitarian Summit*, A/71/353, 23 August 2016.

136 António Guterres, 'Challenges and Opportunities for the United Nations' (4 April 2016) at www.antonioguterres.gov.pt/wp-content/uploads/2016/06/antonio-guterres-vision-statement.pdf.

137 E.g. UN Security Council resolution 1325 (2000): 'Reaffirming the important role of women in the prevention and resolution of conflicts and in peacebuilding'; UN Security Council resolution 2493 (2019): 'to further promote women's participation in peacebuilding efforts, and in the prevention of conflict'.

to and perpetuate conflict and violence.[138] In its 2013 General Recommendation on women in conflict, the CEDAW Committee recognised the importance of effective early warning systems and engaging in preventive diplomacy and mediation.[139] It emphasised that interventions, whether by centralised government or other states, should respect local women's peacekeeping activities and, above all, that preventive efforts should do no harm. The 2015 *Global Study* on the implementation of resolution 1325 (2000) also addressed early warning systems and suggested a three-pronged approach directed at the inclusion of local women: seeking effective and secure ways of enabling women to share their local knowledge, developing gender-sensitive indicators of impending violence and identifying indicators that are specific to gender-based violations against women. As illustration, the *Global Study* explained that higher occurrence of gender-based harassment or violence against women in public places, heightened restrictions on or enforcement of dress codes, and increase in misogynistic expression and propaganda can all serve as warnings of impending generalised violence.

4.6.2 Structural Drivers of Conflict

Early warning systems and preventive diplomacy are limited aspects of conflict prevention that look only to the imminence or likelihood of an outbreak of war. Since at least the 1915 Women's Congress in The Hague, women have looked to the deeper, structural causes of war. The Hague Resolutions called for universal disarmament, women's equality rights and education for peace. Four years later at Zurich, the Congress also recognised that financial and economic measures in the wake of war would condemn 'a hundred million

[138] A 2018 statement by the President of the Security Council recalls that 'a comprehensive conflict prevention strategy should include, inter alia, early warning, preventive deployment, mediation, peacekeeping, non-proliferation, accountability measures as well as post-conflict peacebuilding, and recognizes that these components are interdependent, complementary, and non-sequential'; S/PRST/2018/1, 18 January 2018.

[139] CEDAW Committee, General Recommendation No. 30 on women in conflict prevention, conflict and post-conflict situations, CEDAW/C/GC/30, 18 October 2013, para 29.

people of this generation ... to poverty, disease and despair'.[140] Although women have divided over some issues, notably the validity of pacifism, the need to reduce these drivers of violence – military activity and arms, inequalities and harsh economic policies – has been repeated by women since World War I and many sought their inclusion in resolution 1325 (2000). They were unsuccessful. These objectives are at odds with the masculinist and militaristic ethos of the Security Council and the exercise by its permanent members of coercive foreign policies that foster cycles of violence and reinforce hegemonic masculine values. Without addressing how, inter alia, militarism, imperialism, inequalities, the availability of arms and the political economy all operate separately and in conjunction with each other to maintain insecurity, the WPS resolutions provide an impoverished picture of 'women and security' and reduce their potential for sustainable peace. As was said in the *Global Study*:

> [S]ustainable peace will only be possible when all actors address: the root causes of conflict and violence; a global political economy which prioritizes preparedness for war over peace; continuities in violence and insecurity which are evidenced particularly through the experiences of women and girls; and the growing role of factors such as climate change and natural resource control in creating insecurity.[141]

This could be the transformative value of WPS. Sections 4.6.2.1–4.6.2.3 briefly consider some of these.

4.6.2.1 MILITARISM AND MILITARISATION

Feminists have long exposed the detrimental impact of militarism for women and for peace. A 1915 publication asserted militarism to be 'the curse of women ... Violence at home, violence abroad; ... violence between man and woman ... War has engendered and perpetuated that dominance of man as a military animal which has pervaded every social institution from *Parliament* downwards.'[142]

140 WILPF resolutions, 2nd Congress Zurich, Switzerland 1919, II Treaty of Peace, at https://wilpf.org/wp-content/uploads/2012/08/WILPF_triennial_congress_1919.pdf.

141 *Global Study*, 195.

142 *Militarism versus Feminism: An Enquiry and a Policy Demonstrating that Militarism Involves the Subjection of Women* (April 1915); cited in Jill Liddington, *The Road to Greenham Common: Feminism and Anti-Militarism in Britain since 1820* (Syracuse University Press, 1989) 98–9.

Today, there are numerous instances of how the presence of military and state security forces threatens women's sense of security and well-being. These include the placement of military forces in areas supposedly 'at peace'; the use of military forces to 'protect' mining and other concessions from local resistance in Honduras, Guatemala, the Democratic Republic of Congo and elsewhere; and the presence of the Israeli Defense Force at checkpoints in Gaza and the West Bank. Militarisation changes the local economy, impinging upon peoples' access to land, agriculture, water and resources.[143] But societies do not need to be so explicitly militarised for the gendered ideology of militarism to be pervasive. In a classic exposition, international relations scholar Cynthia Enloe has explained the core beliefs of militarism: armed force as the ultimate resolver of tensions; human nature as prone to conflict; having enemies as a natural condition; hierarchical relations as productive of effective action; a state without an army as naïve, scarcely modern and barely legitimate; in times of crisis, those who are feminine as needing armed protection; and in times of crisis, any man who refuses to engage in armed violent action as jeopardising his own status as a manly man.[144] Enloe explains that this ideology has been normalised as the cornerstone of security through a process of militarisation that digs deep into a society's psyche. Its pervasiveness creates and perpetuates a cycle of insecurity.

The insidious effects of militarisation were resoundingly rejected by the 2015 *Global Study*[145] that urged non-military means of prevention and protection. Similarly, the High-level Panel on Peace Operations sought an 'essential shift' in the design and delivery of peace operations. Through Nyakhat Pal's story recounted in Chapter 3, it reiterated that the UN was created 'to reaffirm faith in fundamental human rights and in the dignity and worth of the human person'. While acknowledging that, in many instances,

143 Report of the Special Rapporteur on the situation of human rights defenders, *Situation of women human rights defenders*, A/HRC/40/60, 10 January 2019, para 32.

144 Cynthia Enloe, 'Understanding Militarism, Militarization, and the Linkages with Globalization Using a Feminist Curiosity', in *Gender & Militarism: Analyzing the Links to Strategize for Peace*, a Women Peacemakers Program Action Pack (24 May 2014), www2.kobe-u.ac.jp/~alexroni/IPD%202015%20readings/IPD%202015_9/Gender%20and%20Militarism%20May-Pack-2014-web.pdf.

145 *Global Study*, 25.

violence and conflict are intractable,[146] the Panel favoured comprehensive political solutions to conflict that integrate human rights: '[P]olitics must drive the design and implementation of peace operations. Lasting peace is achieved not through military and technical engagements, but through political solutions.'

These insights have been lost on members of the Security Council. At the opening of the seventy-fourth session of the General Assembly in September 2019, President Trump boasted that the United States had spent 'over two and a half trillion dollars since [his] election to completely rebuild [the country's] great military' and that the United States is, 'by far, the world's most powerful nation'.[147] NATO – the military alliance for the security of Europe created during the cold war – was not disbanded when that threat retreated, but its membership and reach expanded. The European peace project – the European Communities, now the European Union – is under threat while the military project remains supported and extended. Unsurprisingly, and against the urgings of the *Global Study*, the WPS resolutions are immune to feminist and post-colonial critiques of militarism and the Council relies upon military measures as the primary means of providing protection and promoting security. In consequence, instead of achieving transformation of the international security agenda, resolution 1325 marginalises anti-militaristic feminist advocacy and deprives the WPS resolutions of their transformative potential.[148]

What the Security Council does remain committed to is the greater participation of women in military and security forces,[149] an objective that is promised in a number of National Action Plans

[146] Report of the High-level Independent Panel on Peace Operations, *Uniting our strengths for peace: politics, partnership and people*, A/70/95–S/2015/446, 17 June 2015, paras 8 ff.

[147] Remarks by President Trump to the 74th Session of the United Nations General Assembly, 25 September 2019, at www.whitehouse.gov/briefings-statements/remarks-president-trump-74th-session-united-nations-general-assembly/.

[148] Nicola Pratt and Sophie Richter-Devroe, 'Critically Examining UNSCR 1325 on Women, Peace and Security', 13 (4) *International Feminist Journal of Politics* (2011) 489–503, 493.

[149] UN Security Council resolution 2493 (2019) urges Member States to 'remain committed to increasing the number of civilian and uniformed women in peacekeeping at all levels and in key positions'.

(NAPs).[150] There are different opinions about the rationale for and impact of increasing the number of women in the security sector, but what is clear is that it does not contest the assumption of military solutions. Rather, it sustains militarism with all its downsides for women.

4.6.2.2 INEQUALITIES

Conflict exacerbates 'existing differences of power and access to resources, weakening the position of those who are already without power, whether they are men, women or children'.[151] Violence against women in conflict zones has been recognised as often an extension of the gender discrimination that already exists in peacetime.[152] Existing discrimination also accentuates the likelihood of conflict, and research suggests a correlation between gender equality and a lower likelihood of resort to force. The *Global Study* submits that the security of women is one of the most reliable indicators of the peacefulness of the state.[153] Thus, a commitment to substantive equality across all fields and a concerted and integrated approach that places the implementation of the WPS agenda into the broader framework of CEDAW is a conflict-prevention strategy.[154] The WPS resolutions are not silent on these issues. There are repeated references to gender inequality and women's empowerment and their inclusion in the Sustainable Development

[150] E.g. 'UK National Action Plan on Women, Peace & Security 2018–2022', January 2018, 16; 'United States Strategy on Women, Peace, and Security', June 2019, 7.

[151] Hilary Charlesworth, 'Are Women Peaceful? Reflections on the Role of Women in Peace-Building', 16 *Feminist Legal Studies* (2008) 347–61, 358 citing Judy El Bushra.

[152] E.g. European Parliament resolution, Strasbourg, 25 November 2010 on the 10th anniversary of UN Security Council Resolution 1325 (2000) on Women, Peace and Security, www.europarl.europa.eu/sides/getDoc.do?pubRef=-//EP//TEXT+TA+P7-TA-2010-0439+0+DOC+XML+V0//EN.

[153] See also Jenny Russell and Valerie M. Hudson, 'Gender and Security', in Jill Steans and Daniela Tepe-Belfrage (eds.) *Handbook on Gender in World Politics* (Edward Elgar, 2016) 225–33.

[154] CEDAW Committee, General Recommendation No. 30 on women in conflict prevention, conflict and post-conflict situations, CEDAW/C/GC/30, 18 October 2013, para 26: 'As all the areas of concern addressed in those resolutions find expression in the substantive provisions of the Convention, their implementation must be premised on a model of substantive equality and cover all rights enshrined in the Convention.'

Goals[155] is welcomed. There is acknowledgement that addressing gender inequality and discrimination as root causes of sexual violence in conflict constitutes a conflict-prevention strategy, and states are called upon to protect those who seek to change social norms with respect to gender inequalities.[156] Nevertheless, these provisions remain imprecise and are largely instrumental. They fall short of an unconditional reaffirmation of women's human rights in accordance with CEDAW, as urged by the CEDAW Committee.

A striking omission from the SC resolutions is any reference to economic, social and cultural rights as a means to progressing gender equality and women's and girls' empowerment. This is a severe limitation given their salience as a tool of distributive justice and thus of security. As UN High Commissioner for Human Rights, Louise Arbor drew attention to how inequalities in access to and distribution of economic and social rights fuel insecurity and conflict:[157] '[I]t is hard to feel secure if you are starving, your shack has been destroyed or your water source polluted.'[158] The linkages between women and poverty, the sexual division of labour, the public/private divide that highlights the interrelationship between markets and households, women's unremunerated household work and women's 'caring' ability that keeps them in low-paying, undervalued jobs form no part of WPS: '[F]eminists claim that the operation of the global economy and states' attempts to secure benefits from it are built on these unequal economic relations between women and men which work to the detriment of women's (and certain men's) economic security.'[159]

No transition to peace or security is possible without putting into place an equitable, non-discriminatory, inclusive framework of access

155 UN General Assembly resolution 70/1, 25 September 2015, *Transforming our world: the 2030 Agenda for Sustainable Development.* SDG 5: 'Achieve gender equality and empower all women and girls.'

156 E.g. UN Security Council resolution 2467 (2019), preamble: 'further affirming the importance of promoting gender equality by addressing these and other root causes of sexual violence against all women and girls as part of conflict prevention, conflict resolution and peacebuilding'.

157 Office of the High Commissioner for Human Rights, *Transitional Justice and Economic, Social and Cultural Rights* (United Nations, 2014).

158 Elizabeth Porter, *Peacebuilding: Women in International Perspective* (Routledge, 2007) 26.

159 J. Ann Tickner. 'You Just Don't Understand: Troubled Engagements between Feminists and IR Theorists', 41 *International Studies Quarterly* (1997) 611–32, 628.

to land, resources, livelihoods, and services such as shelter, health, education, clean water and sanitation, in short, access to and delivery of economic and social rights.[160] The WPS resolutions urge provision for non-discriminatory health services, psychosocial, legal and livelihood support and other multi-sectoral services, but these are largely limited to specific women (survivors of sexual violence, including that inflicted by terrorist groups) and for particular ends (humanitarian programming and delivery). They do not extend to long-term food, economic, housing or other forms of social security.

The WPS resolutions are limited in their portrayal of equality. Absent are the many other intersecting inequalities that exist within states and across states, especially the global inequalities of post-colonialism and continuing neocolonialist practices. The resolutions do nothing to challenge the neoliberal economic agenda that has driven post-conflict reconstruction but that undermines security. The international community's post-conflict peacebuilding priorities are to establish law and order, to effect constitutional reform, to hold elections and to reform the security sector. The goal is to secure stable states within well-policed borders that do not constitute a threat to international peace and security. The primary interests are those of the external actors rather than those of local populations. Economic development is left to the international financial institutions, donors' conferences and foreign investors. The last 'tend to focus on infrastructure, markets, extractive industries and commercial agriculture, areas where women are traditionally under-represented'[161] and the former are pursued according to current neoliberal assumptions (free markets privatisation, austerity, cutbacks in public spending and welfare programmes). Their adverse effects fall disproportionately on women and other disadvantaged groups and create a situation of vulnerability to further violence,[162] leaving them at risk of being trafficked and

[160] The Committee on Economic, Social and Cultural Rights has provided guidance on non-discriminatory application of the Covenant; General Comment No. 16, The equal right of men and women to the enjoyment of all economic, social and cultural rights (art. 3 of the International Covenant on Economic, Social and Cultural Rights), E/C.12/2005/4, 11 August 2005.

[161] Report of the Secretary-General, *Women, peace and security*, S/2015/716, 17 September 2015, para 25.

[162] Jacqui True, *The Political Economy of Violence against Women* (Oxford University Press, 2012).

undermined rather than buttressing security in the post-conflict environment.[163]

4.6.2.3 AVAILABILITY OF ARMS

The third systemic basis of insecurity is the production and proliferation of weapons. In their call for universal disarmament, the women in The Hague in 1915 were responding to the weapons of interstate warfare rather than to what is now recognised as the disproportionate impact of small arms on women and girls. Today, the 'urgent need to curb the flow of guns and other weapons, which exacerbate levels of sexual and gender-based violence', cannot be overstated.[164] But it is largely overlooked by the Security Council, where the five permanent members are leading producers and exporters of arms. Three WPS resolutions note article 7 (4) of the Arms Trade Treaty, which provides that, in decision-making about arms export, states 'shall take into account the risk of covered conventional arms or items being used to commit or facilitate serious acts of gender-based violence or serious acts of violence against women and children'.[165] The WPS resolutions do not affirm other attempts to control the flow of small arms that are so destructive to women's security, although, elsewhere, the Council has supported the African Union's commitment to silencing the guns by 2020[166] and reaffirmed the importance of WPS in Africa.[167] Nor has the Council addressed the illicit arms trade other than seeking

[163] For a case study on how this has played out in Bosnia-Herzegovina, see Gorana Mlinarević, Nela Porobić Isaković, Christine Chinkin, Jacqui True, Madeleine Rees and Barbro Svedberg, *A Feminist Perspective on Post-Conflict Reconstruction and Recovery: The Case of Bosnia and Herzegovina* (WILPF, 2017).

[164] Lisa Davis of Madre to the Security Council (2 June 2016) at www.peacewomen.org/e-news/article/inside-open-debate-sexual-violence-conflict.

[165] UN Security Council resolution 2106 (2013) preamble; UN Security Council resolution 2122 (2013) preamble; UN Security Council resolution 2467 (2019) preamble.

[166] E.g. the African Union (AU), *Silencing the Guns by 2020*, adopted May 2013 as part of the Solemn Declaration marking fifty years since the establishment of the OAU; Master Roadmap of Practical Steps to Silence the Guns in Africa by the Year 2020, adopted 28th Ordinary Session of the Assembly of the Union, January 2017.

[167] UN Security Council resolution 2457, 27 February 2019, *Cooperation between the United Nations and regional and subregional organizations in maintaining international peace and security – Silencing the guns in Africa.*

women's participation, in efforts to combat it[168] and, somewhat strangely, to mitigate the risk of their becoming active in the illicit transfer of arms.[169] The CEDAW Committee adopts a more robust stance, seeking 'appropriate control' over 'the circulation of existing and often illicit conventional arms, including small arms', in its approach to conflict prevention,[170] as well as urging states to become parties to the Arms Trade Treaty and regional treaties for the regulation of arms.[171]

If article 7 (4) was taken seriously and applied literally, the Arms Trade Treaty could restrict what is currently regarded as legal arms trading. In general, more men than women are killed and wounded by small arms and weapons, but the different ways in which they are used in violent crimes against women constitute forms of gender-based violence against women. International and regional experts in violence against women have stated that 'a gendered approach to conflict prevention and resolution must include measures to silence the guns by controlling and regulating the arms trade and circulation, including of small arms, which can be used for committing gender-based violence'.[172] The continuing circulation of small arms post-conflict increases the likelihood of violence against women continuing. In light of these facts, the burden on an exporting state to show that there is little or no risk that weapons will be used to commit or facilitate serious acts of gender-based violence must be high, although, in practice, it is ignored.

4.7 Conclusion

The WPS agenda has evolved in the imperfect world of the Security Council and international law where prohibitions against the use of violence are regularly eroded. It is thus unsurprising that its guarantees of women's security are flawed. The Security Council has not

168 UN Security Council resolution 2122 (2013) para 14; UN Security Council resolution 2242 (2015) para 15.

169 UN Security Council resolution 2242 (2015) para 15.

170 CEDAW Committee, General Recommendation No. 30, para 29.

171 E.g. CEDAW Committee, concluding observations to the Democratic Republic of Congo, CEDAW/C/COD/CO/8, 6 August 2019, paras 12–13.

172 'The Platform of United Nations and Regional Independent Expert Mechanisms on the Elimination of Discrimination and Violence against Women' (Platform on EDVAW), Joint Statement (4 February 2020) at www.ohchr.org/Documents/Issues/Women/SR/Statement_conflict_prevention_EDVAW_platform.pdf.

provided any understanding of the world in which issues of 'women and security' play out other than that of militaristic violence, violent extremism and responses to violence that often incur further violence. Further, within this world view, it has concentrated on just one aspect of insecurity for women and girls – the threat to their physical and psychological security through the commission of gender-based and sexual violence – but without placing this in the context of either global inequalities or feminist understandings of hierarchy and power. It has not therefore addressed gender relations, constructions of masculinity and femininity and their interplay, or how social constructions (including gendered social constructions) contribute to and perpetuate violence. Nor has it engaged in any sustained way with the concept of human security as a way of reducing the reliance on national security measures.

5

Conclusions

5.1 Introduction

The Security Council's series of resolutions on Women, Peace and Security (WPS) have not been adopted in a vacuum but operate within the framework of changing international law and institutional activity. In some cases, this is made explicit, as where the Council calls for respect for existing international legal obligations,[1] including those emanating from international humanitarian law (IHL), human rights law, especially the Convention on the Elimination of All Forms of Discrimination against Women (CEDAW) and the Convention on the Rights of the Child (CRC), refugee law, and the law relating to remedies and trading in small arms.[2] In others, it is implicit, as, for instance, with respect to the secondary rules of state responsibility,[3] treaty interpretation[4] and sources of international law.[5] However, apart from generalised references, there is no attempt in the WPS resolutions to explain their relationship to or interaction with other rules and principles of international law, or to make connections

[1] See Chapter 2. [2] The Arms Trade Treaty, New York, 2 April 2013.

[3] UN General Assembly resolution 56/83, 12 December 2001, Annex *Responsibility of States for internationally wrongful acts.*

[4] Vienna Convention on the Law of Treaties, 23 May 1969, articles 31–3. There is no authoritative text on the interpretation of Security Council resolutions; Sir Michael Wood, 'The Interpretation of Security Council Resolutions', 2 *Max Planck Yearbook of United Nations Law* (1998) 73–95; Sir Michael Wood, 'The Interpretation of Security Council Resolutions, Revisited', at www.ilsa.org/Jessup/Jessup18/Second%20Batch/18757413_020_01_s002_text.pdf.

[5] Statute of the International Court of Justice, 1945, article 38 (1).

where to do so would enhance coherence. The resolutions do not engage with complex or controversial questions of international law such as the responsibility of states for the wrongful acts of non-state actors, legal responses by states to such acts,[6] or the responsibility of non-state actors for their own violations of human rights law. The legal categorisations of IHL are absent from the resolutions. In light of the cross-border nature of armed conflict, another omission is any consideration of states' responsibility for the extraterritorial acts of their own agents acting either individually or as members of an international or regional organisation, as donors acting through international financial institutions, or for the acts of non-state actors within their jurisdiction such as private militia, corporate bodies or private military contractors.[7] Instead, the Council makes its recommendations to states and other actors without reference to any international legal complexities.

This final chapter first considers briefly the relationship between the WPS agenda and some complementary areas of international law and policy. It then asks whether the WPS agenda could come to be described as a specialised regime of international law or whether it is more realistically to be viewed as an ongoing institutionalised political agenda. The chapter closes with some concluding comments about the themes that have been raised throughout the book.

5.2 The Language of International Law

When the WPS resolutions employ terms that have been defined in other international legal instruments, the assumption must be that the Council is adopting the accepted definitions of international law, for instance of 'genocide',[8] 'crimes

[6] E.g. does an armed attack by a non-state actor give rise to the right to self-defence, including in the territory of a third state?

[7] See CEDAW Committee, General Recommendation No. 30 on women in conflict prevention, conflict and post-conflict situations, CEDAW/C/GC/30, 18 October 2013, paras 8–17; Committee on Economic, Social and Cultural Rights, General Comment No. 24 (2017) on State obligations under the International Covenant on Economic, Social and Cultural Rights in the context of business activities E/C.12/GC/24, 10 August 2017.

[8] Convention on the Prevention and Punishment of the Crime of Genocide, UN General Assembly resolution 260 A (III), New York, 9 December 1948, article II.

against humanity',[9] 'torture',[10] 'reparation'[11] and 'refugees'.[12] Other terms have become widely accepted through usage in a range of instruments and institutions. For instance, 'gender-based violence' is used repeatedly throughout the WPS resolutions and is central to the pillars on prevention, protection and relief and recovery. It was first defined by the CEDAW Committee in 1992 as 'violence that is directed against a woman because she is a woman or that affects women disproportionately'.[13] The Committee explained that, as such, it is a form of discrimination within article 1 of CEDAW. The following year, the General Assembly resolved that '"violence against women" means any act of gender-based violence',[14] an assertion that was repeated in the Beijing Platform for Action.[15] In 2017, the CEDAW Committee affirmed that states have accepted its interpretation of gender-based violence for twenty-five years and that, through state practice and *opinio juris*, the prohibition of gender-based violence has evolved into a principle of customary international law.[16] The Security Council has not suggested any disagreement with either this proposition or the Committee's definition of gender-based

[9] 'Crime against humanity' is defined in the Rome Statute of the International Criminal Court, 1998, article 7 (1). The International Law Commission has defined it in its Draft Articles on Prevention and Punishment of Crimes against Humanity, adopted by the Commission, on second reading, at its seventy-first session, 2019, chapter IV, article 2.

[10] Convention against Torture and Other Cruel, Inhuman or Degrading Treatment or Punishment, UN General Assembly resolution 39/46, 10 December 1984, article 1. The definition of torture as a crime against humanity in the Rome Statute of the International Criminal Court, 1998, article 7 (2) (e) omits the requirement of involvement of a public official.

[11] UN General Assembly resolution 60/146, 16 December 2005, *Basic Principles and Guidelines on the Right to a Remedy and Reparation for Victims of Gross Violations of International Human Rights Law and Serious Violations of International Humanitarian Law.*

[12] Convention relating to the Status of Refugees, Geneva, 28 July 1951, article 1; Protocol relating to the Status of Refugees, New York, 31 January 1967, article 1.

[13] CEDAW Committee, General Recommendation No. 19, Violence against women, 11th session, 1992, para 6.

[14] UN General Assembly resolution 48/104, 20 December 1993, *Declaration on the Elimination of Violence against Women.*

[15] Fourth World Conference on Women, Beijing Declaration and Platform for Action, 1995, para 113.

[16] CEDAW Committee, General Recommendation No. 35 on gender-based violence against women, updating general recommendation No. 19, CEDAW/C/GR/35, 26 July 2017, para 2.

violence,[17] which, through the WPS resolutions, it has imported into the context of international peace and security. In turn, the Committee has reiterated that conflict places women at heightened risk of gender-based violence by both state agents and non-state actors.[18] There are, however, still some gaps and inconsistencies in the fuller descriptions of what constitutes gender-based violence, for instance with respect to the inclusion of economic violence,[19] that the Council has not addressed.

The Security Council also uses 'sexual violence' without definition or explanation. There is no treaty-based or otherwise authoritative definition of sexual violence. In a report to the Council, the Secretary-General has explained that in the context of conflict it 'refers to rape, sexual slavery, forced prostitution, forced pregnancy, forced abortion, enforced sterilization, forced marriage, and any other form of sexual violence of comparable gravity perpetrated against women, men, girls or boys'.[20] This understanding is essentially in line with the crimes listed in the Rome Statute as war crimes and crimes against humanity when the other required elements of crime are present.[21] The list does not resolve what makes violence 'sexual' and leaves open the possible emergence of a widely accepted definition such as that espoused in the 2019 Civil Society Declaration on Sexual Violence.[22]

[17] This definition is repeated in the Council of Europe Convention on preventing and combating violence against women and domestic violence (Istanbul Convention) 2011, article 3 (d).

[18] The CEDAW Committee asserted the association between wars and armed conflict and increased sexual assault in CEDAW Committee, General Recommendation No. 19, Violence against women, 11th session, 1992, para 16 and fully incorporated the concept of gender-based violence into situations of conflict and post-conflict in its General Recommendation No. 30.

[19] Economic violence was not included in the CEDAW Committee's General Recommendation No. 19 but is in the updating General Recommendation No. 35; see also Protocol to the African Charter on Human and Peoples' Rights on the Rights of Women in Africa (Maputo Protocol), 2003, article 1 (j) and the Council of Europe Convention on preventing and combating violence against women and domestic violence (Istanbul Convention) 2011, article 3 (a), which both include economic harm.

[20] Report of the Secretary-General, *Conflict-related sexual violence*, S/2016/361, 20 April 2016, para 2.

[21] Rome Statute of the International Criminal Court, 1998, article 7 (i) (g); 8 (2) (b) (xxii); 8 (e) (vi). The Secretary-General had added forced abortion.

[22] At https://4genderjustice.org/wp-content/uploads/2019/09/Civil-Society-Declaration-on-Sexual-Violence.pdf.

5.3 Trafficking as Gender-Based Violence

A particular form of gender-based violence is trafficking in women and girls.[23] In 2016, the Security Council for the first time addressed human trafficking as a threat to international peace and security, highlighting the incidence of trafficking in armed conflict and its aftermath, as well as its association with conflict-affected sexual violence.[24] In this sense, trafficking of women and girls in armed conflict fits directly into the substantive content of WPS. However, and despite the evident commonality between the Council's anti-trafficking resolutions and those relating to WPS, the latter made no reference to human trafficking in armed conflict until resolution 2467 (2019) where the Council requested the Counter-Terrorism Committee Executive Directorate (CTED) to include in its country reports information about states' efforts to address it.[25] And, correspondingly, the former do not speak to the suite of WPS resolutions but only to resolution 2242 (2015) as expressing concern about sexual and gender-based violence as 'part of the strategic objectives and ideology of certain terrorist groups'.

The Council reinforces the criminal law approach to combating human trafficking through calling upon states to ratify the Palermo Protocol[26] and to take immediate and decisive steps to criminalise trafficking and prosecute traffickers. Trafficking is (rightly) associated, and thus to be addressed in conjunction, with money-laundering, anti-corruption and anti-bribery measures, as well as counterterrorism. While the Council recognises the violations of human rights entailed in human trafficking, it does not reiterate the

23 UN General Assembly resolution 48/104, 20 December 1993, *Declaration on the Elimination of Violence against Women*, article 2: 'Violence against women shall be understood to encompass (b) Physical, sexual and psychological violence occurring within the general community, including … trafficking in women and forced prostitution.'

24 UN Security Council resolution 2331, 20 December 2016, *Maintenance of International Peace and Security*. The Council adopted a second resolution on human trafficking in 2017; UN Security Council resolution 2388, 21 November 2017, *Maintenance of International Peace and Security*.

25 UN Security Council resolution 2467 (2019) para 29.

26 Protocol to Prevent, Suppress and Punish Trafficking in Persons Especially Women and Children, supplementing the United Nations Convention against Transnational Organized Crime, UN General Assembly resolution 55/25, 15 November 2000 (Palermo Protocol). The definition of trafficking in article 3 (a) is presumably accepted by the Security Council.

centrality of human rights in all efforts to tackle trafficking.[27] Nor does it call for ratification of human rights treaties that address trafficking.[28] Survivors are regarded as victims of crimes who are to be accorded services, including health care, psychosocial care, safe shelter, livelihood support and legal aid. This formulation does not affirm victims' existing entitlement to such services under human rights law; it affirms only the more limited requirement that any such provision must be in full respect of their human rights. Similarly, the WPS resolutions recognise the heightened vulnerability to sexual violence and barriers to receiving support services caused by displacement,[29] but they do not link displacement with the particular risk of being trafficked.[30] The special rapporteur on trafficking has recommended, within the pillars of WPS, preventive measures against trafficking to be taken in IDP and refugee camps.[31]

The primary objective of resolutions 2331 (2016) and 2388 (2017) is to tackle trafficking as a terrorist and a war economy tactic by terrorist and violent extremist groups. While human trafficking is a criminal offence and may constitute a crime against humanity and while its continued incidence threatens international peace and security, this concentration on trafficking as a terrorist activity disregards its other manifestations,[32] some of which are targeted specifically at women and girls.[33] It also further weakens the international discourse on women's human rights. WPS seeks to bring women's experiences of conflict to the fore, including through women's meaningful participation in policy and decision-making. Aligning WPS with the anti-trafficking resolutions would emphasise that such

27 See Office of the High Commissioner for Human Rights, *Recommended Principles and Guidelines on Human Rights and Human Trafficking*, Economic and Social Council, E/2002/68/Add.1.

28 E.g. CEDAW, 1979, article 6; Convention on the Rights of the Child, 1989, article 35.

29 E.g. UN Security Council resolution 2467 (2019) para 31.

30 Special rapporteur on trafficking in persons, especially women and children, A/73/171, 17 July 2018, para 36: 'Women and girls in refugee and internally displaced persons camps are particularly vulnerable to being trafficked.'

31 Ibid., at paras 35–8 (prevention); 46–8 (protection).

32 The Palermo Protocol, article 3 (a) lists 'the exploitation of the prostitution of others or other forms of sexual exploitation, forced labour or services, slavery or practices similar to slavery, servitude or the removal of organs'.

33 Special rapporteur on trafficking in persons, especially women and children, A/73/171, 17 July 2018, para 21.

participation is as applicable to policy- and decision-making about combating trafficking as it is to other forms of conflict-affected gender-based and sexual violence.

The special rapporteur on trafficking has advocated the integration of a 'human rights-based and gender-sensitive approach' to human trafficking into the WPS agenda in order to complement and strengthen anti-trafficking efforts.[34] This would also allow a coordinated and strong reassertion of shared and complementary international norms, which might, in turn, support stronger implementation of WPS.[35] But, at the same time, there must be caution against further securitisation through the linkage that has been made between terrorism and violent extremism and both trafficking and WPS. However, the recent adoption of a survivor-centred approach in preventing and responding to conflict-affected sexual violence[36] could, if adhered to throughout all four pillars of WPS and anti-trafficking efforts, be a counter-balance to securitisation.

5.4 The Environment and Climate Change

International laws and principles relating to the environment have proliferated, especially since the 1972 United Nations Conference on the Human Environment in Stockholm.[37] More recently, climate change and related natural disasters as a threat to international peace and security have been the subject of Security Council debate,[38] presidential statement[39] and resolutions on local and

[34] Ibid., at para 12.

[35] See, further, Christine Chinkin and Gema Fernández, 'Human Trafficking, Human Rights, and Women, Peace and Security: The Sound of Silence', in Paul Kirby and Laura Shepherd (eds.) *New Directions in Women, Peace and Security* (Bristol University Press, 2020) 201–18.

[36] UN Security Council resolution 2467 (2019).

[37] Patricia Birnie, Alan Boyle and Catherine Redgwell, *International Law and the Environment* (Oxford University Press, 3rd ed. 2009); Ruth MacKenzie, Philippe Sands and Jacqueline Peel, *Principles of International Environmental Law* (Cambridge University Press, 4th ed. 2018).

[38] The Council has debated the impact of climate change on international peace and security four times since 2007, most recently in January 2019; Chair's summary of the Security Council open debate on 25 January 2019, 'Addressing the impacts of climate-related disasters on international peace and security', S/2019/113, 7 February 2019.

[39] Statement by the President of the Security Council, S/PRST/2011/15, 20 July 2011.

regional instability.[40] The 2015 *Global Study on the Implementation of Resolution 1325* included the effects of climate change in its analysis of the root causes of conflict.[41] It noted that women and girls are among those most susceptible to harm caused by climate and other disasters for interconnected reasons such as their lack of access to information and resources, entrenched gender stereotypes and inequalities, and cultural restrictions.[42] For instance, women continue to be responsible for food and water provision in most cultures, tasks that are exacerbated by shortages and restricted access contributed to by environmental degradation (itself furthered by conflict and displacement of peoples) and climate change. In conflict, women and girls face heightened risks of violence simply in seeking to perform these daily tasks.[43] The *Global Study* also considered the relationship between climate change and displacement, which, especially when combined with other factors such as depleted natural resources, unequal land distribution, insecure land tenure and inadequate infrastructure, causes further instabilities. Displaced women and girls are vulnerable to sexual and gender-based violence.[44] And, in 2020, violent attacks against both women's human rights defenders and environmental defenders have increased.

Climate security is thus directly relevant to the WPS agenda, but it has made little inroad within it. The need to address the situation of displaced women in IDP or refugee camps has been recognised in many of the WPS resolutions since their outset,[45] but without any

[40] E.g. UN Security Council resolution 2349, 31 March 2017, para 26 recognises 'the adverse effects of climate change and ecological changes among other factors on the stability of the [Lake Chad Basin] Region, including through water scarcity, drought, desertification, land degradation, and food insecurity, and emphasises the need for adequate risk assessments and risk management strategies by governments and the United Nations relating to these factors'. There are also relevant resolutions relating to Somalia, the Sahel, Mali and Darfur.

[41] Radhika Coomaraswamy and others, *Preventing Conflict, Transforming Justice, Securing the Peace: A Global Study on the Implementation of Security Council Resolution 1325* (United Nations, 2015) [hereinafter *Global Study*] 15.

[42] *Global Study*, 211. [43] Ibid., at 212.

[44] UN Security Council resolution 2467 (2019) para 31: 'displaced persons face specific, heightened risks of sexual and gender-based violence'.

[45] UN Security Council resolution 1325 (2000) para 12; UN Security Council resolution 1820 (2008) para 10. The WPS resolutions adopted after it make no linkage with the Report of the Special Rapporteur on the human rights of internally displaced persons, *Internally Displaced Women Progress, Challenges and the Way Ahead,* A/HRC/23/44, 18 March 2013.

reference to the impact of environmental or climate factors. Resolution 2242 (adopted following the high-level review of WPS in 2015 that was informed by the *Global Study*) notes the impact of climate change but makes no relevant recommendations for changed behaviours by states or other actors. Neither of the two WPS resolutions adopted in 2019 makes any further reference to insecurity generated by climate change or environmental degradation, although the preamble to resolution 2467 makes the link between conflict-affected sexual violence in conflict and illicit trading in natural resources. Despite the many calls for women's increased participation in decision- and policy-making with respect to conflict prevention, management and resolution, the WPS resolutions do not bring decision-making on natural resource management in fragile and conflict-affected settings or climate change negotiations into this pillar. The CEDAW Committee, like the authors of the *Global Study*, is aware of the need to integrate women's human rights and thus WPS into all such decision-making. The Committee's General Recommendation No. 37, adopted in 2017,[46] links the climate crisis to other root causes of women's oppression, including but not limited to violence against women, and confirms women and girls as leaders and vital participants in solutions to disaster relief and the climate crisis. The three principles identified by the Committee as fundamental to addressing disaster reduction in the context of climate change are also core WPS principles: gender equality and non-discrimination, participation and empowerment, and accountability and access to justice. But the connection has not been made in the WPS agenda, to its detriment and, more importantly, to that of the women and girls most affected and to the planet itself.

5.5 Humanitarian Intervention and the Responsibility to Protect

When UN Security Council resolution 1325 was adopted in 2000, the debates around the legality of the military action in 1999 by NATO in Kosovo and Serbia were still ongoing.[47] The human rights

[46] CEDAW Committee, General Recommendation No. 37 on Gender-related dimensions of disaster risk reduction in the context of climate change, CEDAW/C/GC/37, 7 February 2018.

[47] E.g. the different views expressed in 49 *International and Comparative Law Quarterly* (2000).

violations committed by the Serbian authorities in Kosovo had highlighted the ambiguities inherent within the UN Charter – a system designed to uphold state sovereignty through non-intervention but that also looks towards justice through the promotion of fundamental human rights. This unresolved tension in the purposes and principles of the Charter is accentuated by the indeterminacy of language that is transported into WPS: what is a threat to the peace and what constitutes security? And, more specifically, was the military campaign in Kosovo legally justified as protection of the human rights of the Kosovo Albanian population or was it an illegal use of force as coming outside the stipulated exceptions to the prohibition on the use of force?[48] Another espoused position was that it was formally illegal but legitimate as upholding international community values.[49] These different opinions were thought by some to expose a gap between formal international law and the ethical principles upon which it is supposedly based. It was also apparent that especially the United States and the UK were using their military power to shift the boundaries of unilateral legitimate behaviour by claiming further exceptions to the UN Charter based on a broad mix of human rights, democracy and national security. Where possible, they sought legality within the terms of the Charter by seeking Security Council authorisation, but where this was not forthcoming, they acted without it, as in Kosovo and four years later in Iraq. In the case of Kosovo, a further veneer of legitimacy was attempted by the decision of a multilateral organisation – NATO – to undertake military action, although a humanitarian justification is not included in the North Atlantic Treaty.[50] Nor did this multilateralism alleviate concerns about neo-imperialist interventions under the guise of humanitarianism.

The debate was widened through formulation of the concept of a Responsibility to Protect[51] in 2001, just over a year after the

[48] UN Charter, 1945, article 42 (UN Security Council authorised action) and article 51 (individual and collective self-defence).

[49] Independent International Commission on Kosovo, *The Kosovo Report: Conflict, International Response, Lessons Learned* (Oxford University Press, 2000).

[50] The North Atlantic Treaty, Washington D.C., 4 April 1949, article 5 provides for armed force only in individual or collective self-defence against an armed attack on one or more member states of the alliance.

[51] International Commission on Intervention and State Sovereignty, *The Responsibility to Protect* (International Development Research Centre, 2001).

adoption of resolution 1325. The new doctrine sought to shift the terms of the debate from the claimed rights of intervening states to the needs of the supposed beneficiaries, those on the ground subjected to serious harms. It is fashioned around the understanding that the state has primary responsibility for protection of its own citizens and that the international community should first support that state in seeking to prevent humanitarian catastrophe and should intervene only in extreme situations where this has failed. Diplomatic, humanitarian and other peaceful means are to be first attempted and military action is to be engaged in only as a last resort. To minimise subjective determinations of the scale of the humanitarian crisis, Security Council authorisation is required. The final pillar of the Responsibility to Protect is the obligation to rebuild following any such intervention.

Even before the International Commission on Intervention and State Sovereignty (ICISS) published its report on *The Responsibility to Protect* in December 2001, the terrorist attacks of 11 September 2001 had led to further claims for the legal use of force in response in Afghanistan. Still further claims were made to support the legality of the invasion of Iraq in 2003. Justifications for military action by a self-appointed 'coalition of the willing' based on reinterpretation of Security Council resolutions, pre-emptive self-defence from the threats of terrorism and weapons of mass destruction, were again merged with those relating to upholding human rights and democracy.

In the changed and changing security environment and intensified militarised response, the Responsibility to Protect has been reiterated, albeit with different articulations. The Outcome Document of the 2005 Global Summit endorsed its key components,[52] which was itself reaffirmed by the Security Council in various contexts[53] and embraced by a substantial academic commentary. It is the subject of regular reports by the Secretary-General[54] and, since 2009, of General

[52] UN General Assembly resolution 60/1, 24 October 2005, *World Summit Outcome*, paras 138–9. The Assembly, however, narrowed the application of the doctrine to genocide, war crimes, ethnic cleansing and crimes against humanity.

[53] E.g. UN Security Council resolution 1674, 28 April 2006, *Protection of Civilians*, para 4; UN Security Council resolution 1894, 11 November 2009, *Protection of Civilians*, preamble; UN Security Council resolution 2171, 21 August 2014, *Conflict prevention*, para 16; UN Security Council resolution 2220, 22 May 2015, *Small arms*, preamble.

[54] E.g. Report of the Secretary-General, *Responsibility to protect: lessons learned for prevention*, A/73/898–S/2019/463, 10 June 2019.

Assembly debates. In 2011, it was cited in the preamble to the resolution in which the Council acted under UN Charter chapter VII to mandate 'all necessary measures, ... to protect civilians and civilian populated areas under threat of attack' in Libya.[55] This appears as a direct integration of the doctrine into a legally binding decision of the Council. But concerns that the resolution was used to enforce regime change in Libya and the ensuing insecurity and violence, as well as the Security Council's inability to prevent ongoing gross human rights abuses in, inter alia, Syria, Myanmar and Yemen, have led to the doctrine becoming less politically prominent.[56] International lawyers are wary of the doctrine, which has been mainly expounded in soft law instruments and has not been subject to consistent state practice. Some lawyers welcome its moral force, while others resist it as legitimating neo-colonial interference by powerful states in the internal affairs of weaker states, including with respect to the pillar for rebuilding a fragile or conflict-torn society. This allows for the presence of humanitarian workers and Western contractors who do not necessarily consult or work with local communities and can fuel further resentment. Nor does the Responsibility to Protect resolve the tension between state sovereignty and human rights,[57] or between military action and recourse to the human rights mechanisms.[58]

As an agenda for the maintenance of international peace and security, WPS is not immune from contestations about when there can be legal recourse to armed force under international law. As such, it would appear to have affinity with the Responsibility to Protect, and the relationship between the two agendas has provoked

[55] UN Security Council resolution 1973, 17 March 2011. See also UN Security Council resolution 1975, 30 March 2011 (Côte D'Ivoire).

[56] It has nevertheless been cited in a handful of other situations; see Alex J. Bellamy and Sara E. Davies, 'WPS and Responsibility to Protect', in Sara E. Davies and Jacqui True (eds.) *The Oxford Handbook of Women, Peace and Security* (Oxford University Press, 2019) 585–97, 588.

[57] Hilary Charlesworth, 'Feminist Reflections on the Responsibility to Protect', 2 (3) *Global Responsibility to Protect* (2010) 232–49, 236.

[58] The ICJ has stated that the use of force was not 'the appropriate method to ensure respect of human rights', for 'when human rights are protected by international conventions, that protection takes the form of such arrangements for monitoring or ensuring respect for human rights as are provided in the conventions themselves'. *Case concerning Military and Paramilitary Activities in and against Nicaragua* (*Nicaragua* v *United States of America*) (Merits) 1986 ICJ Reports, 124, para 267.

much comment, as well as feminist critique. The Responsibility to Protect is not a women's agenda, its language is gender-neutral and resolution 1325 (2000) was not referenced by the ICISS. But there are commonalities.[59] In similar language to the Responsibility to Protect, the WPS resolutions from 1820 (2008) onwards affirm states' basic human rights obligations, that they bear the 'primary responsibility to respect and ensure the human rights of their citizens and subject to their jurisdiction as provided for by international law'. Both agendas address the consequences of the state's failure to uphold this primary responsibility. The WPS pillars on prevention, protection and relief and recovery are echoed in those of the Responsibility to Protect relating to prevention of harms and societal rebuilding.[60] The harms to be prevented and protected against in the latter are ethnic cleansing, genocide, crimes against humanity and war crimes, while the focus of WPS is gender-based and sexual violence. These can, of course, come within the categories encompassed within the Responsibility to Protect.[61] And, in addressing the issues from the perspective of those needing assistance, the Responsibility to Protect explicitly turns the searchlight, inter alia, on the duty to protect women from systematic rape, although not necessarily in conflict-affected situations as is the case with protection from sexual violence in WPS. In both cases, the emphasis is on large-scale abuses rather than on the 'everyday' violence committed against women. Neither the Responsibility to Protect nor WPS upholds the importance of protection from failure to deliver economic and social rights, or discrimination in that regard. Some commentators have urged closer alignment between the two, while others have concluded that they are 'distinct but complementary agendas' that are – or at least could be – mutually reinforcing.[62]

Unlike the Responsibility to Protect where military action is envisaged as allowable in extreme circumstances, the WPS resolutions are

[59] Bellamy and Davies (*supra* n 56) 585–97.

[60] There is no counterpart to the first pillar of WPS – women's participation and empowerment – in the Responsibility to Protect, although the importance of local knowledge and supporting local efforts in seeking to understand the situation is recognised as contributing to the credibility of international actions.

[61] UN Security Council resolution 1820 (2008) notes that 'rape and other forms of sexual violence can constitute a war crime, a crime against humanity, or a constitutive act with respect to genocide'.

[62] Bellamy and Davies (*supra* n 56) 585–97.

silent about this as a means of protection. But this is an artificial silence, and militarism and the possibility of military action imbue the WPS resolutions. As discussed in Chapter 4, a military presence is assumed in peacekeeping operations mandated with civilian protection. The need to protect women from oppression can be readily slotted in as an additional ethical underpinning to military action, especially where the enemy is as notoriously hostile to women's rights as the Taliban or ISIS/Daesh. In Afghanistan in 2001, the 'liberation' of women from the Taliban was lauded by members of the military coalition. Claims based on external security from terrorist attacks were thus fused with those for internal security – the liberation and emancipation of Afghan women. There are counter-arguments that oppose the use of military force to uphold women's rights in general,[63] as well as in the specific case of Afghanistan. The action failed to take account of Afghan women's own history, presenting them only as targets of the Taliban and furthering their racial and gendered stereotyping as victims in need of protection from the outside. There was no follow-up such as ensuring women's full and meaningful participation in the Bonn peace talks, despite the adoption of resolution 1325 the previous year. Women's rights can be and are negotiated away at the behest of those who reject women's equality[64] and in favour of other political imperatives.[65] Nearly two decades later, Afghan women remain insecure and marginalised by peace processes involving the Taliban. Nor does the claim of intervening to uphold gender equality sit well with the emergence of an adverse gender ideology within those 'civilising' states themselves. In addition, any military action is

63 E.g. Karen Engle, '"Calling in the Troops": The Uneasy Relationship among Women's Rights, Human Rights and Humanitarian Intervention', 20 *Harvard Human Rights Journal* (2007) 189–226; Anne Orford, *Reading Humanitarian Intervention: Human Rights and the Use of Force in International Law* (Cambridge University Press, 2009).

64 In 2013, the CEDAW Committee noted the 'climate of persisting and extreme violence, in particular against women' in Afghanistan and expressed its concern that 'women's interests and needs may be compromised in the peace negotiations owing to the deep-rooted patriarchal attitudes in the State party'; CEDAW Committee, Concluding Observations, Afghanistan, CEDAW/C/AFG/CO/1–2, 30 July 2013, paras 7 and 8.

65 The CEDAW Committee has expressly warned against this, recommending that states reject 'all forms of rollbacks in women's rights protections in order to appease non-State actors such as terrorists, private individuals or armed groups'; CEDAW Committee, General Recommendation No. 30 on women in conflict prevention, conflict and post-conflict situations, para 17 (b).

a 'volatile and risky' enterprise for addressing women's inequalities[66] and poses further threats to women's security. It can be questioned whether the requirement of proportionality – a shifting concept in international law – can ever be satisfied.[67] And military intervention is the tip of the iceberg when measured against the prevailing and normalised ideology of militarism that makes talk of peace unpopular and unpatriotic. It was such considerations that led the *Global Study* to reject attempts to use women as instruments in military strategy and to assert a resounding '"No" to militarization'.[68]

5.6 Human Security

During the 1990s, the Security Council grew more ready to accept that threats to international peace and security were not constituted solely through interstate interventions but also arose through massive harms to civilian populations, especially in the 'new wars' of those years. It responded to the deliberate targeting of civilians and the extreme brutality of those attacks by creating new institutions,[69] authorising 'all necessary measures' for humanitarian purposes[70] and expanding the scope and number of peace operations. At the same time, a number of policy-oriented reports and UN General Assembly and Security Council resolutions focused on the need to safeguard the security of individuals rather than just that of the territorial state, for instance the thematic resolutions on the protection of children[71] and of civilians

66 Charlesworth (*supra* n 57) 232–49.

67 E.g. '[T]he protection of human rights, a strictly humanitarian objective, cannot be compatible with the mining of ports, the destruction of oil installations, or again with the training, arming and equipping of the contras.' *Case concerning Military and Paramilitary Activities in and against Nicaragua* (*Nicaragua* v *United States of America*) (Merits) 1986 ICJ Reports, 124, para 268.

68 *Global Study*, 25.

69 E.g. the International Criminal Tribunal for the former Yugoslavia and the International Criminal Tribunal for Rwanda.

70 UN Security Council resolution 688, 5 April 1991 led the way by insisting that 'Iraq allow immediate access by international humanitarian organizations to those in need'; UN Security Council resolution 794, 3 December 1992 authorised the use of all 'necessary means' for the establishment of a secure environment for humanitarian relief operations in Somalia.

71 The General Assembly first addressed this subject; UN General Assembly resolution 51/77, 12 December 1996 followed publication of the Report of the Expert of the Secretary-General, Ms Graça Machel, *Impact of Armed Conflict on*

in armed conflict.[72] The underlying ethos of these developments is perhaps best captured by the prominence accorded to the emerging concept of human security, although no consensus has evolved about either its scope or its formulation.[73] A broad form of human security, encompassing development and disarmament, was pioneered by UNDP. The 1994 *Human Development Report* emphasised material security – freedom from want – although the link with physical security – freedom from fear – was also acknowledged. A narrower form of human security was more directly concerned with freedom from physical harm and drew on the growing influence in international affairs of the link between security and protection of human rights, primarily civil and political rights. The Responsibility to Protect, as articulated by the ICISS, embodied this approach to human security.

As with the Responsibility to Protect, human security was endorsed by the General Assembly in its 2005 World Summit Outcome document. The Assembly recognised that all individuals 'are entitled to freedom from fear and freedom from want' and to 'fully develop their human potential',[74] thus aligning itself with both the wide and the narrow positions on human security. The Assembly has furthered its understanding of human security in subsequent resolutions as a 'people-centred, comprehensive, context-specific and prevention-oriented [tool]' for the 'protection and empowerment of all people and all communities'.[75] It has stressed that human security and the Responsibility to Protect are two separate agendas and that the former 'recognizes the interlinkages between peace, development and human rights', meaning all human rights – civil, political, economic, social and cultural rights. Following its transportation into the General Assembly, human security, like the Responsibility to Protect, has received somewhat piecemeal repetition and institutional application.

Children, A/51/306, 26 August 1996; UN Security Council resolution 1261, 30 August 1999.

72 UN Security Council resolution 1265, 17 September 1999.

73 See Christine Chinkin and Mary Kaldor, *International Law and New Wars* (Cambridge University Press, 2017) chapter 11.

74 UN General Assembly resolution 60/1, 24 October 2005, *World Summit Outcome*, para 146.

75 E.g. UN General Assembly resolution 66/290, 25 October 2012, *Follow-up to paragraph 143 on human security of the 2005 World Summit Outcome.*

There is no explicit cross-referencing between the WPS resolutions and human security, although, in their similar emphasis on prevention of and protection against harms to the individual, there are evident associations, as well as differences. The WPS focus is on physical harm (and that of a particular form of harm – gender-based and sexual violence). There is little mention of protection from want and minimal reference to livelihood support except as a component of humanitarian relief. As mentioned previously, the WPS resolutions are silent as to the provision of economic, social and cultural needs as entitlements under human rights law. Further, neither the Responsibility to Protect nor human security accounts pay much heed to the importance of civil society and the need to engage with and support local communities,[76] especially women's, efforts at protection, prevention or peacebuilding. The General Assembly's understanding of human security does incorporate the need for 'greater collaboration and partnership among Governments, international and regional organizations and civil society', but this is less than the commitments to civil society expressed in the WPS resolutions, both procedurally[77] and on the ground in conflict-affected territories.[78] But, above all, what differentiates WPS from human security is the inclusion of women. Although largely contemporaneous, each of WPS, the Responsibility to Protect and human security has a different genesis. The Responsibility to Protect was a response to mass atrocities, spearheaded by an elite group of public figures. Human security was framed within an institutional environment as a deliberate move away from a concentration on state security but still requiring

[76] See, however, *A Human Security Doctrine for Europe: The Barcelona Report of the Study Group on Europe's Security Capabilities* (2004), which argued for a 'bottom-up' approach; http://eprints.lse.ac.uk/40209/1/A_human_security_doctrine_for_Europe%28author%29.pdf.

[77] E.g. UN Security Council resolution 2242 (2015) where the Council expressed its intention to 'invite civil society ... to brief the Council in country-specific considerations and relevant thematic areas'.

[78] E.g. UN Security Council resolution 2467 (2019) where the Council expressed its intention to 'make better usage of periodical field visits to conflict areas, through the organization of interactive meetings with the local women and women's organizations in the field about the concerns and needs of women in areas of armed conflict; ... and engage with victims, affected communities and civil society, including women's organizations'.

national ownership.[79] In contrast, resolution 1325 grew out of and gave institutional legitimacy to the goals of the global women's movement going back to 1915. While the WPS agenda has been tamed and subordinated to the Security Council's political agenda in ways discussed throughout these chapters, it nevertheless retains its distinct perspective. WPS as the transformative agenda envisaged by women's civil society may indeed be loosely described as human security for women.

5.7 Sustainable Development Goals

Many of the ideas of WPS, human security and the non-military aspects of the Responsibility to Protect have been brought together through the UN General Assembly's 2030 Agenda for Sustainable Development with its vision of a world 'free of poverty, hunger, disease and want, where all life can thrive ... a world free of fear and violence' and where no person is left behind.[80] The Sustainable Development Goals (SDGs) provide a blueprint – a 'plan of action for people, planet and prosperity' – for transformative economic, social and environmental development. They are not an overtly security agenda, but they recognise that sustainable development depends upon peace and security, which in turn require sustainable development.[81] The SDGs are not in legally binding form, but, since they are said to be grounded in human rights law, to that extent they represent legal obligation. The nexus with CEDAW and WPS is especially evident in Goal 5 on gender equality and the empowerment of women. Goal 16[82] with its focus on ending violence, promoting the rule of law, strengthening institutions and increasing access to justice[83] also resonates with the WPS

[79] UN General Assembly resolution 66/290, 25 October 2012, *Follow-up to paragraph 143 on human security of the 2005 World Summit Outcome*, para 3 (f): 'Human security is based on national ownership.'

[80] UN General Assembly resolution 70/1, 25 September 2015, *Transforming our world: the 2030 Agenda for Sustainable Development*, para 7.

[81] Ibid., at para 35.

[82] SDG 16: 'Promote peaceful and inclusive societies for sustainable development, provide access to justice for all and build effective, accountable and inclusive institutions at all levels.'

[83] Report of the Secretary-General, *Special edition: progress towards the Sustainable Development Goals*, E/2019/68, 8 May 2019, para 37.

agenda. The CEDAW Committee[84] has regularly engaged with the High-level Political Forum on Sustainable Development[85] to emphasise the need to integrate women's rights across Agenda 2030 in its entirety and its oversight function in monitoring the Agenda's implementation. To this end, in its concluding observations on their periodic reports, the Committee routinely reminds states of their obligation to advance Agenda 2030 in accordance with the provisions of CEDAW,[86] as it similarly does with implementation of WPS.

This discussion has centred on the linkages and overlap between WPS and other security agendas (the Responsibility to Protect and human security) and the SDGs as the most important contemporary development agenda. They have many common objectives, but each is distinct and there is little coordination either conceptually or between their practitioners. The question that arises is as to the best way forward. There are different possibilities: should the agendas be integrated for their mutual and reciprocal strengthening through enhanced coherence or should they remain separate with the risk of different, even contradictory development? Are there risks of greater securitisation, for instance through bringing the General

[84] As has the Committee on Economic, Social and Cultural Rights (CESCR) that sees economic, social and cultural rights as a fundamental pillar of the SDGs: CESCR, *The pledge to leave no one behind: the International Covenant on Economic, Social and Cultural Rights and the 2030 Agenda for Sustainable Development*, E/C.12/2019/1, 5 April 2019.

[85] E.g. CEDAW Committee, Contributions to the 2030 Agenda for Sustainable Development, 16 May 2018, at https://tbinternet.ohchr.org/_layouts/15/treatybodyexternal/Download.aspx?symbolno=INT%2fCEDAW%2fINF%2f8697&Lang=en.

[86] The CEDAW Committee includes as a standard paragraph in its concluding observations to state reports that it:

> welcomes the international support for the Sustainable Development Goals and calls for the realization of de jure (legal) and de facto (substantive) gender equality, in accordance with the provisions of the Convention, throughout the process of implementing the 2030 Agenda for Sustainable Development. The Committee recalls the importance of Goal 5 and of the mainstreaming of the principles of equality and non-discrimination throughout all 17 Goals. It urges the State party to recognize women as the driving force of the sustainable development of the State party and to adopt relevant policies and strategies to that effect.

See, e.g., CEDAW Committee, Concluding observations on the fourth periodic report of Côte d'Ivoire, CEDAW/C/CIV/CO/4, 30 July 2019.

Assembly's agenda for sustainable development into the Security Council's WPS agenda, and would this further distance the various agendas from both human rights and the primacy of gender? And, from the perspective especially of WPS, should we seek its alignment with these other agendas and thereby risk it becoming so top-heavy as to be meaningless? These and other questions require reflection as WPS reaches its twentieth anniversary in 2020. It is clear that, despite spawning a welter of activity at the national, regional and international levels, the WPS agenda has failed to enhance security for women and girls on the ground during conflict and its aftermath. Is this possible while it is located within the Security Council where militarised and neoliberal economic thinking prevails? Either radical repositioning within the Council or an orientation away from the Council back to women's and peace organisations, in conjunction with like-minded states, is needed. In the political environment of 2020, the former is unlikely. The latter would allow for greater coherence and a coordinated basis for resistance to the current push-back against gender equality and women's rights.

5.8 WPS: A Special Regime of International Law?

WPS, like the other agendas discussed throughout this chapter, is framed as a policy agenda, not as legal obligation, except for its association with or grounding in the UN Charter and other special regimes of international law. But could these different agendas represent new ways of making international law through their repetition in resolutions adopted in different institutions, substantial academic commentary, expert reports, institutional practice, generation of new positions, political commitments at the international, regional and national levels and active involvement of civil society? Determination of legal status has to be made separately in each case, but what is apparent is that the classic analysis of how international obligations are formed is inadequate for the complexities of contemporary international life. Nor does a binary distinction between law and 'soft' law or 'hard' and 'soft' obligations resolve the question.

A further consideration is whether WPS could emerge as a 'special regime' of international law with further evolution of legal obligation. The concept of a self-contained regime was advanced by the International Court of Justice (ICJ)in the *Tehran Hostages* case[87] and further developed by the International Law Commission (ILC) in its study of fragmentation in international law.[88] The ICJ 's identification of diplomatic law as a self-contained special regime centred on the existence of rules agreed through the Conventions on Diplomatic and Consular Relations[89] that applied in case of breach in place of the general rules of international law relating to breach of a treaty obligation. WPS evidently does not come within this model; it has no bespoke regime for non-compliance or breach. But the ILC identified a further model of a legal regime that has its own experts, ethos, preferences and structural bias. Such regimes emerge from the informal activity of lawyers, diplomats, pressure groups, shifts in legal culture and in response to the practical needs of specialisation rather than through conscious acts of regime creation.[90] They are, in the view of the ILC, institutionally 'programmed' to prioritise particular concerns over others. The ILC gave examples of such regimes – international criminal law, humanitarian law, trade law, environmental law. It explained that special regimes of this sort 'mirror the functional diversification of the international society or, more prosaically, the activities of particular caucuses seeking to articulate or strengthen preferences and orientations that seem not to have received sufficient attention under the general law. The application of special "principles" by specialized implementation organs is a visible feature of such regimes.'[91]

WPS is already grounded in some of these regimes recognised by the ILC and cannot be understood without reference to them. It has its own notable features that are compatible with this broad model of a special regime. It has evolved through the activities of civil society, notably women's human rights and peace organisations, in response to the long-term neglect of women within international law in

[87] *Case Concerning United States Diplomatic and Consular Staff in Tehran* (*United States of America* v *Iran*) 1980 ICJ Reports 3, para 86.

[88] *Fragmentation of International Law: Difficulties arising from the Diversification and Expansion of International Law*; Report of the Study Group of the International Law Commission, finalized by Martti Koskenniemi, A/CN.4/L.682, 13 April 2006 [ILC, Study Group].

[89] Vienna Convention on Diplomatic Relations, 18 April 1961; Vienna Convention on Consular Relations, 22 April 1963.

[90] ILC Study Group, at para 158. [91] Ibid.

general and particularly in legal regimes relating to conflict, violence and security. It has been supported by diplomats and international institutions. WPS now has its state champions ('friends of 1325'); its institutions (the Special Representative of the Secretary-General on conflict-affected sexual violence,[92] the Informal Experts Group[93]); its institutional champions (CEDAW Committee, UN Women); its procedures (annual open debates at the Security Council); its language and ethos ('gender perspective', 'gender-based violence', 'peacebuilders', 'survivor-centred'); its principles (gender equality, the four pillars of WPS). A body of academic and NGO research and writing has developed and teaching curricula have been introduced. It also has its own potentially transformative priorities: ensuring that the experiences of women and girls in conflict-affected situations are brought into international law and policy-making in accordance with principles of women's human rights. Accepting that WPS might evolve into such a special regime would allow for a more fluid idea of international law-making and what creates a distinct subject or regime of international law.

Another approach is potentially to understand the WPS agenda as a 'holistic body of law'. Sandesh Sivakumaran has explained the emergence of what he identifies as a law of international disaster relief from a range of instruments, statements and practices. He argues that, while this might appear to be an unorthodox way of making international law, this mix of techniques is in fact not unusual and allows international law-making to be flexible and to develop according to the needs of the international community.[94] WPS fits well into this analysis. The international community has identified conflict-affected sexual violence as a violation of IHL and of human rights, as an international crime and as a threat to international peace and security. There is a range of relevant instruments. The need for an effective and holistic response thus combines state interests with those of individuals subject to the immediate harms of sexual violence. Coordinated action by a range of actors is envisaged: the Security Council, states, international personnel, international

[92] The position was mandated by UN Security Council resolution 1888 (2009).

[93] The Informal Experts Group was mandated by UN Security Council resolution 2242 (2015).

[94] Sandesh Sivakumaran, 'Techniques in International Lawmaking: Extrapolation, Analogy, Form and the Emergence of an International Law of Disaster Relief', 28 *European Journal of International Law* (2018) 1097–1132.

civil society, local communities, women and girls, men and boys, those who reject the gender binary. This approach is premised on accepting that international law can be and is made by other actors than states[95] and without the formalities and piecemeal approach of treaty-making and the uncertainties of customary international law. It can fill the gaps that are left by states in law-making. There are other advantages to the suggested holistic approach. To paraphrase Sivakumaran: the rights and obligations are not contingent on where in the world the conflict takes place, the type of conflict, the type of harm experienced or of assistance required, or the identity of the state or other actor seeking to provide assistance. It would obviate the need for debates about formal legal status of particular norms and would bring order to a rather messy area of international life.[96] It would also give effect to the expertise women have built up in over a century of activism, writing and practice. Sivakumaran's analysis assumes, as a starting point, the existence of a multilateral treaty to which there is wide adherence. There are relevant multilateral treaties – the Geneva Conventions and Protocols, CEDAW – and there are other instruments, including the final documents of global summit meetings and a succession of ten Security Council resolutions, adopted over twenty years, generally by consensus. Recognition of the WPS agenda as a comprehensive and holistic framework with normative status would also provide some protection against backlash and a basis for resistance against regressive tendencies by leading members of the Council.

5.9 Conclusion

This book has provided an overview of the principles of WPS within the framework of contemporary international law. A theme throughout has been the tension between a women's human rights and peace agenda that was inspired and motivated by civil society and supported by the UN human rights bodies, notably CEDAW and its monitoring Committee, and the security agenda of the UN Security Council. At the twenty-year milestone, it is apparent that the security dimension predominates, with little attention given to any understanding of peace, let alone a peace that delivers for women, beyond cessation of armed conflict. WPS has been

[95] Ibid., at 1131. [96] Ibid.

harnessed by the UN and the bureaucrats. It has become a top-down process that is too often not known about on the ground by those who need it, while those at the top either are insufficiently cognisant of the voices from below or, when they hear them, fail to heed their messages. As a vehicle for bringing feminist and other marginalised voices into international law, it has had some small successes but little structural impact. On the one hand, adoption of UN Security Council resolution 1325 in 2000 was a triumph for women activists and the adoption of nine further resolutions was a continuation of that success. But, on the other hand, the Security Council has flattened and tamed the transformative potential of the WPS agenda. At the same time, for some Council members, the agenda has gone too far by overstepping the Council's authority or challenging the patriarchal structures of society by upholding gender equality, particularly women's sexual and reproductive rights and non-binary gender roles. That progress through international law cannot be assumed has exposed by the WPS agenda even as that agenda could acknowledge and celebrate gender fluidity. As Di Otto has posited, perhaps the goal of seeking a Security Council resolution on women and peace and security in 2000 was asking for too much. Even a succession of resolutions was never going to be able to subvert the power politics of the Council while allowing the Council to further shore up and legitimate that power through its apparent commitment to gender equality. To me, it symbolises the dilemma that Hilary Charlesworth, Shelley Wright and I faced in our first critique of international law through a feminist lens:[97] do we continue to fight for the enhancement of the lives of women and others marginalised by the state-centred, imperialistic and flawed processes and structures of international law and institutions or do we recognise that this can never amount to more than tinkering around the edges and celebrate small gains? WPS is such a gain and, in the right hands, it provides a tool of resistance, but, in its current location, it is not going to bring peace or security for women and girls, for men and boys, for all those who do accept a gendered binary, or indeed for all life on this planet.

[97] Hilary Charlesworth, Christine Chinkin and Shelley Wright, 'Feminist Approaches to International Law', 85 *American Journal of International Law* (1991) 613–45.

Index

Index

Index

Index

Index

Index

For EU product safety concerns, contact us at Calle de José Abascal, 56–1°, 28003 Madrid, Spain or eugpsr@cambridge.org.

www.ingramcontent.com/pod-product-compliance
Lightning Source LLC
LaVergne TN
LVHW011814200926
848484LV00005B/1193